BRITISH EAST AFRICA
VICTORIA NYANZA
3900 Ft.
ALBERT NYANZA
2300 Ft.
ALBERT EDWARD NYANZA
3307 Ft.
GERMAN EAST AFRICA
Longitude East of Greenwich
30°
32°
34°
North Latitude
South Latitude
Equator
2°
SOMERSET NILE
Karuma Falls
Murchison Falls
Mahagi (Tungura)
Magungo
Shoa Meru
Atada Deanu
Fauvera
Rapids
Magungo Melizsa
Kasija
Kisuna
Rionga's
Koki
Chorobezi
Masindi
Kikunguru Hill
Isakh
Marusi Hill
R. Masansi
M'ruli (Komrasi's)
Aggusi
Kisiwihe
L. Kioga
L. Salisbury
Kabora
Kavalli's
Inde sura
Fort Budo
Barego
R. Dui
R. Ihuru
R. Ituri
R. Ibina
Waterfall 1000 ft. (Wahamba Falls)
Taigeri R.
Kabarega's
M'Bahovia
Parhani
Kijamba
Kayango
Ft. Kafu
Kiggagaru
Karchi
M'Base
Duberge
L. Ibrahim
Niamiongo
R. Nogombwa
NILE (KIVIRA)
Nsussi R.
Lugogo
Kahura
Tabingwa's
Gabula's
Urondogani
Miro's
U. S. O
Mt. Azif
Mboga
Wakusura
Maanja
Ft. Grant
Ft. Lugard
BULLAM WEZI
Baxigaxi
BRITISH EAST AFRICA
SINGO
Busindi
AWAMBA MATARA
Kasagama's
Ft. Gerry
R. Mpanga
Kisisi R.
Ft. de Winton
Lwekula
Mt. Edwin Arnold (Sababa)
Matiana
Ft. Raymond
Gomba
Bira
Mwera
Ft. Kampala
Ripon Falls
Napoleon G.
Mtala
Mtsora
Ft. Edward
16400
MENGO
Bweya
Gulama
Ziba
Kawaligoma
Mondo's
Chikahema
Vuma
Murchison Bay
Port Alice
KITARWENDA
BWERA
Katonga R.
USONGORA
Ft. George
Salt Lake
Kaxinga
Runsuma
Equator
ALBERT EDWARD NYANZA
3307 Ft.
Kwa Kaihuru
ANKOLE
Mtali's
Masaka
Kiango
Bali
Lulamba I.
Kaganda I.
SEWAIA
SEMAGAI
Sesse
Archipelago
VICTORIA NYANZA
3900 Ft.
Kagegi Gulf
R. Oso
R. Lowra
R. Lulu
Vichumbi
RUWENZORI
ORU
Ruampara Mts.
R. Ruwezi
Kamswaga's
Ruhanga
Igoro
Rujumbira Mt.
BUTUMBI
Makowalis
country
Buhora
Sango
Nyangoma
R. Semliki

THE PERFECT VICTORIAN HERO

To
Kathleen and Ian

THE PERFECT VICTORIAN HERO

Samuel White Baker

by

Michael Brander

MAINSTREAM

This edition published by
MAINSTREAM PUBLISHING COMPANY (EDINBURGH) LTD.
25 South West Thistle Street Lane
Edinburgh EH2 1EW

ISBN 0 906391 24 5

Cover design by James Hutcheson

Title page photographs show Sir Samuel White Baker and his second wife, Florence.

Typeset, printed and bound in Great Britain by
Spectrum Printing Company, Edinburgh

Contents

Acknowledgements

My thanks are due to many libraries, as usual, but in particular to the staff of the National Library of Scotland, especially for access to the Grant Letters; to the Central Library in Edinburgh; to Mr. Brian M. Gall and the staff of the East Lothian District Library; to the Director of the Sheffield City Libraries for access to the Wharcliffe Correspondence and to the Rt. Hon. Earl of Wharncliffe for permission to quote from the letters: also to the Royal Geographical Society for access to the Baker Diaries with Dr. John Baker's consent, particularly to Mr. G.S. Dugdale, the Librarian, and Mrs C. Kelly, the Archivist, for their help. I would also like to thank the Baker family, particularly Dr. and Mrs John R. Baker and the late Colonel and Mrs. E. Baker for their generous help and hospitality in allowing me free access to their homes to inspect family manuscripts, diaries and other material in considerable quantities, also for reading and commenting on the finished manuscript. Finally, I am most grateful to Kenneth H. Grose, M.A., and to my wife Evelyn, for their help in the tiresome task of reading the typescript and commenting on it. I must, however, make it clear that any views, or interpretations, as well as any mistakes, or omissions, are mine alone.

Foreword

The very varied spellings used for native names and places in India, Egypt and Africa between 1850 and the present day are liable to cause confusion to the reader to say the least. As far as possible I have adhered throughout to the spellings, often somewhat original, used by Samuel White Baker himself. For the same reason I have used the maps, or copies of the maps, which were the ones he used to illustrate his books. In the same way I have used the illustrations that he himself drew, or used, in his own works. Apart from the fact that these last are the only illustrations suitable they add a very distinctive flavour of their own.

By the same author

Biography
The Country Divine: Twelve Self-Portraits: St. Andrew Press:

Military History
The Tenth Royal Hussars: Seeley Service & Cooper
The Highlanders & Their Regiments: Seeley Service & Cooper:
Scottish & Border Battles & Ballads: Seeley Service & Cooper:

Directories & Lexicography
A Dictionary of Sporting Terms: A & C Black:
An International Encyclopedia of Shooting: Editor: Peerage Books:
A World Directory of Scottish Associations: Editor: Johnston & Bacon:

Travel
Over the Lowlands: Bles:
Ho for the Borders: Bles:
Around the Highlands: Bles:
Soho for East Anglia: On de Rochefoucald's Tour of 1784: Bles:
A Hunt Around the Highlands: On Thornton's Tour of 1784: Standfast Press:

Social History
The Emigrant Scots: Constable:
The Portrait of a Hunt: Hutchinson:
The Hunting Instinct: Oliver & Boyd:
The Georgian Gentleman: Saxon House:
The Victorian Gentleman: Saxon House:
The Making of the Highlands: Constable:
The Life & Sport of the Inn: Gentry Books:
The Original Scotch: A History of Scotch Whisky: Hutchinson:
Hunting & Shooting: A History of Field Sports: Weidenfeld & Nicolson:

Guides & Manuals
Groundgame: Tideline:
The Roughshooter's Sport: Tideline:
The Roughshooter's Dog: Gentry Books:
The Gameshot's Vade Mecum: A & C Black:
A Guide to Scotch Whisky: Johnston & Bacon:
Gundogs: Their Care & Training: A & C Black:
An Introduction to Trout Fishing: Spurbooks:
Scottish Crafts & Craftsmen: Johnston & Bacon:
The Complete Guide to Horsemanship: A & C Black:

Preface

Surprisingly there have only been two full length biographies of Samuel White Baker since his death in 1893. The first, in 1895, was an authorised biography by his friends Douglas Murray and Silva White. The second in 1949 was by Dorothy Middleton. It is unfortunate that Richard Hall's book, published in 1980, started only at the age of 37, but with the author's bias towards Africa this was perhaps not surprising. The most balanced portrait of Baker, albeit only two chapters long, is possibly that by Alan Moorehead in *The White Nile*, where he described him as a 'kind of fulcrum in African exploration.' Understandably, perhaps, all these biographers, except the last, have concentrated on Baker's exploits as an explorer and suppressor of the slave trade, only cursorily, if at all, covering his feats as the greatest hunter of his age, or indeed any age, before or since, and ultimately as the forerunner of the modern conservationists.

From an early age Samuel White Baker was what can only be termed 'adventure prone.' With a powerful physique and great stamina as well as a good ear for languages he was a natural leader of men of any race. Born in the Georgian age and reared in the Georgian tradition at a grammar school and under private tuition, rather than at one of the developing public schools in the Arnold mould, he was always an individualist and never a team man. Yet conversely he was brought up in and lived through the period when the narrow Victorian mentality, exemplified by 'the dear Queen' formed a mental straitjacket for many people in Britain. To these minds he was the epitome of the perfect Victorian hero.

Caught between the Georgian and Victorian ideologies he is not at first sight an easy person to define. There were unexpected depths and apparent contradictions in his character. Although the son of an apparently typical Victorian conservative and wealthy middle class merchant, he himself did not become a businessman. Instead he formed an agricultural settlement in the hinterland of Ceylon. He was highly adaptable, an animated coversationalist, wrote extremely readable books and was something of a linguist. At the same time, whilst not in the least dull, he was extremely practical and an excellent long term planner on both small and large scale. Yet while apparently forthright and straightforward he was also not without guile when required.

Although his first wife was the daughter of the neighbouring vicar, by whom he raised a large family in the Victorian tradition, it seems almost certain that his second wife, seventeen years his junior, was bought in a slave market on the lower Danube, while he was on a hunting expedition with the Maharajah Duleep Singh. With her he explored Abyssinia and the sources of the Nile for five years, before returning to England and presenting her to a hero-worshipping public. He then went on at the behest of the Khedive of Egypt to attempt to suppress the slave trade in the Sudan, being rewarded with the rank of Pasha.

It was, however, above all, throughout his life, as a hunter that he excelled, for that was his consuming passion. In Ceylon he re-discovered the method of 'par force' hunting employed by the Norman kings, wherein the greatest feat was to kill a boar, or buck, hunting single-handed with hounds armed only with a knife. This he did many times. He also hunted large numbers of animals, from elephants to antelopes, with a muzzle loading gun, but he was unusual in his time that he did not kill for the sake of slaughter. He later shot big game all round the world, in Africa, India, North America and elsewhere. As is often the case, however, his hunting was allied to a love of the quarry he hunted. He foresaw the day when the vast quantities of animals then to be seen would need to be conserved and acted accordingly. In North America, for instance he refused to kill any bison after he had shot his first specimen and merely stalked them for the pleasure of watching them at close quarters to the annoyance and bewilderment of his American guides. Considering the life he led the most remarkable feature of it was that he died in bed at the age of seventy two.

1

Background

Samuel White Baker's family came originally from Kent, where they had a family seat at Sissinghurst, near Maidstone. In Tudor and Stuart times they produced their share of courtiers and minor nobility. Sir John Baker was sometime Attorney-Gerneral and Recorder of London, Chancellor of the Exchequer and Speaker of the House of Commons during the reigns of Henry VIII, Edward VI and Mary. His brother James was Samuel White Baker's lineal ancestor on the male side. Sir Richard Baker was author of the *Chronicle of the Kings of England*, republished for the third time as late as 1660. Later the branch of the family from which Samuel White Baker stemmed moved to an estate near Poole in Dorset, settling down to produce a line of adventurous and enterprising seafaring Englishmen of the same stamp as Hawkins and Drake.

His grandfather, Valentine Baker, born in 1737, started life in the Royal Navy, like his father and grandfather before him. On the outbreak of the American War of Independence, having resigned his commission, he took command of the eighteen-gun privateer, the sloop *Caesar*. In 1782, by which time England was at war with France, Spain and Holland, as well as with the emergent American nation, he encountered a thirty-two gun French frigate in the mouth of the English Channel. Despite the large discrepancy in size between the two ships, Valentine Baker, in the best English tradition, instantly gave battle, sailing into the attack without hesitation.

So magnificently did he fight his ship and inspire his men that the French frigate, severely mauled, struck her flag. By this time the *Caesar*, with all her boats smashed to splinters and her rigging in a poor state, was unable to board her prize. Disregarding the established rules of warfare, the French then re-hoisted their flag and made their escape as best they could. They were, however, so crippled that the following day they were easily captured by an English frigate and escorted into Portsmouth harbour.

It was also to Portsmouth that Valentine Baker steered his badly damaged sloop to re-fit and repair the ravages of battle. On seeing the erstwhile enemy vessel lying at anchor there he immediately claimed her as his prize. The French captain, guilty of mis-conduct in transgressing the rules of war and mortified at seeing how greatly inferior was the ship to which he had struck his flag, promptly shot himself.

To show their appreciation of their fellow citizen's courage and determination the merchants and insurers of Bristol presented Valentine Baker with a suitably inscribed silver vase in memory of his victory.As this was far from being the only prize he captured in the course of the war he accumulated a considerable fortune. This he invested in estates in Jamaica and Mauritius, setting up a merchant trading fleet and ending his days as a highly respected Bristol merchant venturer.

Such was the infant mortality of those late Georgian and early Victorian days, however, that while Valentine Baker had seven sons and two daughters, only two of those sons married and of those only the youngest, Samuel, successfully raised a family. Prior to his marriage, Samuel was shipped off to Jamaica in 1815 to gain experience of that end of the family ventures. He did not travel in luxury, but in a small merchantman, and noted in his diary somewhat ruefully that he considered himself "an unlucky young dog taking the voyage, he hardly knows why, but imagines it may be partly to keep him from an idle winter and to strengthen a sickly constitution."

On his arrival he was surprised to find, contrary to much of the propaganda being disseminated in England, that the plantation slaves were a great deal better treated than many so-called free-born Englishmen of his acquaintance. He wrote: "Mr. Wilberforce should certainly be sent to Jamaica to witness the Christmas gambols of these poor slaves. For ten successive nights I could scarcely sleep for the infernal noises of the 'enslaved mortals'."

Following their victory at Waterloo in 1815 the British were undisputed world leaders in every field of endeavour. This was the age of the burgeoning British Empire. It was also the age of the Industrial Revolution in Britain. All round the world British merchants, with a merchant fleet second to none sailing under the security of the British Ensign backed by the might of the Royal Navy, were busy making their fortunes by selling the products of the Industrial Revolution from centres such as Manchester, Birmingham and Sheffield to a receptive world as yet incapable of emulation. In return they bought the raw materials they required such as cotton, coconut fibre, linseed oil and similar items, or luxury goods such as silks, spices, coffee, sugar and wines.

Proving to have an aptitude for business it was not long before Samuel Baker returned from the West Indies and settled down to become a thriving merchant with estates in Mauritius and his own trading fleet. To this end he was forced to spend a good deal of time in London and bought a house in Whitehall Yard. While still a young man he married the daughter of Thomas Dobson of Enfield and bought a house there as well, named "Ridgeway Oaks". It was there that a large part of his family of eight children was raised, but in 1833 he moved to the west again to Gloucestershire and ended his days as a director of the Great Western Railway and Chairman of the Gloucester Bank.

On the 8th of June, 1821, a few weeks before the coronation of George IV, Samuel White Baker was born in London at the house in Whitehall Yard, the second of five sons and three daughters. His earliest years in the nursery, in petticoats as was the custom until the age of four or five, were spent in Enfield. There he appears to have been taught by his mother rather than the more customary governess, if we are to take an eyewitness account literally: "In the lessons learnt at his mother's knee . . . Geography was his delight and as a mere baby he had learnt the names of all the countries then known and had acquired some knowledge of their capitals and their special characteristics . . ."

Young Samuel White Baker spent a happy and carefree childhood at Enfield between his own home and that of his maternal grandfather, with his brothers, Thomas the eldest, who died young in 1832, John, Valentine and James. With their three sisters they formed a particularly united family, growing up with unusual freedom and developing foreceful and original characters. Samuel appears to have been forever investigating anything that interested him, frequently leading his companions with him and frequently ending in trouble. His pocket knife was often in use, cutting open any object of note to see what was inside. His pockets were generally bulging with oddments including beetles, caterpillars and similar natural treasure troves.

His interest in nature was almost unbounded. He is reported to have rescued drowned puppies and kittens with a view to resuscitating then and, on finding it beyond his powers, to have buried them with full funeral honours. It was, perhaps, carrying matters too far when in such a spirit of natural enquiry he buried his small sister up to her neck in a flowerbed to see if this would make her grow any faster. After this escapade he was sent to a preparatory school at Rottingdean, a small village near Brighton. A description of him at this time may have been somewhat idealised in typically florid

Victorian manner, but it is nevertheless probably near enough to
form a reasonably close picture of him as he was then:

> "He was of the Saxon type; a noble looking boy, with very fair
> complexion, light hair and fearless blue eyes. He was enterprising,
> mischievous, for ever getting into scrapes and leading others into
> them; but he was never known to tell a lie nor to do a mean thing. He
> was very affectionate and fond of his home; always tearful on leaving it
> for school; but a plucky little fellow, ready to fight much bigger boys
> than himself on the slightest charge of homesickness or for any
> infringement of his rights . . ."

What the school itself was like is not stated, but the general
standard of such schools in the late Georgian and early Victorian
period was extremely low. They were usually run by clergymen as an
addition to their stipend with indifferently educated and sadistic or
drunken assistant ushers in charge of the boys. Accommodation was
generally poor and sanitation, as everywhere else at that time, either
inadequate or non-existent. Regular caning, or birching, was to be
expected and such education as there was generally consisted of
mere learning by rote. Bullying by the older boys was part of the
natural order of things and there were, of course, no organised games
at that time. Not altogether surprisingly, he does not appear to have
learned a great deal there. He seems to have learned more in the
holidays, as on the occasion during a visit to his maternal grandfather's house at Enfield, when he made his first close acquaintance
with the highly explosive qualities of gunpowder. While he was
experimenting with the manfacture of squibs on the kitchen table,
watched by an admiring audience of younger brothers and sisters,
one of the newly made fireworks ignited and sparks landed on the
heap of gunpowder on the table. The resulting explosion rang all the
bells in the house, blew out the kitchen windows and deposited him
at the far end of the room. Apart from burns on his bare arms and
being temporarily blinded by the flash, he was none the worse.
Fortunately for his brothers and sisters one of the kitchen maids saw
what was about to happen and thrust them through the door in time
to save them from sharing in the effects. No doubt grandfather
Dobson, like Queen Victoria subsequently, was not amused, but in
view of the injuries he had suffered it is unlikely that Samuel was
punished unduly for the offence. There is little doubt that he was able
to provide an eloquent defence of his experiment, for even then he
was capable of expressing himself well both verbally and in print.

The earliest example of a letter written by him, which is still extant,
is dated 1832, when he was aged eleven and still at school at
Rottingdean. Already George IV was dead and William IV had been

on the throne for two years:

> My Dear Aunt,   Rottingdean. 25th March, 1832.
> I have not been very well since I last came back from home, which is about a week ago, but I am now much better. Tell me in your next letter whether you forgot to take the piece of metal that I found with a piece of flint in the middle to London, because since you left us I have found several bits of the same sort in the house, which I suppose had been broken off the same lump . . . Give my love to Aunt Maria and Grandpapa.
> I remain,
> Your affectionate nephew, Sam. W. Baker."

The contents of the letter are relatively unimportant, but they indicate that even by that age he had learned to express himself with a clarity and ease which was later to make him such an eminently readable author of books on sport and travel.

In the same year, 1832, his elder brother Thomas died and he thus became the eldest of the family. The following year, 1833, they moved to Highnam Court, about two miles from Gloucester, leasing the house and estate from Sir John Guise. The house itself, surrounded by a beautiful park of 56 acres with a further 2,000 acres around it, was a very considerable change from Enfield. Here there was much more room for a boy of twelve to develop a naturally powerful physique. With excellent shooting on hand Samuel was not backward in taking every advantage of the opportunities for sport. It was here that he first developed fully the love of the gun and the chase, of dogs and other animals, both domestic and wild, which was to last him throughout his life.

His closest companion at this time, and throughout his life the closest of his family to him, was his younger brother John, who shared his enthusiasm and interests. The two boys soon made the acquaintance of the neighbouring family of the Rev. Charles Martin, Rector of the adjacent parish of Maisemore. The rectory itself was only separated from the grounds of Highnam Court by a stream, and the boys soon rigged up an arrangement for pulleys to haul a tub backwards and forwards so that the two families could meet more easily. Thereafter they all became close friends as they grew up together.

Between 1833 and 1835 Samuel was sent to school at Gloucester College, close by the Cathedral, for his father had an obstinate Georgian prejudice against the growing popularity of the public schools and preferred his sons to be educated amongst the local boys of the neighbourhood, where he could keep an eye on them. It says much for Samuel's physical development at this period, or else for the puny size of the ushers, that fifty-five years later he recalled that while it was not an agreeable interval in his life, "I believe that I was the only boy who never received corporal punishment, an exception amongst 96 individuals. The solitary exception of myself from the cane, or birch, was not the result of any superior merit on my part; I was only a size too big and too strong."

He had certainly already learned to use his fists effectively and he was later an excellent boxer and fencer. On one occasion when he was just seventeen he was involved with a notorious local bully in Gloucester. Intervening to protect an innocent victim from the clutches of this powerful oaf, Baker was forced to take firm action. His first blow, shrewdly placed on the jaw, laid the man prostrate on the ground. He did not attempt to come back for more. In after years the well-known late-Victorian author of boy's books, G.A. Henty, who used Baker as the inspiration for many of his heroes, was to incorporate this incident in one of his plots. To judge by Baker's later accomplishments such a feat would have been well within his powers as a well-grown seventeen-year old on the verge of manhood. By the time he was full-grown he stood a matter of five foot ten inches, with very broad shoulders and deep chest, weighing in his prime some fifteen stone, but always very agile and quick on his feet. Even as a youngster he must have been a formidable opponent.

His schooling had almost ended in 1837 when the death of William IV and accession of the young Queen Victoria heralded an entirely different way of life, even if this may not have been immediately apparent. The old easy immorality of the Georgian period was already passing and with the spread of Methodism a much narrower form of Christianity positively encouraging hypocrisy and double standards was not long in developing. Throughout the period the developing pubic schools consciously devoted themselves to educating 'Empire Builders' to govern the ever spreading outposts of the British Empire while British merchants continued to introduce the products of the Industrial Revolution to the furthest corners of the world with, of course, satisfactory returns. The outcry against slavery abroad continued while the conditions of the poor in Britain's industrial slums were often far worse, but none of this was immediately obvious to anyone brought up in the rising middle classes of the time of which the Baker family were a typical example.

Whether Samuel Baker would have benefited from the guiding hand of someone like Thomas Arnold, who was headmaster of Rugby from 1827 to 1842, and who may be fairly said to have revolutionised the educational system of the country during that period, as well as fostering a much narrower outlook, is another matter. The probability is that even at this early stage Samuel Baker was too much of an individualist to take kindly to regimentation in any form. He was already self-reliant and scornful of discipline, unless self-applied. When something interested him he was always prepared to master it. He certainly profited little from his sojourn at Gloucester College, although he gained much practice with rifle and shotgun in the grounds of the estate, or sometimes further afield in the Forest of Dean and the New Forest, then teeming with deer and other wildlife. He was more interested in the study of ballistics and the mechanism of rifle or shotgun than in ordinary schooling. Even at the age of seventeen he was trying to persuade seasoned military men that some form of rifle would be more effective for army use than the old smooth bore "Brown Bess" musket still in general use.

Scarcely surprisingly in the circumstances his father decided that the time had come to obtain some form of private tuition for his eldest son. After some deliberation he chose the Curate of Tottenham, the Rev. Mr. P.H. Dunster. If his ideas on schooling may not have been successful, there is very little doubt that Samuel Baker Senior's choice of tutor was an excellent one. The Rev. Mr. Dunster subsequently wrote:

> In the spring of 1838 I had an interview with Mr. Baker, who told me how disappointed he was at the backward state of his son Samuel's education. He mentioned that he had extensive and valuable estates in the Mauritius which would form an excellent provision for his two eldest sons; and said that he wished his son Samuel to go out as soon as possible and take over the management of the property.
>
> The result was that the future Sir Samuel came to me as my resident pupil. He was at that time a strong, well-made, lad with a very gentlemanly bearing, a florid complexion, bright auburn hair, and an open, honest countenance, full of life and animal spirits. We took to each other from the very first; and continued fast friends to the day of his death.
>
> My pupil was certainly deficient in subjects of general education. I tried him in Latin and Greek; with the former he was fairly conversant, but the latter was new to him. He was much interested, I remember, with Xenophon's stirring narrative of the Retreat of the Ten Thousand. He also read Caesar and Livy with me.
>
> It was the dull process of school routine that had discouraged him. My chief aim was to cultivate in him a taste for reading and to make the acquisition of general knowledge as easy as I could.
>
> My father had an excellent library, containing works by the best English authors—History, Travels, Fiction, etc. Here my pupil and I worked together. He was much interested in scientific subjects, some of which we illustrated by actual experiments. But the books in my father's library pleased him most, chief among them being, curiously

> enough, Balzoni's *Travels in Egypt and Nubia,* and two volumes of Dr.
> Madden's *Travels,* one of which was described as A Twelve Months
> Residence in the West Indies, during the transition from slavery to
> apprenticeship.
>
> Sam. Baker had plenty of natural ability, and had been well
> grounded in earlier years. He read fluently, spelt correctly, wrote a
> good hand and could express himself well and easily.
>
> In our neighbourhood, there was a Circulating Library, containing
> some three thousand volumes, from which he kept himself supplied
> with books, selecting Travels, tales of adventure, and the best works of
> contemporary Fiction. There was little in the way of sport or out-door
> amusements. Occasionally he took his gun on the Tottenham marshes,
> with a fine old English spaniel of ours,—a most excellent water dog
> and high in favour with him. Sometimes in open weather he had a
> run with a pack of beagles belonging to a friend in the village. In the
> summer his chief amusement was bathing in the river; and he soon
> became a strong swimmer.
>
> During the two years that Sam. Baker was with me, he was more my
> companion than my pupil. His education consisted in the development
> of that which was in him, rather than the acquisition of book
> knowledge.

If he had not already read it, Samual White Baker's reading during
his sojourn with the young curate of Tottenham must certainly have
included that sporting classic of the day, Colonel Peter Hawker's
Instructions to Young Sportsmen, which ran through numerous editions.
No doubt he also read other books on the subject of guns and rifles,
for about this time, on his return to Highnam Court, one of his first
actions was to get George Gibbs, the gunsmiths in Bristol, to make
him a rifle to his own design.

Pursuing his somewhat haphazard and unorthodox course of
education for his eldest son, Samuel Baker Senior had decided that
he should next go the Frankfurt to learn the German language under
the nominal care of a banker, Herr Behrens. The Germans, like most
continentals, were keen on rifle shooting, and the rifle in most
common use there was a weapon weighing some sixteen pounds, but
with a comparatively small ball and weak charge of powder. Young
Samuel resolved to improve on this continental weapon.

The rifle he designed weighed a massive twenty-one pounds with a
barrel thirty-six inches long and carried a belted ball of three ounces,
or a conical bullet of four ounces with a charge of no less than sixteen
drachms of powder. Since breech-loaders were not introduced until
the late 1850s, this was, of necessity, a muzzle-loader with two
grooves of rifling. As a rifle of this weight with such a charge would
be liable to knock down any weakling who tried to fire it, he was

given to understand, scarcely surprisingly, that it was "preposterous in the professional opinions of the trade". Only those with the breadth of shoulder and powerful build of someone like Samuel White Baker himself could hope to fire such a weapon with any chance of accuracy after carring it for any distance. In fact he was to use it and others modelled on it with great effect on elephant and buffalo as well as other big game in later years, when he was to write with justified pride:

> The twist was one full turn in length of the barrel. The rifling was an exceedingly deep and broad groove (two grooves), which reduced the difficulty of loading to a minimum, as the projecting belt enabled the bullet to catch the channel instantly, and to descend easily when wrapped in a greased silk patch without the necessity of hammering. The charge of powder was inserted by inverting the rifle and passing up the loading rod with an ounce measure screwed to the end; this method prevented the powder from adhering to the sides of the barrel and thus fouling the grooves.
>
> An extraordinary success attended this rifle, which became my colossal companion for many years in wild sports with dangerous game. It will be observed that the powder charge was one-third the weight of the projectile, and not only a tremendous crushing power, but an extraordinary penetration was obtained, never equalled by any rifle that I have since possessed.
>
> This weapon was in advance of the age, as it foreshadowed the modern Express, and the principle was thoroughly established to my own satisfaction, that a sporting rifle to be effective at a long range must burn a heavy charge of powder, but the weight of the weapon must be in due proportion to the strain of the explosion.

How he fared in shooting with this rifle is not recorded, but it is typical of his pertinacity that after attending a series of lectures for a period of some eighteen months he returned to England having learned to speak and write German. With this accomplishment his nominal education came to an end. His father's plans for the future were that he should join him in his London office in Fenchurch Street, although all concerned should have realised that this scheme was foredoomed to certain failure.

Despite the fact that by an accident of fate he had been born within the sound of Bow Bells and was thus able to claim with pride throughout his life that he was a Londoner by birth, Samuel White Baker was never a man fond of living in towns. The narrow lanes and smoke-filled city chop and coffee-houses, the poky offices and clerk's life perched on a high stool behind a desk, were simply unsuited to him in every way. His upbringing and background were those of a countryman. He belonged to the open spaces and fresh air, rather than the cramped life of the town dweller. It soon became obvious that if he was to take any part in his father's business it would not be in the offices in the city of London, but in some more active role.

At this stage, however, Samuel White Baker and his brother John, whose tastes were generally alike, announced their desire to marry their boyhood playmates, the daughters Henrietta and Elizabeth of the Rev. Charles Martin, the Rector of Maisemore. On the 3rd of August 1843, when Samuel was just twenty-two and his brother only twenty-one, the two couples were married in a joint ceremony by the Rector in Maisemore Church. Both young grooms then drove off with their brides on a sunny summer evening for a joint honeymoon in Clifton, then a pleasant village close to Bristol.

Poor John and Elizabeth were not allowed to linger long in England. It had already been decided that the two brothers and their young wives should go out to Fairfund, the large family sugar plantation in Mauritius, which was in need of competent administration. Within a month the younger brother and his bride were aboard the *Jack* of one hundred tons and sailing for their destination, round the Horn.

Samuel and Henrietta stayed in England a further eighteen months, long enough for their first son, Charles Martin, born in August 1844, to be weaned. Then Samuel, with Henrietta by this time heavily pregnant once again, set off to join his brother. Their second son, John Lindsay Sloane, was born in Mauritius in June of 1845, to be followed by a sister in the ensuing year.

Although the brothers were the closest of their family and the two young brides were delighted to be together again, it is very clear that they did not enjoy life in Mauritius. Despite the fact that it was in many ways very beautiful—mountainous and well wooded, with on the whole a reasonable climate—they found it a stultifying place in which to live, not least because of the inhabitants.

During the Napoleonic Wars Mauritius had proved a useful base for the French to harass English shipping in the Indian Ocean, until occupied by the British in 1810. Although in 1814 it passed to the British under the Treaty of Paris, it remained basically a French colony, subject to French laws, with the majority of the inhabitants French-speaking, either of French descent or half French half-native Creoles. Thirty years later, despite a succession of British governors very little had changed. As Samuel was quick to note, when the French arrived in a colony they behaved as if they intended to spend the rest of their life there and never return to their native land, building houses with gardens and fruit trees, making due provision for their children's education and in every way putting down roots.

The British, on the other hand, he noted, always behaved as if they intended to return in due course to their old homes in Britain. In such circumstances, with French the predominant language, inevitably the English formed their own clique and the French-speaking settlers remained at a distance from them. This hardly made for a comfortable existence. No doubt the Bakers were high on the guest list in the complex protocol of Government House, but that would not make them any the better liked by their French neighbours, or their Creole employees.

To complicate matters further the old negro slaves had been freed, and to cultivate the plantations the British had imported coolie labour from India, with inevitable friction resulting. The most that could be said for this from Samuel's viewpoint was that he learned for the first time how to get the best out of native labour. In handling the coloured plantation workers and the coolie labour force he gained experience which was to be invaluable to him in later years.

But the aspect which must have exasperated Samuel more than any other, with his inborn hunting instinct, was the almost total absence of any fauna worthy of the name. The dodo, which had once been a notable feature of the island, along with other species of flightless birds, was long extinct. There was nothing left beyond a few monkeys and some recently imported deer. With little sport available and virtually no social life there was practically nothing to occupy their spare time once the day's work on the plantation was over. In such circumstances it is understandable why many similarly placed took refuge in rum, the universal panacea; but neither Samuel nor John, nor indeed any of the Baker family were ever heavy topers, so that this relief too was denied to them.

2

Ceylon

The death of Samuel White Baker's eldest son, Charles Martin, in the early part of 1845, contributed to a general hardening of his dislike for the life in Mauritius. He later wrote that the "spirit of wandering . . . allured me towards Ceylon." He also admitted that it was only after reading accounts in *Blackwood's Magazine* and similar publications depicting the thrills of elephant hunting in Ceylon that he decided to investigate the interior and the sport to be had there for himself. It was primarily his love of adventure and the thought of using his massive rifle on the largest beast known to man that attracted him to the Ceylonese jungles. Whatever his motives, there was never with him a great gap between thought and action, so that he was soon making arrangements to spend some months there to see what it was like. Before the year was out he took ship for Colombo, leaving his brother John behind to supervise the estate at Fairfund and look after his wife and family.

Ceylon proved a considerable contrast to Mauritius. The Dutch had ceded control of the island to the British in 1796 during the Napoleonic Wars'. When, in 1815, the local chieftains protested to the British about the tyranny of the Kandian King, a minor Colonial War was waged against him and in due course, after his defeat, he was exiled, thus ending a dynasty which had lasted 2,000 years. The island thus became part of the still expanding British Empire and the rich interior highlands were opened up for development. The earlier production of cinnamon, which had been favoured by the Dutch, was gradually replaced by the much more profitable production of coffee resulting in a considerable boom. Although an estimated £3,000,000 had been invested during the coffee boom between 1837 and 1845, much of this investment was by planters using borrowed capital, ignorant of the first principles of agriculture and content to oversee their plantations in the interior from the comparative comfort of Colombo. When the protective duty was withdrawn and foreign competition intervened the price of coffee slumped from £7 to £3 and not surprisingly the boom ended with a slump in 1847 when many fortunes were lost and estates changed hands at a fraction of their costs a few earlier. With the advantage of hindsight eight years later, Baker was to write of Ceylon:

> . . . a coffee estate in a good situation in Ceylon will pay a large interest for the capital invested, and will ultimately enrich the proprietor, provided that he has *his own capital* to work the estate, that he gives it his own personal superintendence, and that he *understands* the management . . . but a coffee estate is not infrequently abused for not paying—when it is worked with borrowed capital, at a high rate of interest, under questionable superintendence . . . A rapid fortune can never be made by working a coffee estate.
>
> . . . In the coffee districts of Ceylon there is little or no level ground . . . and the steep sides of the hills offer many objections to cultivation. The soil, naturally light and poor, is washed by every shower . . . Thus it is next to impossible to keep an estate in a high state of cultivation, without an enormous expense in the constant application of manure.
>
> Many estates are peculiarly subject to landslips . . . produced by the violence of the rains . . . A good well managed estate should produce an average crop of ten hundredweight án acre, leaving a nett profit of fifteen shillings per hundredweight. Unfortunately . . . the inclemency of the seasons and the attacks of vermin are constantly marring the planter's expectations . . .

Samuel White Baker's prime interest in visiting Ceylon initially was hunting elephants, not coffee planting, although it was typical of him that he took the trouble to become fully informed about it. His first impressions of the island were far from favourable, for Colombo seemed to him considerably inferior to Port Louis, with a harbour almost empty of shipping and "a peculiar dullness throughout the town,—a sort of something which seemed to say, 'coffee does not pay' ". After several enquiries as to which was the best hotel he finally selected the Royal, which he found airy, light and clean, but barn-like. He wrote:

> A good tiffin concluded, which produced a happier state of mind, I ordered a carriage for a drive . . . The general style of Ceylon carriages appeared in the shape of a caricature of a hearse . . . Those usually hired are drawn by a single horse, whose naturally vicious propensities are restrained by a low system of diet. In this vehicle, whose gaunt steed was led at a melancholy trot by an equally small-fed horse-keeper, I traversed the environs of Colombo . . . across the flat Galle Face (the race course) . . .

He was not impressed by his first tour of Colombo and at breakfast the next morning was pleased to see several fellow guests in the room. He soon got into conversation with a couple of them and noted subsequently:

> . . . one of my first questions naturally turned upon sport. *"Sport!"* exclaimed the two gentlemen simultaneously, *"sport!* There is no sport to be had in Ceylon!—at least the race week is the only sport I know of," said the taller gentleman . . . "I have an estate in the interior and I have never seen a wild elephant. There may be a few in the jungles of Ceylon, but *very* few, and you never see them!" I began to discover the stamp of my companion from his expression "you never see them". Of course I concluded he never looked for them . . . I subsequently discovered that my new and non-sporting acquaintances were coffee planters of a class then known as the Galle Face planters, who passed their time cantering about the Colombo race-course and idling in the town, while their estates lay a hundred miles distant, uncared for, and naturally ruining their proprietors.

Fortunately for him, that afternoon he encountered an old friend from Gloucestershire, Lieutenant de Montenac, who was serving with the 154th Regiment of Foot in Ceylon. He immediately agreed to join him in a sporting expedition into the interior. With his experienced assistance Baker had soon rented "a good airy house in Colombo as headquarters, and the verandahs were soon strewed with jungle-baskets, boxes, tent, gun-cases, and all the paraphernalia for a shooting trip". In those days of muzzle loaders, with ladles, bullet moulds, loading rods, powder flasks, percussion caps, greased patches and all the multifarious items necessary just for shooting, paraphernalia was indeed the word to describe the equipment required for a shooting expedition. In addition to all this there were such necessities as food, drink, clothing, bedding and similiar essentials, quite apart from harness and fodder for the horses and food for the numerous servants accompanying them. Equipping such an expedition successfully required considerable experience of the conditions likely to be encountered and Baker was fortunate to have such a friend on hand to guide him.

It is more than probable, however, that he would have managed very successfully by himself. Throughout his life he was notably thorough in all his preparations, whatever the task he was undertaking. It was typical of him that he made a particular point of checking for himself the anatomy of the elephant before he started hunting them. He wrote later:

> When I arrived in Ceylon, one of my first visits was to the museum at Colombo. Here I carefully observed the transverse sections of an elephant's skull, until perfectly acquainted with its details. From the museum I went straight to the elephant stables, and thoroughly examined the head of the living animal; comparing it in my own mind with the skull, until I was thoroughly certain of the position of the brain, and the possibility of reaching it from any position . . .

His first shooting expedition with his friend de Montenac was a considerable success. He shot elephants, buffalo and deer and returned to Colombo highly satisfied with the sport he had enjoyed. Even if this expedition had not proved successful it is unlikely that he would have stayed in Mauritius any longer. As it was he had enjoyed himself so much that he sent for his wife and family to come over to Ceylon to join him. Unfortunately his daughter, Jane, still a babe in arms, was taken ill at the start of the 2,500 mile voyage and was buried at sea off the Maldive Islands in September 1846. The family re-union was to be tinged with sadness.

It was not long, however, before Samuel had persuaded his brother John and his wife to join them. After hearing of the sport Sam had been enjoying it may be imagined that he did not need a great deal of persuading. Nor was it long before they were off on another hunting expedition into the interior, leaving their wives behind in Colombo. On this occasion, Sam recorded, he "tried the rough system of travelling, and started off with nothing but my guns, clothes, a box of biscuits, and a few bottles of brandy—no bed, no pillow, no tent, nor chairs or table, but, as my distressed servant said, 'no nothing' . . . I literally depended upon my guns for food, and my cooking utensils consisted of one saucepan and a gridiron, a 'stew' and a 'fry' being all that I looked forward to in the way of gourmandism. Sleeping on the bare ground in native huts, dining cross-legged upon mother earth with a large leaf as a substitute for a plate, cocoa-nut shell for a glass, my hunting-knife comprising all my cutlery . . ."

Both he and his brother appear to have enjoyed themselves beyond measure. On their first day's stage, when they were still within thirty miles of Kandy, they stopped at 2p.m. for a bath in the river, leaving their guns in the post-holder's hut. They had barely started to dress again when a native ran up to tell them that elephants were devouring his crop of korrakan, something akin to clover seed. Sending for their guns they set off in pursuit at once, but the elephants winded them and a hard chase through the thorny jungle followed. By 5p.m. in oppressive heat they had almost given up, when they realised that the female elephant they were pursuing had turned back for the very field of korrakan in which they had first been seen. They heard the alarm call of the elephant within a hundred yards and ran at full speed in pursuit, getting so close behind her "that I could have slapped her". He continued:

> At length, losing all patience, I fired my barrel under her tail, giving it an upward direction in the hope of disabling her spine. A cloud of smoke hung over me for a second and throwing my empty gun on one side, I put my hand behind me for a spare rifle. I felt the welcome

barrel pushed into my hand at the same moment that I saw the infuriated head of the elephant with ears cocked charging through the smoke! . . . I had just time to cock the two-ounce rifle and take a steady aim. The next moment we were in a cloud of smoke, but as I fired I felt certain of her. The smoke cleared from the thick bushes, and she lay dead at *six feet* from the spot where I stood. The ball was in the centre of her forehead . . . Had she been missed I would have fired my last shot. This had been a glorious hunt . . .

John, who had fired over his brother's shoulder at exactly the same moment as he had fired, so that each was unaware of the shot, had placed his ball within three inches of Sam's. They were both very pleased with themselves after the lengthy chase, but Sam was to remark at a later date:

> One great cause of danger in shooting in thick jungles is the obscurity occasioned by the smoke of the first barrel; this cannot escape from the surrounding bushes for some time, and effectually prevents a certain aim with the remaining barrel. In wet weather this is much increased. For my own part I dislike shooting in thick jungles and I very seldom do so. It is extremely dangerous, and is like shooting in the dark . . . "

It was only later on that Sam was to appreciate the errors they committed on these early hunting expeditions. Although they were extremely successful as novices in pursuit of big game they were both guilty of the same fault. They were contemptuous of the game they shot and ignored the very real dangers to which they were exposing themselves, principally through ignorance. It was not very long before Sam learned his lesson, while shooting buffalo.

Two days later they first encountered a herd of buffalo. They had gone ahead of their servants and, still only some eighty miles from Kandy, they broke out of the jungle in full view of Minneria Lake, which was some twenty miles round the perimeter. It was a lovely afternoon about 4p.m. and they enjoyed the beautiful scene in silence for some time. Then, although only armed with shotguns and a few balls, they became bored with waiting for their servants to catch up with them, and decided on a "stroll". They soon enountered a herd of around a hundred buffalo on the open plain.

Seven large bulls came forward in an ugly temper prepared to show fight, but the brothers ran up within thirty paces. One bull charged but turned sideways on the last moment and was hit in the shoulder by both brothers firing, as usual, as one. With a broken shoulder blade it fell to the ground, then tried to retreat on three legs, but was gored by another bull. Leaving John to finish off the bull that had been hit, Sam went in full chase after the other. Although cantering off and occasionally stopping, as if to show fight, this beast would neither stand nor charge. Finally Sam managed to cut him off by running round a creek into which the animal had entered. By this time, however, he had only two balls left. At a distance of some fifteen paces Sam fired at his chest and, when the smoke cleared, saw the buffalo bull standing in exactly the same position with only a trickle of blood running from the hole where the ball had entered to show that he had been hit. "Annoyed", as he put it, at this, Sam then fired his other barrel and his last ball, with precisely the same lack of effect except that by this time the beast was looking extremely enraged.

It was then for the first time that Sam realised his danger, but, standing his ground resolutely, he put his fingers in his mouth and blew a resounding whistle—a recognised signal for help between the brothers. For nearly a quarter of an hour he and the bull faced each other. Then Sam suddenly remembered that he had a purseful of small change to pay the coolies. Pouring a double charge of powder down the barrel he wrapped three shillings worth of sixpences in a piece of his shirt and rammed this down the barrel on top of it. This was hardly driven down when the bull advanced. Sam promptly cocked his gun and prepared to shoot, but the animal checked yet again, although by this time only seven paces from him.

At this point he heard his brother approaching breathlessly, having run all the way on hearing his whistle. Unfortunately he had only one ball left. Sam just had time to warn him to aim for the head, when the beast finally charged. John fired with no effect and Sam, waiting until the bull's head was within inches of his barrel, fired the charge of small change into the centre of his forehead.

The bull was bowled over by this shot and both Sam and John turned and ran for their lives, heading for a large fallen tree about half a mile away where they would be safe. The bull rose to its feet and followed them slowly. Reeling after them at a slow canter it finally fell to the ground, yet again within about two hundred yards of them. They then retreated under cover of the forest to the place they had left their horses. The bull remained "stunned by the collision with her Majesty's features upon the coin which he had dared to oppose", but when they returned the next morning, fully expecting to find him dead, there was no sign of him and they never saw him again. All the same, the young Bakers had learned a valuable lesson.

By breakfast time the following morning at 8a.m., however, Sam had amply revenged himself. Using his four-ounce rifle he had bagged no less than four buffalo bulls and one cow. The brothers had, however, faced a massed charge of a herd of buffalo and had they not killed two of the leaders as they charged down on them they would have been overwhelmed. Sam was quick to note that the same shot at the junction of throat and chest, which had been useless with the light gun the previous day, was deadly with the four-ounce rifle. He wrote of this occasion:

> Although I have since killed about two hundred wild buffaloes I have never witnessed another charge by a herd. This was an extraordinary occurrence and fortunately stands alone in buffalo-shooting. Were it not for the two heavy rifles our career might have terminated in an unpleasant manner.

It was not long before Sam came to have considerable respect for the buffalo. On numerous occasions he found that they would attempt to charge regardless of mortal wounds. Their courage and determination to press home their attacks won his complete admiration. He warned that their character could never be relied upon and that caution and good shooting, together with heavy rifles, were essential when shooting them.

The brothers were fully occupied for the next few months on various shooting expeditions, the sport in the jungles and plains of Ceylon being very much to their liking. In the same day they might shoot elephant, buffalo, deer, crocodile, duck and snipe, or peafowl for the pot. Whether living rough in native huts, or in more luxurious style in tents, with their servants in attendance, they thoroughly enjoyed the life in the wild, with the whole of Ceylon as their hunting ground and no-one to say them nay. Indeed it was the very lack of population which enhanced their pleasure and made it such a perfect game preserve.

Then, towards the end of the year, tragedy struck the Baker family again when John Lindsay, Sam's surviving much-loved son, was poisoned by an evil-minded servant and died soon afterwards. Immediately on learning of his son's illness, Sam hastened back to Colombo on board a coasting vessel, the fastest means of travel available. The craft capsized, but he continued the journey without bothering to put on dry clothing. The result was that he himself arrived dangerously ill with fever, to find that he was too late. Thoroughly depressed and still seriously ill, he withdrew to the highland resort of Newera Eliya, some 115 miles inland from Colombo. There, at an altitude of 6,000 feet, in the government rest house, such as it was, he recovered his normal rude health within a fortnight. He wrote subsequently:

> A poor miserable wretch I was upon my arrival at this elevated

station, suffering not only from the fever itself, but from the feeling of an exquisite debility that creates an utter hopelessness of the renewal of strength.

I was only a fortnight at Newera Eliya. The Rest-house or inn was the perfection of everything that was dirty and uncomfortable. The toughest possible specimen of beefsteak, black bread, and potatoes were the choicest and only viands obtainable for an invalid. There was literally nothing else; it was a land of starvation. But the climate! What can I say to describe the wonderful effects of such a pure and unpolluted air? Simply, that at the expiration of a fortnight, in spite of the tough beef and the black bread and potatoes, I was as well and as strong as I ever had been; and in proof of this, I started instanter for another shooting excursion in the interior.

Later on he somewhat modified his description thus:

The station then consisted of about twenty private residences, the barracks and officers' quarters, the Rest-House and the Bazaar; the latter containing about 200 native inhabitants. Bounded upon all sides but the east by high mountains, the plain of Newera Eliya lay like a level valley of about two miles in length by half a mile in width, bordered by undulating grassy knolls at the foot of the mountains. Upon these spots of elevated ground most of the dwellings were situated, commanding a view of the plain, with the river winding through its centre. The mountains were clothed from the base to the summit with dense forests, containing excellent timber for building purposes. Good building stone was procurable everywhere; limestone at a distance of five miles . . . How often have I thought of the thousands of starving wretches at home, who here might a earn a comfortable livelihood! . . . I have scanned the vast tract of country; and in my imagination I have cleared the dark forests and substituted waving crops of corn, and peopled a hundred ideal cottages with a thriving peasantry!

Discussing their future plans together round the camp fire after a successful day's hunting, both he and his brother John considered the idea of investing some of their capital in a settlement in these, to them, seemingly ideal surroundings. The collapse of the coffee boom in that same year, 1847, meant that there were numerous estates available at a fraction of the price they had previously made. It must have seemed to them that they had found the right place and the perfect opportunity, but first they had to return to England to convince their father that this was a better plan than returning to the family plantation in Mauritius, or settling down at home to run the family business.

With their future still undecided they returned to England by ship round the Cape. It was a fateful period in Europe. On their return home in the year 1848 there were revolutions in France, Germany,

Austria and Italy and an attempt at rebellion in Ireland, which was firmly suppressed. At home there were Chartist riots and talk of Karl Marx's newly published *Communist Manifesto.* Nor was the international situation promising with the threat of war against Russia looming in the background. Yet it needed a great deal more than these events to shake the deeply ingrained complacency of the British upper and middle classes in the mid-eighteenth century.

One major change Sam and John found little to their liking, for their father had sold Lypiatt Park and moved to London because of their mother's deteriorating health. No doubt this move added to their general feeling of discontent with Britain. Barring their strong family feeling there seemed little to hold them at home and Sam found his mind constantly returning to his days of sport in the jungle and the plains of Ceylon.

He wrote nostalgically of how "Scenes of former sports and places were continually intruding themselves upon my thoughts; and I longed to be roaming once more at large with the rifle in the noiseless wilderness of Ceylon."

To anyone with as pronounced a hunting instinct as Sam the opportunities available in Britain were pitiful when compared with those to be had in Ceylon. In addition, the noise and tumult of London, the cries of the itinerant street vendors, the rumble of metal wheels on the cobbles and the echo of horses' hooves, the stink of dung and sweat, the smoke and the fogs, were all anathema to anyone like him, longing for the freedom and peace of the jungle or the plains. He had tasted the pleasures of hunting with rifle and hound in the vast hinterland of Ceylon and quite naturally he wanted to return as soon as humanly possible. He kept finding himself gazing into the windows of various gunmakers' shops and sometimes entered to look at the various rifles for sale. He would then, he admitted, spend an hour or so boring the wretched assistants by suggesting various improvements that might be made in their design,. This, he wrote, with his usual wry humour, "as I was not a purchaser, must have been extremely edifying".

Finally he and his brother decided to make their own settlement somewhere in the region of Newera Eliya. Nor, it seems, was their father disposed to argue with them, for no doubt with his shrewd business sense he saw that this was a suitable time to invest money in land in Ceylon. It must also have been plain to him that little he could say would make any difference to his sons' plans. Sam himself, while paying lip-service to his ideals of transforming Newera Eliya into a thriving arcadia, wrote more realistically concerning his personal intentions:

. . . I determined to make a regular settlement at Newera Eliya, sanguinely looking forward to establishing a little English village around my own residence . . . I trusted to be enabled to effect such a change in the rough face of Nature in that Locality as to render a residence at Newera Eliya something approaching to a country life in England, with the advantage of the whole of Ceylon for my manor, and no expense of gamekeepers.

3

Newera Eliya

What the brothers really had in mind at Newera Eliya was the best of both worlds. They wanted a small piece of England snugly laid out around them, with all the advantages of the hunting and shooting available at hand in Ceylon. This of course, has been the ideal of almost every wealthy Englishman who has decided to set up home outside his native land. There have been many in the Antipodes, in North and South America and in Africa, who have had the same ideal in mind. The younger sons of squires, or landowners, who have not inherited the land themselves and have been forced to emigrate have often had similar ideals at the back of their heads. In general most of them have had to put up with second best.

As far as Sam and John were concerned they were more interested in the sport available, which they had already sampled, than they were in reproducing an English background to go with it. Nevertheless they certainly did their best to provide that as well. Once their decision was taken, with Sam the leader as usual, the brothers set about the business of making preparations for their settlement with typical Baker wholeheartedness. There were never any half measures about any of Sam's actions. As ever he proved himself a considerable organiser and administrator. Since it was their intention to have a thoroughly up-to-date farming settlement, if run on somewhat feudal lines, he set about it systematically. He noted:

> I purchased farming implements of the most improved descriptions, seeds of all kinds, saw-mills, etc., and the following stock: A half-bred bull (Durham and Hereford), a well-bred Durham cow, three rams (a Southdown, Leicester and Cotswold), and a thoroughbred entire horse by Charles XII; also a small pack of foxhounds, and a favourite greyhound ('Bran').

Sam also enjoyed himself at the gunsmiths, choosing Mr. Beattie of 205 Regent Street to make him four double-barrelled Number 10 rifles to his own design. Each weighed fifteen pounds with two grooves in the rifling. The sights were platinum at the muzzle and blue steel with a platinum strip with a broad and deep letter 'V' cut in the breech sights. The bright metal foresight was to counter the gloom of the jungle and the broad 'V' allowed for rapid aim when necessary. They were made with double bolts and a silver plate let into the stock under the breech to prevent wear. For these rifles he used six drachms of powder for elephants and four drachms for deer and general shooting.

He also had a hunting knife made to his own pattern by Paget of Piccadilly. The blade was a foot long, two inches broad at the widest part and slightly concave in the middle. The steel was of the finest available quality and with handle it weighed three pounds. Double-edged for three inches from the point, it could inflict a fearful wound, and Sam was to use it frequently when hunting with his hounds to give the quietus to a stag or wild boar at bay before them.

He also arranged for quantities of powder, caps, shot and similar essential supplies for his favourite sport. All in all he was certain of one thing—he would not lack for the necessary stores. Already he was developing that all-important ability to anticipate future requirements which was to become such an important feature of his life when planning expeditions into the unknown. This was his first major problem in logistics of this nature and it was by no means an easy one.

His brother John took charge of their combined families, with their brother Valentine, a bailiff, his wife and daughter, a blacksmith and his wife and eight other emigrants, including a coachman, Henry Perkes, all of whom embarked together on "the good ship *Earl of Hardwicke*" in September 1848. Sam himself went ahead choosing the overland Cairo to Red Sea route which had been increasingly used since the 18th century by travellers in a hurry wishing to avoid the long sea voyage round the Cape. It was his self-appointed task to choose the site of their settlement and after considerable deliberation he selected a thousand acres in Newera Eliya at the eastern edge of the plain. This land he duly purchased from the government at a matter of £1 an acre.

Although the monsoon was still sweeping the countryside he employed a force of eighty natives to clear the ground and by the time the main party had arrived there were some neat white cottages awaiting them, while the Bakers themselves shared a rented house. Transporting the machinery and other gear from Colombo to Newera Eliya over the 115 miles of indifferent road from sea level to over 6,000 feet inevitably involved some casualties. Prominent amongst these was a carriage sent out from England and pair of useful Australian horses, which were driven over a precipice by the groom,

Henry Perkes, who was both one-eyed and a confirmed drunkard. Some years afterwards Sam recorded the ill-spelt missive he received from Perkes on this occasion as closely as he could remember it:

> Honord Zur
>
> I'm sorry to hinform you that the carrige and osses has met with a haccident and is tumbled down a preccippice and its a mussy as I didn't go too. The preccippice isn't very deep being not above heighty feet or therabouts—the hosses is got up but is very bad—the carrige lies on its back and we can't stir it nohow. Mr. —— is very kind and has lent about a hundred niggers, but they ain't more use than cats at liftin. Plese Zur come and see whats to be done.
>
> Your Humbel Servt. H. Perkes.

Somewhat naturally Sam was not best pleased to lose both his carriage and a pair of good horses before they had even reached Newera Eliya. After investigating the crash and finding that it was due to Perkes galloping the horses while intoxicated, he sent the blacksmith in charge of a gang to haul the remains of the carriage up the precipice, rather than leave it to rot. He also sent a mahout with a trained elephant to help if necessary and as an afterthought sent Perkes as well. This was the cause of another disaster.

Perkes, more accustomed to riding than walking, insisted on riding on the elephant and, despite the mahout's protests, in goading it into a trot, which he kept up for fifteen miles to the scene of the accident. Finding the elephant was not required he then refreshed himself with brandy and water, and in his own words "tooled the old elephant along till he came to a standstill". The mahout then returned to report to Sam that his elephant had died as a result of the groom's treatment. As Sam put it with considerable restraint:

> Mr Perkes was becoming an expensive man; a most sagacious and tractable elephant was now added to the list of his victims; and he had the satisfaction of knowing that he was one of the few men in the world who had ridden an elephant to death. That afternoon Mr. Perkes was being wheeled about the bazaar in a wheelbarrow, insensibly drunk, by a brother emigrant who was also considerably elevated.

Drunken scamp that he was with his black patch over one eye notwithstanding, the near-illiterate one-eyed Perkes was also a devil with the maid-servants, proving himself a most successful Lothario. In spite of all his failings, however, Sam was forced to admit that he was both honest and industrious. It was all too much, just the same, and Henry Perkes was the first to go, leaving Newera Eliya to become a groom in Colombo, where he seems to have prospered exceedingly.

There were also inevitable casualties amongst the livestock, which could not be so readily replaced. The pure-bred cow was unable to stand the strain of being driven up to the settlement with the other cattle and died on the way. The Southdown ram died from a surfeit of fresh clover and the Leicester ram fought and killed the Cotswold ram. There was an epidemic amongst the cattle, and twenty-six bullocks died, as well as five good Australian horses, in the first year. But Sam refused to be downhearted by these setbacks. When Nature was not involved and he could control the issues he was not a man to allow matters to get out of hand. He wrote:

> I shortly experienced great trouble with the emigrants: they could not agree with the bailiff, and openly defied his authority. I was obliged to send two of them to gaol as an example to the others. This produced the desired effect and we shortly got regularly to work.

Towards the end of the first year Mrs. Fowler, the wife of the bailiff, a woman of very amiable disposition, died as the result of an illness of long standing. After this final sad event things began to improve steadily. Thanks largely to the Bakers' determination, the settlement began to prosper despite indifferent soil, lack of manure and the depredations of wild animals. Before the first year was out a church and a public reading room had been added to the settlement. Sufficient corn had been grown to merit building a brewery, and with the liberal use of guano a reasonable crop of vegetables was produced. Sam, John and Valentine found plenty of time to hunt; deer, duck, snipe, partridges, peacocks and peahens were useful additions to the larder. The flock of sheep also prospered, providing both wool and mutton.

Although at first, inevitably, the settlement proved a financial dead loss, with perseverance it began to thrive reasonably well. The livestock, despite depredations from leopards and other wild animals, steadily increased in numbers. Later, Sam was able to recall:

> The fields were green; the axe no longer sounded in the forests; a good house stood in the centre of cultivation; a road two miles in length cut through the estate; and the whole place looked like an adopted "home". All the trials and disappointments of the beginning passed away and the reality was a picture, which I had ideally contemplated years before . . .

Sam's daughter, Edith, and John's son, Julian, came out to the settlement with them. Then Henrietta bore two more daughters, Agnes and Constance, while John's wife, Elizabeth, had a son, Arthur, and a daughter Mary. While their husbands were away hunting, as they often were, Henrietta occupied herself with sketching the countryside and making furniture to her own design, with the help of a native carpenter, and Elizabeth painted finely detailed flower pictures on native pottery and plates.

Valentine, destined for a military career, joined the Ceylon Rifles, but found plenty of time to accompany his brothers on their frequent hunting expeditions. Sam and John spent most of their time when not at home away in the forests or plains with rifle or hounds in search of game. For the next seven years this was to be Sam's principal occupation and in the process he developed into a big game hunter and naturalist capable of spending days on end in the jungle without coming to any harm. The understanding of hunting and the ways of wildlife as well as the sheer ability to survive which he learned by trial and error in the jungles of Ceylon were to stand him in good stead throughout the rest of his life in many remote corners of the world. He also learned a simple basic background of doctoring skills, which were always to be useful to him. His hounds were frequently the worse for wear in their battles with deer, or wild boar at bay, and after the hunt his first task was stitching up their sometimes frightful wounds. Nor was he averse from dealing with the numerous complaints of those natives or others who came to him in the settlement, physicking them as he thought fit, although not always with the desired results.

A case in point was the Irish nanny who complained of toothache, whereupon Sam agreed to extract the tooth for her. He applied the pliers and with a quick twist of his powerful wrists whipped out the molar. "The Lord be praised!" exclaimed his patient. "Yer Honour did it iligant; but it's the wrang tooth."

Although he usually set off hunting on an empty stomach with his belt tightened two notches and continued throughout the day without eating, Sam was by no means a masochist. he liked to eat well whenever possible and learned to carry suitable condiments with him so that if benighted he could light a fire and cook himself a reasonable meal with steaks from a deer or similar quarry, and provide himself with a comfortable makeshift bed and encampment. It was not all hardship by any means, although the risks he ran were often hair-raising in the extreme. Sam soon learned that only a fool is uncomfortable when he has no need for it. He reckoned by this time to travel with every comfort and convenience and yet still enjoy good sport. After a strenuous day's hunting he liked, if possible, to be able to relax and discuss the day with his companions over a glas of port and a cigar.

The first essential to comfortable travel, he maintained, was a good waterproof tent, light enough to be carried by two bearers. His own was built like an umbrella, fifteen-feet in diameter, big enough to shelter three people comfortably. A circular table fitted in two halves round the tent-pole and there was ample room for three folding chairs, with the three beds arranged against the walls. All clothes and necessaries were stowed in boxes under the beds and he even included a dressing-table and a gun-rack.

The second essential item, in his view, was a good canteen, made of japanned block tin, containing complete dinner and breakfast services for three people. This he had transported on a bamboo pole slung between two coolies. It included "everything that can be required in an ordinary establishment". His clothes were packed in tin boxes to prevent them being eaten by white ants. The scale of his normal hunting retinue may be gauged from his comments on the other items to be taken with the party:

> Cooking utensils must be carried in abundance, together with a lantern, axe, bill-hook, tinder-box, matches, candles, oil, tea, coffee, sugar, biscuits, wine, brandy, sauces, etc., a few hams, some tins of preserved meats and soups, a few bottles of curacoa, a glass of which in the early dawn, after a cup of hot coffee and a biscuit, is a fine preparation for a day's work . . .

He also built a primitive hunting lodge in a sheltered corner of the Newera Eliya plains, which he dignified by the name of "Elk Lodge". In fact this was quite a substantial building since it had a verandah twenty-eight feet by eight in front and a dining room twenty feet by twelve with a fireplace eight-feet wide dominating it. There were also two bedrooms each twenty feet by eight. The floor was carpeted with deer hides pegged to the wood and the walls were covered with talipot leaves, the universal substitute for thatch in Ceylon. There were also stables for three horses, a kennels, a kitchen and a shed for twenty coolies and servants. He wrote of it:

> The fireplace was a rough piece of art, upon which we prided ourselves extremely. A party of eight persons could have sat before it with comfort. Many a roaring fire has blazed up that rude chimney; and dinner being over, the little round table before the hearth has steamed forth a fragrant attraction, when the nightly bowl of mulled port has taken its accustomed stand. I have spent many happy hours in this said spot, the evenings were of a decidedly social character. The day's hunting over, it was a delightful hour at about seven P.M.— dinner just concluded, the chairs brought forth before the fire, cigars and the said mulled port. Eight o'clock was the hour for bed and five in the morning to rise, at which time a cup of hot tea and a slice of toast and anchovy paste were always ready before the start . . .

It did not take Sam long to discover that the small pack of foxhounds he had specially selected from the Duke of Beaufort's pack and that of Lord Fitzhardinge, although excellent thoroughbred foxhounds, were completely hopeless in the jungle, where, of course, it was impossible to ride. They ran riot on every sort of vermin, from cats and genets to little mouse deer and there was no controlling them. Furthermore by giving tongue as soon as they came on a scent they warned their quarry of its danger long before they could hope to come up with it.

By degrees, through trial and error, Sam evolved his own pack which was perfect for hunting in the jungle and plain on the large Sambur deer, generally misnamed elk in Ceylon, or on wild boar. Some were pure-bred foxhound, some a cross between pointer and foxhound, foxhound and blood-hound, mastiff and blood-hound, also mastiff and blood-hound crossed with kangaroo-hound from Australia and English greyhound and kangaroo-hound. His aim was to produce three types of hound, namely a slow hunting hound able to find a cold scent and work it out tenaciously, which he called finders, then a faster hound able both to follow a scent at speed and bring the deer to bay, which he termed finders and seizers, and finally there were long-legged powerful hounds for coursing the quarry in view and seizing it. With these three types of mixed hound his pack was complete, working in concert with him. Without apparently being aware of the fact, what Sam was achieving was re-creating the old method of hunting in which the Norman Kings had delighted in the early Middle Ages. William Twici, huntsman to Edward III, wrote a book in Norman French in 1327 entitled *Le Art de Venerie*. In this he described exactly this method of hunting deer "Par Force", as it was termed.

By his various hound crosses Sam in effect was breeding back to the same types of hounds used by the Normans for their sport in the forests of early England, which in many ways must then have much resembled those in Ceylon. There can be little doubt, however, that Sam's form of hunting was a good deal more dangerous; far from being accompanied by numerous followers, he was at most accompanied by one other companion, generally his brother John, and his only weapon was his trusty hunting knife. Furthermore it was probably a great deal more strenuous for he frequently had to follow his hounds up and down steep mountainsides on foot without being able to use horses. Indeed he was seldom able to ride more than short areas on the plain. Once the stag took to the hills he had to follow on foot, willy nilly.

The Sambur's habits were to feed at night in the plain, then, after gorging throughout the night, to drink its fill at a stream before withdrawing by dawn to the depths of the forest, generally lying up high on the mountainside. The method of hunting therefore was to visit a secluded plain and set the hounds on to a stream. The foxhounds crossed with blood-hound or pointer would then take the lead and soon would strike a scent and give tongue. As soon as this happened the other hounds, which had been held in couples, would be released and would run off mute at speed, following the scent hard and fast. On the mountainside the stag, already lying up with a paunch full of green food and a gallon or so of water inside him, would hear the sound of the slow old hounds on the scent. Listening to them about half a mile away he would think himself safe enough, unaware of the mute hounds fast approaching him. Then suddenly they would burst into view and he would be forced to head up the hill as fast as could move, and since the hounds were travelling on empty bellies and he on a full one it usually happened that he was forced to turn downhill to make his best pace.

Listening to the voices of his hounds Sam, like a good huntsman of the Elizabethan school, subsequently copied by the coonhunters of Kentucky, able to distinguish each hound in a pack by sound alone, could tell roughly how the hunt was faring. Guessing as to the direction the deer was taking he would run as fast as possible that way with two fresh seizers, or greyhounds. If he was lucky the sound of crashing twigs and branches would herald the approach of the hunted stag in full view. Then the straining greyhounds would be released, and moving at full speed they would soon catch up with the stag, as yet unaware of these fresh hounds close upon him. Sam would give a loud view halloo and the other hounds would then head eagerly for him, knowing they could now abandon the scent. Meanwhile the greyhounds would have seized the stag and soon the pack would be round him baying him in a fast running stream.

This was the moment for Sam to move in himself, encouraging his hounds with a cry and joining in the fray. As soon as the seizers had fastened on an ear and distracted the quarry he would step in with his faithful hunting knife. Generally it only required one good thrust with his blade in behind the shoulder and the hunt was over, the deer falling dead amidst a tangle of hounds. For a minute or so Sam would allow the general rush on the body to continue to encourage the hounds, but then they were whipped off and sat in a circle expectantly waiting. He would then gralloch the stag, removing the paunch and viscera to one side along with the heart and lungs. The liver was cut into small pieces and fed to the young hounds, each being called by name to receive his portion. When he was ready the halloo was given for a worry and the entire pack fell on the spoil like wolves.

Should any hounds have been wounded by the stag at bay Sam would do his best to provide suitable first aid on the spot. Bran, his favourite greyhound, being thin-skinned, was especially liable to rips and tears and eventually Sam described him as being virtually a patchwork of stitches. Then came the long trek back to the camp or hunting lodge, sometimes burdened with the head of the quarry, or a choice haunch of venison. Only too often there was the sad business of attending to a dying hound, which had been over-eager in the fray. All in all it was testing work for hound and huntsman.

The Count of Foix and Bearn in the Pyrenees, Gaston III, who lived in the fourteenth century and was perhaps the greatest huntsman of his day, thought that facing a charging boar was the finest form of hunting. At the same time he was under no illusions about the dangers involved, indicating that he had often seen a boar "slit a man from knee up to the breast and slay him all stark dead at one stroke so that he never spoke thereafter". Sam and his brother John frequently found themselves faced with a boar which their hounds had brought to bay. On one occasion they killed a boar between them which weighed over four hundredweight. On another occasion Sam killed a boar weighing two and a half hundredweight,—"a middling-sized boar"—with a single downward cut of his hunting knife, which severed its spine. In these mêlées both hound and huntsman were at risk. While carrying on this particularly strenuous form of hunting Sam and his brother adopted their own highly individual, but extremely practical, garb. He described it thus:

> This woven dress consisted of tights, similar to ordinary elastic drawers, with a short jacket of the same material that fitted like a jersey. These were dyed green. A pair of rather high ankle boots, which laced in the usual manner, the soles not more than a quarter of an inch thick, with about a dozen large nails in each, and the same around the heel. A rather broad leather belt. with a very large and strong buckle, and my hunting knife, completed the outfit. A small helmet-cap protected the head.

Inevitably Sam became immensely fond of many of his hounds and recalled in particular "Smut", whose sire was a Manilla Blood-hound, and whose temperament was ferocious. Seamed with scars all over his body, he was the hero of at least four hundred deaths of elk and boar. Another excellent dog he owned was an Australian greyhound of great courage appropriately named Killbuck. Yet another Australian greyhound, wire-haired like a Scottish deerhound, was named Lena, also courageous and powerful. Mated with Bran, his own favourite greyhound brought out from England with his family, she produced a notable dog named Lucifer, who combined his parents' courage, speed and beauty. There were many more, but, as Sam noted, they had to combine superlative courage with discretion if they were to survive.

Quoting from his game book during four months of 1852, from March to June, Sam noted that he and his hounds killed twenty-eight elk, or Sambur deer, eleven bucks and seventeen does, in addition to four hogs, two boars and two sows. Since his pack only hunted three times a week in the dry season and on every fine day in the wet months throughout the year, this was a very fine show of game. It also gives some idea of how fit Sam himself must have been. He himself wrote from experience:

> No person can thoroughly enjoy elk-hunting who is not well-accustomed to it, as it is a sport conducted entirely on foot and the thinness of the air in this elevated region is very trying to the lungs in hard exercise. Thoroughly sound in wind and limb, with no superfluous flesh, must be the man who would follow the hounds in this wild country—through jungles, rivers, plains and deep ravines, sometimes from sunrise to sunset without tasting food since the previous evening, with the exception of a cup of coffee and a piece of toast before starting. It is trying work, but it is a noble sport; no weapon but the hunting knife; no certainty as to the character of the game that may be found; it may either be an elk, or a boar, or a leopard, and yet the knife and the good hounds are all that can be trusted in . . .

With the rifle both Sam and his brother John were deadly shots. They thought little of running amidst a herd of elephants and killing as many as ten at one time. At this date the Ceylon government was paying a bounty for every elephant killed as they were causing considerable damage to crops and habitation. Inevitably in such work both brothers had many narrow escapes and on more than one occasion each saved the other's life by killing a charging elephant with a single shot when to have missed would have meant that the other was trampled to death.

All in all this was an excellent training for the rigorous years he was to spend in Africa and elsewhere. His body was toughened by the regular physical exercise he took. His senses were quickened by constant contact with nature, studying wildlife of all kinds. He learned also to deal with natives, although in general he considered the Cingalese a useless and indifferent decadent race. Amongst the few who accompanied him hunting for whom he had any regard was a half-caste named Wallace. He tended to take both men and animals as he found them, and he found the Cingalese sadly lacking in courage.

Describing his surroundings and his activities with his usual vivid pen, he wrote:

> Here, then, I am in my private sanctum, my rifles all arranged in their respective stands above the chimney piece, the stags' horns round the walls hung with horn-cases, powder flasks, and the various weapons of the chase. Even as I write the hounds are yelling in the kennel. The thermometer is 62°F and it is midday. It never exceeds 72° in the hottest weather, and sometimes falls below freezing point at

night. The sky is spotless and the air calm. The fragrance of the mignonettes and a hundred flowers that recall England fills the air. Green fields of grass and clover, neatly fenced, surround a comfortable house and grounds. Well-fed cattle of the choicest breeds, and English sheep are grazing in the paddocks. Well made roads and gravel walks run through the estate. But a few years past and this was all wilderness . . . The monkeys and parrots are even now chattering among the branches, and occasionally the elephant in his nightly wanderings trespasses upon the fields unconscious of the oasis within his territory . . . The still starlight night is awakened by the harsh bark of the elk; the lofty mountains, grey with the silvery moonlight, echo back the sound; and the wakeful hounds answer the well known cry by a prolonged and savage yell. This is Newera Eliya, the sanatorium of Ceylon, the most perfect climate of the world . . .

The adjacent country, of comparatively flat table land, occupies an extent of some thirty miles of length, varying in altitude from 6,200 to 7,000 feet forming a base for the highest peaks in Ceylon, which rise to nearly 9,000 feet. Alternate large plains, separated by belts of forest, rapid rivers, water-falls, precipices and panoramic views of boundless extent, form the features of this country, which combined with the sports of the place, renders a residence at Newera Eliya a life of health, luxury and independence

Independent and healthy, from his viewpoint, it certainly was, but luxury must always be a matter of taste. Thinned down to pure muscle and sinew, fit and powerful as the animals he hunted, Samuel was able to stand up to days on end of gruelling exercise and to injuries which would have disabled lesser men for months. On more than one occasion he was very close to being killed. His description of one such incident gave full play to his narrative powers. His party had already bagged nine elephants and, as he wrote:

I had one barrel still loaded, and I was pushing my way through the tangled grass towards the spot where the dead elephants lay together, when I suddenly heard Wallace shriek out, "Look out, sir! Look out!— an elephant's coming!"

I turned round in a moment; and close past Wallace from the very spot where the last dead elephant lay, came the very essence and incarnation of a "rogue" elephant in full charge. His trunk was thrown high in the air, his ears were cocked, his tail stood erect above his back as a poker, and, screaming exactly like the whistle of a railway engine, he rushed upon me through the high grass with a velocity that was perfeclty wonderful. His eyes flashed as he came on and he had singled me out as his victim.

I have often been in dangerous positions, but I never felt so totally devoid of hope as I did in this instance. The tangled grass rendered retreat impossible. I had only one barrel loaded, and that was useless, as the upraised trunk protected his forehead. I felt myself doomed; the few thoughts that rush through men's minds in such hopeless positions flew through mine, and I resolved to wait for him until he was close upon me before I fired, hoping that he might lower his trunk and expose his forehead.

He rushed along at the pace of a horse in full speed; in a few moments as the grass flew to right and left before him, he was close upon me, but still his trunk was raised and I would not fire. One second more and at this headlong pace he was within three feet of me; down slashed his trunk with the rapidity of a whip thong, and with a shrill scream of fury he was upon me.

I fired at that instant; but in the twinkling of an eye I was flying through the air like a ball from a bat. At the moment of firing I had jumped to the left, but he struck me with his tusk in full charge upon my right thigh and hurled me eight or ten paces from him. That very moment he stopped and turning round, he beat the grass about with his trunk, and commenced a strict search for me. I heard him advancing close to the spot where I lay still as death, knowing that my last chance lay in concealment. I heard the grass rustling close to me; closer and closer he approached, and he at length beat the grass with his trunk several times exactly above me. I held my breath momentarily expecting to find his ponderous foot upon me. Although I had not felt the sensation of fear while I stood opposed to him, I felt like what I never wish to feel again while he was deliberately hunting me up. Fortunately I had reserved my fire until the rifle almost touched him, for the powder and smoke had nearly blinded him and had spoiled his acute power of scent. To my joy I heard the rustling of the grass grow fainter; again I heard it at a still greater distance; at length it was gone!

At that time I thought that half my bones were broken, as I was numbed from head to foot by the force of the blow. His charge can only be compared to a blow from a railway engine going at twenty miles an hour.

Not expecting to be able to move, I crept to my hands and knees. To my delight there were no bones broken and with a feeling of thankfulness I stood erect. I with difficulty reached a stream of water near the spot, where I bathed my leg, but in a few minutes it swelled to the size of man's waist.

Despite this he was back hunting the herd two days later and killed four more, two with a right and left from his double rifle. In five days he bagged thirty-one elephants and his largest score for a single day was fourteen. Nevertheless he regarded elephants as the supreme quarry and accorded them rather than the lion the title of "King of Beasts". He wrote:

The king of beasts is generally acknowledged to be the lion but no one who has seen a wild elephant can doubt for a moment that the title belongs to him in his own right. Lord of all created animals in

> might and sagacity, the elephant roams through this native forests. He
> browses upon the lofty branches, upturns young trees from sheer
> malice and from plain to forest he stalks majestically at break of day
> "monarch of all he surveys" . . .

At this time the hinterland of Ceylon was overrun with elephants
and, despite the rewards offered by the government, until Baker's
arrival there had been little serious attempt to bring their numbers
under control. During his years there he killed several hundred and
began to bring them under a measure of control. In the manner of all
hunters who have a real understanding of their quarry, he came to be
more fond of elephants than almost any other beast. In later life he
could truthfully write:

> There is no one who more admires or is so foolishly fond of
> elephants. I have killed some hundreds in my early life, but I have
> learned to regret the past and nothing would now induce me to shoot
> an elephant unless it were either a notorious malefactor, or in self-
> defence.

The method of catching elephants on a large scale by driving them
into a "keddah", or large bamboo stockade in the jungle with a long
gradually tapering entrance had not been introduced to Ceylon from
India at this time. Occasionally youngsters were caught by using tame
elephants to distract them and lassooing their hind legs, then binding
them to the nearest tree. Sam was involved in this highly dangerous
method of catching wild elephants on at least one occasion. On the
whole, however, when he first went to Ceylon there were simply so
many elephants that their numbers militated against catching them
and it was merely a matter of controlling the herds by culling as
many as possible. Even so, Sam noted with foreboding:

> Every year increases the number of guns in the possession of the
> natives, and accordingly diminishes the number of animals. From the
> change which has come over many parts of the country within my
> experience of the last eight years, I am of the opinion that the next ten
> years will see the deer-shooting in Ceylon completely spoiled and the
> elephants very much reduced. There are now very few herds of
> elephants in Ceylon that have not been shot at by either Europeans or
> natives, and it is a common occurrence to kill elephants with
> numerous marks of old bullet wounds . . . at the report of a gun every
> herd within hearing starts off for the densest jungle.
>
> A native can now obtain a gun for thirty shillings; and with two
> shillings'-worth of ammunition, he starts on a hunting trip. Five
> elephants at a reward of seven shillings per tail, more than pay the
> prime cost of his gun; to say nothing of the deer and the other game
> that he has bagged in the interim.
>
> . . . there is no rest for the animals; in the daytime they are tracked

up, and on moonlight nights the drinking places are watched and an unremitting warfare is carried on. This is sweeping both deer and buffalo from the country and must eventually annihilate them . . .

The Moormen, he noted, were the best hunters among the natives. They killed buffaloes, pigs and deer indiscriminately and dried the flesh, smoking it over fires of green wood. Since many castes of native would not eat buffalo meat and others would not eat pork, all their meat was then sold as venison and found a ready market.

Within a decade or so of Sam writing in this vein, Game Laws perforce had to be introduced in Ceylon, since the elephants and other animals were diminishing so rapidly. How much Sam and his friends were responsible for this is another matter. In November 1851, for instance, he chronicled a three-week-long hunting expedition consisting of himself, his brother Valentine on a fort-night's leave from the Ceylon Rifles, the Hon E. Stuart Wortley (afterwards Lord Wharncliffe and a lifelong friend of Sam's) and another friend Edward Palliser. They shot fifty elephants, five deer and two buffaloes. Wortley killed two deer and ten elephants, Valentine, who left early had only two elephants, but Edward Palliser shot sixteen elephants and two buffaloes. Sam recounting the expedition, modestly left the reader to calculate that he himself shot three deer and twenty-two elephants, by far the largest share of the bag. This was a particularly luxurious trip as they took two tents and used his own simply as a dining tent. Sam wrote:

> There was nothing wanting in our supplies. We had sherry, madeira, brandy and curacoa, biscuits, tea, sugar, coffee, hams, tongues, sauces, pickles, mustard, sardines en huile, tins of soups and preserved meats and vegetables, currant jelly for venison, macaroni, vermicelli, flour and a variety of other things that add to the comfort of the jungle including last, but by no means least, a double supply of soap and candles. No one knows the misery should either of these fail, dirt and darkness is the necessary consequence.

It all sounded a perfect Paradise for the hunter, but Sam was honest enough to mention the drawbacks as well as the advantages of the country. He recorded:

> Ceylon is, at all times, a frightful place for vermin; in the dry weather we have ticks: (These little wretches, which are not larger than a grain of gunpowder, find their way to every part of the body, and the irritation of their bites is indescribable. Scratching is only adding fuel to fire; there is no certain prevention or relief from their attacks; the best thing I know is cocoa-nut oil rubbed daily over the whole body, but the remedy is almost as unpleasant as the bite.); in the wet weather mosquitoes, and, what are still more disgusting, "leeches", which swarm in the grass and upon the leaves of the jungle. These creatures

insinuate themselves through all the openings in a person's dress—up
the trousers, under the waistcoat, down the neck, up the wrists and in
fact everywhere, drawing blood with insatiable voracity and leaving an
unpleasant irritation for some days after.

All these annoyances form great drawbacks to the enjoyment of the
low-country sports . . . When the day is over and the man, fatigued by
intense heat and a hard day's work, feels himself refreshed by a bath
and a change of clothes, the incurable itching of a thousand tick bites
destroys all his pleasure; he finds himself streaming with blood from
leech-bites, and for the time feels disgusted with the country. First rate
sport can alone compensate for all these annoyances.

Inevitably there came the day when even his iron frame and
constitution gave way. In 1854, after a particularly strenuous hunting
expedition in an unhealthy part of the island, which had resulted in
the death of his favourite horse Jack and of one of his coolies, Sam
contracted a severe fever and nearly died. When he had recovered,
the families held a council and decided that the time had perhaps
come to return to England. Not only were their children in need of
schooling, but they themselves had been abroad for nearly a decade
and there were numerous pressing family matters at home needing
their attention.

Sam, himself, climbed to the top of Pedrotallagalla, the highest
mountain in Ceylon, some 8,280 feet high, and looked down from
there on his settlement at Newera Eliya. He decided that he was
satisfied with his work. He wrote:

How wonderful the alteration made by man on the face of Nature!
Comparatively but a few years ago, Newera Eliya was undiscovered,—
a secluded plain among the mountain tops tenanted by the elk and
bear . . . How changed! The road encircles the plain and carts are busy
in removing the produce of the land. Here, where wild forests stood,
are gardens teeming with English flowers; rosy faced children and
ruddy countrymen are about the cottage doors; equestrians of both
sexes are galloping round the plains; and the cry of the hounds is
ringing on the mountainside! And the church bell sounds where the
elephant trumpeted of yore . . .

Feeling that he had achieved what he had set out to do and accepting that it was time that he returned to England to take over the
responsibility for his family affairs, Sam left the estate at Newera Eliya
in the charge of his brother John, ably assisted by their bailiff. He and
his family sailed again for England. The first apprentice hunting
interlude in Sam's life was over. He had enjoyed himself, apparently
haphazardly, for some eight years and in the process, unwittingly, had
prepared himself well for the more serious years to come.

$$4$$

After Ceylon

Not all Sam Baker's time in Ceylon was spent hunting, or in organising the settlement at Newera Eliya. He also developed his latent talent for writing and in 1852 sent Longman in London the manuscript of his first book *The Rifle and Hound in Ceylon*. This contained vivid accounts of numerous hunting expeditions from Newera Eliya and other parts of Ceylon. It also had plenty of advice for the would-be sportsman, written with humour and good sense. Longman accepted it with alacrity and published it the following year, with drawings by a professional artist based on Sam's own sketches and descriptions, for in those days before the general introduction of the camera almost everyone was taught how to draw in reasonable perspective as a matter of course. The book proved an instant success, for his racy style and his exciting accounts of his remarkable hunting feats were very much to the taste of the average armchair British sportsman. The book was re-printed no less than six times, the last in 1892.

Before they left Ceylon, early in 1855, he was already, at Longman's urgent request, nearing the end of a somewhat similar account of life at Newera Eliya entitled *Eight Years Wanderings in Ceylon*. This was a slightly more mature book containing further excellent accounts of hunts in which he had been engaged and also an entertaining record of the founding of the settlement at Newera Eliya. He included some interesting details on Ceylon's economic background and prospects, as well as on the natural history of the island. Throughout the book he made various uninhibited comments both on the government of Ceylon and the standards set, or not set, by the various governors, together with his own ideas and suggestions for improvements. This book was even more successful than the previous one and went into seven editions by 1894.

It is doubtful if either of his books had much real impact on the government of Ceylon. Although between them they went into thirteen editions over forty-one years, they were neither of them the sort of book which any government would be prepared to recognise officially. Since his suggestions for improved government were in the main very sensible, however, the majority of them came to be accepted in due course, much to his and his family's satisfaction.

When they first returned to England, Sam was still not fully recovered and Henrietta was heavily pregnant once again. In the meantime Samuel Senior had remarried after being left a widower in 1851, while his eldest sons were still away in Ceylon. He was now living at Thorngrove in Worcestershire with his second wife. In the circumstances it was perhaps natural that Sam and Henrietta moved in this direction, settling down at Fladbury in Worcestershire, where his youngest daughter, Ethel, was born. It was there that he finished his second book.

Although Sam himself soon recovered his usual robust health, Henrietta, having been delivered of seven children in their twelve years of marriage, was no longer strong enough to stand the strain of childbirth. It was soon clear that the birth, combined with abrupt change of climate, had had a thoroughly adverse affect on her health. As is clear in the letters she wrote to her sister still at Newera Eliya, she was also missing her greatly, as well as finding the damp English climate very trying. It was decided to move the entire family—Sam, Henrietta, accompanied by her younger sister Charlotte Martin, and their four daughters—to Bagnerers-de-Bigorre in the Pyrenees, where the climate was considered suitable for the invalid. Here incidentally, Sam also hoped to shoot a bear, only to find on his arrival that the local *Maire* had already shot the sole bear in the area a few days earlier. The nearest he approached to it was eating some of the resulting stew, which he declared "excellent".

Then abruptly came tragedy, when Henrietta, already in a weakened state of health and in no condition to withstand a serious illness, contracted typhus. For a fortnight, during which she was mostly in a coma, he never left her bedside. On the 29th of December she died and Sam was left desolate. With four motherless daughters, one still a babe in the care of its nurse, he remained completely grief-stricken and utterly unable for once to cope with the situation in which he found himself.

Fortunately for him and for the children, Charlotte Martin, Henrietta's younger sister, although only twenty-two, assumed command of matters in the calm manner of those indomitable Victorian English women who survived sieges, famines, wars and natural disasters all round the world with unconquerable common sense. She took charge of the sorrowing widower and his four children and brought them back to England. Once returned to the bosom of the Baker family there were plenty of loving aunts and resourceful uncles to care for the children and provide help and comfort for Sam, although it was to be many months before he was to return to anything like his old self.

Before long, however, he decided that he must go abroad again. The Crimean War was still continuing fitfully, and his brothers Valentine and James were serving in the 12th Lancers and 8th Hussars respectively. Having arranged for the care of his daughters, Sam went off to join them, hoping to see some action before the war was over, but as it was he arrived in Shuktari only a few days before the Peace concluded. He had evidently contemplated joining the Turkish contingent but changed his mind fairly promptly after his arrival, describing them as "a sort of refuge for the destitute". He then thought he might "make a tour through Circassia, and judge of the facilities for a Russian attack upon India", which he felt might be useful in view of the seemingly high probability of war with Russia breaking out again.

Instead he made a short expedition with his brother Valentine and a friend to Sabanja on the edge of the Sea of Marmora. Here he found a considerable variety of sport available—at that time anything might be encountered from bear, boar, wolves, red deer or roe, to partridges, duck and other wildfowl. It was perhaps the varied hunting, or maybe just the wildness of the area, where few Europeans ever penetrated, that attracted him, but he was to return there in happier circumstances only four years later. On this occasion it was not long before he returned to London.

Here he was re-united with John and his family, who had by this time also returned to England. John had found a home near Rugby where he enjoyed the splendid foxhunting available in the Shires. Being a first-class horseman, he excelled at the sport. No such ready anodyne was available for Sam since boar and deer hunting on foot armed only with a knife had vanished with the Normans. He was now thirty-five and reasonably wealthy, but utterly unsettled; so much so that for a while he contemplated entering the Church, writing to a friend:

> . . . as you justly observed, in your last letter, afflictions serve to wean us from the world and draw us to more sacred things. No one has felt this more keenly than myself; but you may nevertheless be astonished by my future intentions—*to enter the Church*, if the difficulty of age can be got over, which I think will be no great obstacle . . .

Second thoughts, or sound advice, or obstacles other than age, must have combined to thwart this impulse, but for the moment he remained without any real object or interest. The Indian Mutiny, in which he might ordinarily have been expected to take some active part, brought little more reaction than pained interest at a distance. His customary enthusiasm and drive seemed to have deserted him and his family bemoaned the fact that he no longer appeared to be going to fulfil the earlier promise of a useful life.

It was, however, around this time, following the news of the imminent departure of Richard Burton and John Speke, a young Captain with whom he had become friendly on the voyage home, for a second expedition into the interior of Africa, that his attention first turned towards the exploration of the sources of the Nile. In 1857 when a further expedition was planned to explore the Zambezie, led by Dr. David Livingstone and sponsored by the Government, Sam used his friend Lord Wharncliffe's political influence to try to join it. This approach was referred through 'the usual channels' to Livingstone via the Royal Geographical Society and was firmly rebuffed. Sam promptly proposed to the Royal Geographical Society and Livingstone himself that he formed his own expedition financed by himself and 'auxiliary' to Livingstone's expedition. Almost predictably the Foreign Office vetoed this idea on the grounds that the Portuguese in Mozambique might object. Sam then withdrew gloomily.

During 1857 and 1858 he spent much of the Autumn and Winter months stalking deer, shooting game and fishing in Scotland, keeping himself fit, but accomplishing nothing in the rather aimless fashion of many wealthy young men of the time. It may be that unconsciously he felt that in the country house parties in the Highlands he might encounter another suitable mate to fill the gap in his life. He was a man who needed a wife and without Henrietta much of his old drive and enthusiasm for life were missing.

This is not to say that he did not enjoy himself on occasions. One of his exploits while in a large house party as a guest of the Duke of Athol at Blair Castle makes that clear. It was the custom there to release deer hounds to bay any wounded stag, which was then shot with a rifle. A discussion arose as to whether these hounds, if encouraged to do so, would seize and hold a stag as Sam had described his hounds doing in Ceylon. In a minority of one, Sam stoutly held they would do so. It is easy to picture the various members of the house party mischievously baiting the author of *The Rifle and Hound in Ceylon*. Eventually a trial was agreed on:

> The arguments had interested the ladies of the party, and it was arranged that I might select any two of the deer-hounds and hunt down a fresh stag, run it to bay, and kill it with a knife. To myself the affair appeared exceedingly simple . . . but others disbelieved that the

> two hounds would bring a fresh deer to bay, as they had always been
> accustomed to follow animals that were wounded . . . By the advice of
> the head forester, Sandy MacCarra, I chose my old friend Oscar and
> another hound . . . We were a large party . . . The afternoon was
> perfect . . . the presence of many ladies brought us luck . . . we were
> suddenly delighted by the almost magical appearance of a stag . . .
> about 1,000 yards distant. It was . . . decided . . . I should walk on until
> . . . out of the deer's sight . . .

With the two gillies and the deer-hounds he climbed the hill to a
position above the stag, where they could see the carriages and
spectators waiting beneath them on the road. They managed to get
within a hundred yards of the stag before it sprang up. Then they
slipped the deer-hounds and an exciting chase ensued.

> This must have been a lovely sight from the carriages . . . For a few
> seconds the stag took up the hill, but the hounds ran cunning and cut
> him off; he now took a straight course along the face towards the
> direction where the carriages were waiting below. The hounds were
> going madly and gaining on him . . . and away we went as hard as we
> could go . . . towards . . . the carriages. As we drew near we could see
> the hunt. The deer . . . now turned down the hill towards the river
> with the two dogs within yards of his heels . . . and after running about
> a quarter of a mile down the road we heard the bay and shortly
> arrived at the spot where the stag was standing in the middle of a
> rapid and the hounds were baying from the bank . . . Patting both the
> excited hounds upon the back, and giving them a loud haloo, I jumped
> into the water, which was hardly more than hip deep, but the stream
> was very rapid. The stag, upon seeing my advance ran down the bed
> of the river and halted again after a short run of 50 or 60 yards. The
> two keepers had followed me and Oscar and his companion no longer
> thought of baying from the bank, but carried forward by the torrent,
> together with ourselves were met by the stag with lowered antlers. I
> never saw dogs behave better, although for a moment one was beneath
> the water; Oscar was hanging to the ear. I caught hold of the horn to
> assist the dog and at the same moment the other dog was holding by
> the throat. The knife had made its thrust and the two gillies were
> holding fast by the horns to prevent the torrent carrying away the
> dying animal. This had been a pretty course which did not last long,
> but it was properly managed and in my opinion ten times better sport
> than shooting deer at bay.

Predictably, the head keeper, Sandy MacCarra, did not agree with
Sam's estimate of the day. With the outspokenness of the old
Highland retainer he did not hesitate to make his views plain on the
matter: "Weel, you've just ruined the dogs for ever, and there'll be
nae haudin' them frae the deer noo. They'll just spoil the flesh and
tear the deer to pieces." Reporting this remark, Sam was forced to

comment in all fairness: "This was the keeper's idea of what I thought was good sport. Certainly the venison did not belong to me, neither did the dogs."

There can be little doubt that he found the sport available in Britain more than a little tame after his years in Ceylon. The time soon came when he could not resist the temptation to go abroad once more. This decision, although taken lightly enough, was to bring about the most momentous change in his life.

As some people are naturally accident-prone, so he was adventure-prone. He was the true *Boys' Own* hero and G.A. Henty did well to use him as his story-book prototype. He would "go for a stroll", one of his own favourite phrases covering anything up to a twenty-mile journey through virgin jungle, and inevitably he would find himself involved in some sort of happening not normally experienced by lesser mortals. The anachronism was that, although he was un-doubtedly the epitome of the Victorian story-book hero, he was by no means a typical Victorian Englishman. He was much more an Englishman of the Georgian period than of the Victorian age in which he lived. To begin with he was educated in the Georgian manner at a grammar school and with a private tutor, rather than at one of the new public schools in the Arnold mould. Thus team games had no attraction for him whatsoever. He was also always an individualist and something of an eccentric, never afraid to be different, in the true Georgian manner, not a conformist in the approved Victorian style. Furthermore the bulk of his life was spent outside England, although of course this was true of a great many during the nineteenth century when the British Empire was still in the making. Yet, characteristically, when he did serve in an official capacity abroad it was not in the service of Britain. It is certainly easy to believe that one of the reasons he spent so much time abroad was that he found himself cramped and confined by the English way of life in the Victorian era.

His companion during this particular journey abroad was himself unusual, none other than the Maharajah Duleep Singh. During 1858, while shooting in Scotland, Sam had made the acquaintance of this wealthy young exile from the Punjab, whom the British government in India had seen fit to send to England with a pension of over £50,000 a year to prevent the danger of any popular rising in his favour. As the locally famed "Black Prince" of Elveden in Suffolk, where he held court and shot extensively each year, he was later to become an intimate of the Prince of Wales. In 1876 he established the dubious record of killing 789 partridges with 1,000 shots in a single day and later in the same season killed 2,350 partridges in nine days. At this time he was still only some twenty years old and a keen sportsman, no doubt flattered to have the company of a big game shot of Sam's reputation.

According to letters in the possession of the Baker family they originally planned a hunting trip in Hungary from November 1858 to March 1859 in the great plains where there was available a tremendous variety of game from partridges and great bustards to wild boar, bear and wildfowl in profusion. Once in Budapest they decided to make a voyage down the Danube, despite much advice as to the dangers involved. Although steamers were no longer operating in the winter months, this presented little obstacle to men of their considerable wealth. As Sam wrote to his brother John:

> We hired a covered boat, 60 or 70 feet long and fitted her comfortably at Pesth, and with a crew to row we descended the Danube, everyone prophesying all kinds of miseries and dangers. It was of course cold, but we had three good stoves on board, lots of wood and champagne, two casks of splendid beer and wine on deck, three English servants of the Maharajah, fowls, turkeys, guns, etc., therefore we were always jolly . . .

Whether the ample supplies of beer and wine proved too much for the oarsmen or the navigator, or whether it was simply that in the end the weather conditions proved their undoing, their boat was eventually holed by ice near the small fortress town of Widdin, on the lower Danube, around a hundred miles from the Hungarian frontier. While their boat was being repaired, Sam and the Maharajah were forced to make the best of what hospitality and entertainment this remote Turkish town could provide. They began by paying a visit to the Pasha, whom Sam reported as being "very civil".

The area was full of Hungarian refugees from the Austro-Hungarian uprisings. The revolutions of 1848, which convulsed Europe, led chiefly by the new emergent middle-class intelligentsia against the excesses of the old decayed aristocracy, were in the main successful. Throughout central Europe the numerous tiny principalities and dukedoms which proliferated were amalgamated into larger autonomous states. Modern Europe was in the making, but like so many social convulsions it was not all accomplished either painlessly or at once. There was an immediate enormous upsurge of homeless European emigrants to the New World in the West, the land of promise across the Atlantic, which continued for more than ten years before noticeably diminishing. Many thousands of refugees, especially those in eastern Europe, were forced to turn to the east rather than the west for refuge. Some fled to Russia and some to Turkey, already at odds with each other and neither of them greatly interested in refugees of dubious origins.

In the case of the old Austro-Hungarian Empire of Metternich the tottering process of dissolution lasted a decade or more, with numerous uprisings, revolts and counter-measures, bloody and unpleasant on both sides. Whole villages were put to the sword, men were shot in front of their wives and families, women and children had their roofs burned over their heads. Frequently whole families, both peasants and aristocrats, were slaughtered by opposing factions. Atrocities of this nature were commonplace. It was a time when the young grew up quickly and learned to survive in a world temporarily insane, where normal values had ceased to exist.

Amongst the human flotsam swept up by the tide of revolution was Florence Finnian Von Sass, who was to become Sam's second wife. Left with no family and no home, although, according to family legend, sheltered at first by a faithful nurse, she had survived amongst many other Hungarian refugees under the nominal protection of the Turkish government. By the time she met Sam she had no doubt already lived a lifetime of a kind undreamed of by delicately nurtured English girls of her own age.

This young Hungarian girl, then aged only seventeen, some twenty years his junior, speaking at that time only German in common with him, seemed an unlikely match for the bearded English widower of thirty-six. Even to the end of her days her English was spoken with a strong German accent and they often conversed together in German. Yet theirs was undoubtedly a love match which survived tests far beyond those normally expected of a marriage in more ordinary circumstances. Within the Baker family the occasion of her first meeting with Sam and details of her upbringing and background were seldom discussed during her lifetime. It was generally accepted that her family had died in tragic circumstances and that she wished to forget the past and make a new life with her husband and his family. The Bakers, once they had met her, ever ready to support their own, rallied round her willingly, accepting her at once for Sam's sake, although soon coming to appreciate her for her own undoubted worth.

In practice she proved the perfect wife for Sam. She was good-looking, handsome rather than pretty, with good bones and fine eyes under a broad brow. She was intelligent, her humour matched Sam's own, and she had dignity, courage and strength of character far beyond the average. Sam had found in her exactly the woman he required to support him in his venturesome life.

Inevitably outside the family there was much lurid and romantic speculation as to her origins. It was said that she had been part of a Pasha's harem and had been presented to Sam as a reward for services rendered. It was also rumoured that she was a natural daughter of Franz Joseph, the Austrian Emperor, and had been brought up by a noble family on the Hungarian border, where Sam met her while on a hunting trip and swept her off her feet. According to Robin Baily, a nephew of Sam's who served in the Sudan, his aunt Beatrice became Florence's *confidante* in her later years. From this source we learn that Florence's earliest memories were of yells, fire, shots and blood. Her version of her meeting with Sam is, on the face of it, quite as improbable as any of the other unsubstantiated fictions, but due allowance must be made for Sam's undoubted ability to achieve the improbable. Even so, in this instance, he may be said to have excelled himself, for it would appear that he bought her in the local slave market.

It seems that Sam and the young Maharajah, with little else to do while stranded in Widdin, paid a visit to the local slave market. There Sam saw this beautiful young Hungarian girl, who, on the death or marriage of her erstwhile nurse had fallen into unscrupulous hands. She was about to be put up for sale. He was unable to take his eyes off her and when the bidding started he outbid the wealthiest Turkish merchants present, including, it would appear, an emissary of the Pasha. Since the Pasha could readily have prevented them leaving with their prize it was necessary for Sam and the Maharajah to put as much distance between themselves and the Turkish authorities as possible, without further delay. This would explain why they immediately abandoned their boat and the proposed hunting expedition and, with twenty-four fast horses and three carriages, galloped over the border across the plains of Wallachia to Bucharest. Willy-nilly the Maharajah, playing an unaccustomed and no doubt protesting role as Cupid, accompanied him thus far, but here they finally parted company. The Maharajah left for the fleshpots of Rome, doubtless marvelling at the impetuosity of the English, while Sam and Florence for the moment at least remained in Hungary.

It was probably only when he had time to stop and think about matters deeply that Sam began to appreciate the highly dubious position into which his precipitate actions had landed him. Whether he intended to marry her from the moment he first laid eyes on her, as he later claimed, or whether he was merely infatuated with her beauty, his position was a difficult one. He could hardly, in either case, take her back to England with him. As he subsequently pointed out, Florence was a Roman Catholic. He was a Protestant. Any form of marriage he might go through in Hungary or Turkey was unlikely to be recognised in England. She was unable to speak English and was only a few years older than his own eldest daughter. To take her back to England in those circumstances, before she could even speak the language, seemed unthinkable and unfair both to her and to his family. Clearly he could hardly return and explain that he intended to marry a girl young enough to be his daughter, whom he had bought in a slave market. Whether they considered themselves bound in marriage by a mutual exchange of vows, as he later explained to his close friend Lord Wharncliffe, hardly affected the issue. This was one of the occasions when the truth simply would not suffice.

He had to have a breathing space and fortunately for him a suitable if slightly improbable, reason for prolonging his stay abroad appeared to hand almost at once. An English company had been formed to build a railway across the Dubrushka from Cernavoda on the Danube to Kustanje on the Black Sea, a distance of some forty miles, saving an immense detour round the south of the Danube. One of the directors of this typically Victorian enterprise was none other than William Price MP, who was not only brother-in-law to Sam's stepmother, but had been shooting with him in Perthshire the previous year. On learning that a Managing Director was required to supervise proceedings on the spot Sam wrote to Price and through his influence obtained the post.

Well aware of the family criticism of his lack of occupation since Henrietta's death, he wrote a carefully phrased letter to his eldest daughter from Bucharest on March 11th, which was clearly intended for general consumption:

> I had a great struggle with myself as to whether I should accept my present appointment; for, of course, it will detain me for some time out here and away from you all. But I felt sure that, though away, you would not forget me; and as man was not made to be idle, I thought it advisable to undertake the present work . . .

To his friend Lord Wharncliffe he wrote from Kustanje on the 30th March:

> When I left England, I fully expected to have returned in the Spring .
> . but I have now accepted the post as General-Manager of the Company . . . I shall be obliged to remain here for two years, after which I shall return to England . . .

With his old enthusiasm fully aroused once more he threw himself into the task he had taken on and in April wrote to his sister Min, who was looking after his daughters:

> We are progressing rapidly; the earth works of the railway are advancing daily: the necessary buildings have been commenced; and 1,200 workmen are hard at it . . . My staff will soon be organised. My office is being built as fast as possible; and I am daily expecting the arrival of book-keepers and clerks. Imagine my being anxious for the

completion of the Office! I hear you say, "Saul also among the Prophets!" or, in modern phraseology, "Sam among the clerks". So it is nevertheless. I mean to make this a model concern if I can, and have all the arrangements in perfect order.

Nor was it all work by any means. He had his silver sent out from home to furnish the somewhat bleak "Director's House" he had built for Florence and himself at Constanza. Naturally he also had his guns and dogs and found time to shoot wildfowl in the marshes and to fish. The immense skeins of wild geese and duck on the Danube marshes and exotic fish such as the Zander, the giant pike-perch of the Danube waters, must have provided him with excellent sport when he could spare the time away from the railway. Wherever he might be and however fully occupied, he could always find time to sample the sport available locally.

But his sporting activities did not meet with the approval of his four principal assistants, the somewhat strait-laced sons of a Norfolk parson named Barkley. Jack the eldest, aged thirty, was a self-taught engineer, accustomed to working in Turkey, who had brought his brothers, George, Robert and Henry, on to the company payroll. Nor was it only his sporting activities of which they disapproved. In May 1859 Henry Barkley wrote home to the effect that his brother Jack was "not fond of having much to do with *the Bakers*". From this it may be inferred that Sam had introduced Florence as his wife, but having regard to her youth and inability to speak English the brothers imagined the worst and were combining to cold-shoulder this intruder with his influence at boardroom level, whom they clearly saw as a threat.

While at Constanza at the Black Sea end of the railway, a small ship was wrecked off-shore in a severe storm in December 1859. Seeing a survivor floating helplessly on a spar, Sam entered the water, in spite of the high seas and icy conditions, and hauled him ashore to safety. Florence was amongst the spectators, but it hardly needed a deed such as this to convince her of Sam's heroic qualities. She must already have begun to appreciate, however, that he simply could not avoid situations of this kind. It is indicative of their hostility that although the Barkley brothers were also spectators of the ship-wreck they made no mention of Sam's gallant action either in their letters or in subsequent memoirs.

From the middle of May 1859 the British papers had been filled with John Speke's claims to have discovered the source of the Nile during his expedition with Burton. The two men had quarrelled violently during their exploration and Speke had no real grounds for claiming that the lake he had discovered and named Lake Victoria was indeed the source of the Nile. Furthermore although he had returned before Burton he had agreed to say nothing of their discoveries until they were together again. In the event he seems to have felt entirely justified in publicising his claims because of his deep conviction that he was right. When Burton arrived with a scientific report on Lake Tanganyika, it was largely ignored. In a very short time Speke was backed to the tune of £2,500 with the Royal Geographical Society's blessing for another expedition on which his chosen companion was not Burton, but Captain James Grant. In due course, however, Burton was to exact full vengeance.

The news gleaned from the newspapers was enough to turn Sam's thoughts eagerly to Africa once more. By early 1860 the railway was showing signs of being finished well ahead of schedule, whether owing to Sam's energy and drive or the Barkley brothers' expertise, or a combination of both. Although still acting as high-level negotiator for the company, Sam was increasingly passing the administration to Jack Barkley. In May Sam left for London for month's visit.

He was too late to have a word with Speke, who had already left, but he made a point of seeing others who might be helpful. Amongst these was William Cotton Oswell, the famous African elephant hunter, who gave him a gun to add to his already large armoury. Another was John Petherick, the consul at Khartoum, who was about to get married. Sam had already obviously made up his mind as to his future actions.

Without waiting for the official opening of the railway, Sam virtually gave up his job in June and moved inland. He did not attend the lavish opening ceremony in October which was presided over by his relative by marriage, the MP William Price. In November, however, he was writing to the Royal Geographical Society President, Sir Roderick Murchison, announcing his intention of visiting the little-known region of the Sudan beyond Khartoum and asking for advice. He was advised to explore the eastern tributaries of the Nile on the borders of Abyssinia and he gave the impression that it was his intention to investigate this area—known to be excellent elephant country.

He next engaged rooms in the Armenian quarter of the town of Sabanja. These were beyond the Turkish and Greek quarters and lay at the foot of the densely afforested mountains. The rooms were extremely primitive, being above a cow byre which was visible and audible through the cracks in the floor. These also proved no barrier to the smell. They arrived in December of 1860 and their room was warmed only with a charcoal brazier.

With the first fall of snow almost immediately after their arrival, the brazier and the warmth of the cow byre beneath them were no doubt both welcome. More to the point, from Sam's viewpoint, the woods close to their house were filled with woodcock. he wrote of their quarters:

> This was a sporting residence on the margin of the forest that extended for an unknown distance. I could leave the house and expect a shot at woodcocks within 150 yards from the door. Wolves and jackals were howling close to our windows during the night and wild hogs actually broke the fences and invaded the gardens with an impudence that proved the difficulty of procuring their usual food. The game of the forest included bears (these had hibernated), wolves, boars, red-deer, roe deer, pheasants, woodcocks; while snipe and ducks were found along the borders of the lake.

He clearly enjoyed enormously this varied hunting and noted particularly how well the Greeks and Armenians mixed with each other and with the Turks. The favourite day for a mass hunt was Friday, the Mohammedan sabbath. The Turkish governor of the town invariably enquired on Thursday evening when Sam wanted to shoot the next day and on his appearance at around 9 o'clock he would find all classes of the various races ready and waiting to join him, all apparently in excellent humour.

With some fifty guns of various nationalities posted throughout the forest one would have expected any number of accidents, but as he very sensibly pointed out, the people in most parts of the world know best how to order their own sport without advice from strangers. Apparently this method worked well enough, for he noted that there had never been any report of an accident. The beaters were mainly Turks and the game was driven to the waiting guns. If the Turks killed a boar they gave the meat to the Christians, whereas if the Greeks or Armenians killed a deer this was presented to the Turks. Thus, he noted, the utmost harmony prevailed.

Vegetables were plentiful and cheap and the boars were fat and good eating. Their favourite dish soon became wild boar stewed with leeks, onions and cauliflowers. By way of variety he recorded that this was occasionally changed to "leeks, onions and cauliflowers, stewed with wild boar".

He recorded with interest how the Greek professional woodcock hunters, who supplied the market in Constantinople from the plentiful supply of birds to be found in the wild rose thickets four or five miles from Izmir, used pointers with bells round their necks. When the hunter heard the bell cease to tinkle he knew the dog was on point and searched for it accordingly. The woodcock when shot

were then transported to Constantinople on the daily steamer from
Izmir. He could not help suggesting that a pair of clumber spaniels
working within twenty feet of the handler would have done a better
job, but he obviously enjoyed the sport just the same, for he always
liked any sort of hunting with dogs. He wrote of one typical occasion:

> I had hired a Turkish sportsman, who possessed a little nondescript
> dog with only a stump of two inches to represent a tail. We were
> passing through a thick rose jungle, when we suddenly missed the cur;
> a minute later, we heard vigorous barking within 150 yards of our
> position. Upon arrival at the spot, there was a very large wild boar
> standing at bay, with the little dog before it in a frantic state of
> excitement, but far too sensible to risk a close approach. I had been
> expecting woodcocks, but knowing the uncertainty of the forest, I
> fortunately had a bullet in the left-hand barrel; a shot through the
> shoulder dropped the boar upon the spot, to the intense delight of the
> little dog, which immediately seized it by the snout and endeavoured
> to shake the body twenty times heavier than itself. This was a low-born
> cur, but a jolly little dog, that must, upon the principle of heredity,
> have had some unknown, but heroic ancestor.

It is easy to imagine Sam and Florence laughing together at this
little dog's behaviour, for, although it is nowhere specifically stated, it
is probable that, unlike most English women of the day, she
accompanied him on all his sporting expeditions during those weeks
in Sabanja. There can have been little to keep her in their poky little
rooms above the cow byre with only the charcoal brazier for warmth.
She was never far from his side in later years and it may be assumed
that, especially in their first year together, they were seldom apart.
Acting as gun-bearer, game-carrier, or spare dog-handler, it seems
likely that she enjoyed the sport as much as he did. Unconventional
their behaviour may have been but it obviously gave both of them a
chance to appreciate their extraordinary good fortune in finding each
other.

Florence was one of those rare women who can share a man's
enthusiasms to the full, and Sam was every inch an enthusiast in
whatever he undertook. Full-blooded male that he undoubtedly was,
he still required the solace and backing that only a woman could
provide and without it he was lost. He needed a woman also to
discuss with him his ambitions, hopes, progress and future plans.
Fortunately for him, in Florence he found someone who appreciated
him to the full, who knew when to speak and when to remain silent,
or when to laugh and share a joke; in short someone who could and
did share his every mood.

The expedition to Sabanja may well have been rather more than just a somewhat eccentric sporting holiday. It could have been Sam's way of finding out whether Florence was capable of accompanying him on the explorations he planned. It could, of course, be argued that, besotted with his young mistress, however acquired, Sam merely chose at this stage to head for the interior of Africa as the one place he was unlikely to encounter any criticism, rather than return to England as he had originally planned and desert her. This is to suggest that his expedition was based on little more than a desire to continue an ephemeral amour, whereas he had certainly been considering some such plan for several years. It is also to do him less than justice as a man. Writing in December 1860 he stated firmly to his brother:

> I intend to be in Alexandria in the first week of March, I am going to Khartoum, and from thence, God only knows where, in search of the sources of the Nile. I shall very likely meet Speke, who is working up that way from Zanzibar . . . You know that Africa has always been in my head.

Despite the instructions from the Royal Geographical Society it is plain Sam planned from the outset to meet Speke if possible, but although he confided these plans to his family he was, quite understandably, reticent about making them public. He behaved outwardly as if he had little more in mind than a shooting expedition into the interior, starting from Khartoum and progressing up the Nile. Thus he wrote to his friend and fellow sportsman, Lord Wharncliffe, who had hunted with him Ceylon:

> I cannot tell you with what pleasure I am looking forward to this journey (up the Nile). It will be new ground; and the diversity of animals, with the chance of discovering a new species, will be a source of additional interest.

Baker was, of course, among those great Victorian naturalist explorers, whose interests lay in classifying birds and beasts and noting their way of life and habitat, as well as in exploring new ground and mapping it for future generations. To do so they were prepared to accept extraordinary hardships and face the dangers of hostile tribes and wild animals with unshakeable determination. Their curiosity about the unknown and unexplored was sufficient to drive them on indefatigably.

Neither his family nor his friends were told that he intended to take Florence with him on his exploration. This was a point he kept entirely to himself. Later he was to say that he had tried to get her to return to England to make herself known to his family, but, of course, for her the perils of Africa were no greater than those of the unknown family in England. Scarcely surprisingly, she insisted on accompanying him.

Fortunately for him he was a man of sufficient wealth to be able to turn his enthusiasms into something at least satisfyingly close to his desires. If he felt like exploring the Nile he could afford to equip an expedition to do so. The execution might depend on his determination to carry through his intentions to the bitter end, every bit as much as his ability to foot the bills, but Sam was never short of either money or of determination.

Although, like so many enthusiasts, he liked to make directly for his objective, in this case he had learned from experience. He saw that it would be impossible to progress far into the desert amongst the Arab tribes unless he was in a position to speak the language. The first necessity therefore, as he saw it, was to learn to speak Arabic fluently. Whereas he might have stayed in Cairo and learned to speak with perfect grammar he decided instead to journey into the interior while doing so, thus, at the same time, gaining experience of travel in Africa and the Sudan. His first journey was intended as nothing more than a trial expedition in order to learn what was required and to prepare him for the real thing.

Whether it took place at Sabanja, or during that first year they spent acclimatising themselves to African exploration, it is possible that Florence may have had a miscarriage at some point. There is a reference to such an event in the only piece of fiction Sam ever wrote; his book for boys entitled *Cast up by the Sea* written in 1869 after their safe return from their African explorations. The book is clearly based on events that happened to him in real life and this could be the explanation for their failure to have children.

In any event Sam and Florence were to find that first year in Abyssinia and the Sudan a good preparation for their later expedition to the source of the Nile. At the time they were entirely unaware of what lay before them. They set off from Cairo heading for the unknown. Sam was exceptional even amongst his fellow explorers in many ways, but not least in that he was accompanied throughout all his expeditions by Florence, who shared with him all his hardships and dangers. They made a formidable combination.

5

Into Africa

The first fifty years of the 19th century had seen the domination of the old decaying Ottoman, or Turkish, Empire in Egypt replaced by the independent rule of Mehemet Ali, founder of a dynasty which was to have a profound effect on the country. Hailed by the French as 'the pioneer of European civilisation' the fact remained that under his dynasty Egypt was still ruled in very much the same manner as before with the slave trade from Africa one of the principal sources of income and bribery and graft commonplace at all levels of government. Both the French and the British, vying with each other, kept a close watch on Egyptian affairs, not least since peace in Egypt ensured safe transit of goods overland from Europe to India. In 1856 Said Pasha, Mehemet Ali's favourite son, who had by then succeeded him was persuaded by French influence to grant de Lesseps a concession for construction of the Suez Canal. Lord Palmerston jealous of any apparent undermining of British influence almost inevitably in the circumstances opposed the project and delayed the start for two years.

Throughout the 19th century British influence was considerable throughout the world and the British Empire was still being extended round the globe. This was perhaps one of the basic reasons for British interest in exploration, backed by a natural human curiosity and a desire to fill in the empty spaces on the map of the world, preferably in the colour red to denote a British possession. So far the exploration of the sources of the Nile from the African end had produced somewhat disappointing results. Burton and Speke's expedition had ended in Speke's unsubstantiated statements as to what exactly had been discovered being generally accepted despite Burton's disagreement. Now the Royal Geographical Society was basing its hopes on Speke and Grant's new expedition, which they were backing. No-one at this stage, including those few who had some inkling of his intentions would have considered that Sam had any chance of exploring this still unknown area from the opposite direction without any backing. Had they been aware that he intended travelling with Florence as his sole companion, even his closest friends would have regarded the venture as totally insane. In the circumstances it is understandable that Sam kept his plans very much to himself.

True to the timetable he had set, Sam and Florence began their epic travels in 1861. It was later to become his custom to write books describing his various expeditions based on the journals he kept at the time. On this occasion, with that supreme self-confidence which characterised his actions, whether standing up with his rifle to face the charge of a maddened rogue elephant, or dressing down a hostile native chieftain in front of his massed warriors, he began thus:

> In March 1861, I commenced an expedition to discover the sources of the Nile, with the hope of meeting the East African expedition of Captains Speke and Grant, that had been sent by the English Government from the South via Zanzibar, for that object. I had not the presumption to publish my intention as the sources of the Nile had hitherto defied all explorers, but I had inwardly determined to accomplish this difficult task or die in the attempt.

His first year, however, was spent in thorough preparation for the hardships and dangers which were to come. Sam Baker was always an interesting mixture of the practical man and the enthusiast with the practical side generally predominant. For his first expedition he started with little beyond his confidence in himself, which was ultimately to carry him to success. He wrote with an element of truth:

> My impedimenta were not numerous. I had a *firman* from the Viceroy, a cook and a dragoman. The *firman* was an order to all Egyptian officials for assistance; the cook was dirty and incapable and the interpreter was nearly ignorant of English, although a professed polyglot. With this small beginning, Africa was before me, and I thus began the search for Nile sources.

Armed with the Viceroy's passport he and Florence set off from Cairo by boat to Korosko. There he bought sixteen camels and set off across the Nubian desert. At the half-way stage, at Murat, where they found only a well of bitter water, Florence was ill. Despite this, the full two-hundred-and-thirty-mile journey to Abu Hamed only took ninety-two hours' actual marching time and their camels averaged twenty-five miles a day. On the final stage to Berber they were again held up by Florence falling ill, but they promptly made up for it the next day, as he noted in his journal:

> May 27. Marched four hours and forty-five minutes, when we were obliged to halt, as F is very ill. In the evening I shot two gazelles, which kept the party in meat.

> May 28. Marched fifteen hours to make up for the delay of yesterday
> Shot a buck on the route . . .

Despite the delays caused by Florence's illnesses they had made very good time. They reached Berber, the final stage after Abu Hamed, in a further fifty-seven hours. This was decidedly good going for inexperienced desert travellers and can only have been achieved at the cost of considerable personal discomfort, which Florence accepted uncomplainingly.

It is a noticeable feature throughout his diaries, written during his travels, that he never mentioned Florence by name, merely, occasionally, noting some comment or action by "F" using only the initial. This apparently strange omission becomes particularly marked when the diaries themselves are compared with his published accounts of his journeys, where mention of Florence, as his wife, is frequent. The explanation for this seemingly strange divergence between the journals written at the time and the books published after the event is comparatively simple. While writing his journals, Sam was, of course, by no means sure that he was going to survive what by any standards was an extremely hazardous expedition. It is more than probable that in their initial "exchange of vows" taken soon after their strange meeting, Florence with typical Hungarian passion had sworn that should he die she would immediately kill herself rather than live without him. Thus, had his journals been recovered after his death, he had no wish for mention of a female companion, at that time still undisclosed even to his nearest relatives, to be found in them and cause embarrassment to his family.

Sam was seldom anything but consistent. Well aware how his position must appear to the Victorian concept of morality, he took good care to stay as far away as it was possible to be from any likely critics, until he was in a position to present Florence as the perfect wife for an adventurous Englishman. At the same time she also had to learn to speak English and comport herself as a Victorian lady with a ready-made family of four daughters, the eldest of whom was not far short of her own age. No doubt in the somewhat carefree existence they led it was often simpler to converse together in German, or later in Arabic, rather than for Sam to insist continually on her speaking in English with him.

During that first year Sam's diaries often read more like game books' than a record of exploration. It is also clear that Sam often behaved more like a young carefree lover than a responsible Victorian explorer of the unknown already approaching middle age. A large part of this, of course, was due to the fact that they did not encounter a great deal in the way of difficulties during their first year.

Sam wrote early on in his travels that "At present there is no more danger is travelling in upper Egypt than in crossing Hyde Park after dark, provided the traveller be just and courteous."

After the rigours of crossing the Nubian desert, however, both he and Florence were happy to rest for a week in Berber, where they were hospitably received by the venerable ex-governor, Halleem Effendi, and where Sam noted particularly that ". . . innumerable ring-doves were cooing in the shady palms; and the sudden change from the dead sterility of the desert to the scene of verdure and life, produced an extraordinary effect upon the spirits . . ." When, over a ceremonial coffee, Sam divulged his plans to search for the sources of the Nile, both Halleem Effendi and the Governor did their best to dissuade him from what they termed this "mad scheme". Needless to say Sam was not to be swayed by any such advice once his mind was made up, although he appreciated their good intentions. He was impressed by the point they made that he could not hope to succeed until he could dispense with an interpreter. He therefore determined to learn Arabic as quickly as possible.

The interpreter, Mahomet, accustomed merely to guiding parties of tourists from Cairo as far as the second cataracts, was in any event already proving to be more of a liability than an asset. A tiresome, vain and often impudent braggart, Mahomet frequently and loudly bemoaned his fate at joining their expedition. Sam was in turns amused and infuriated by him, occasionally being reduced to punching his head for some exceptional outburst.

Sam was never averse to taking physical action when he was sure it was necessary. He noted at one point with obvious experience:

> I cannot agree with some writers in believing that personal strength is unnecessary to a traveller. In these savage countries it adds materially to the success of an expedition, provided that it be combined with kindness of manner, justice and unflinching determination. Nothing impresses savages so forcibly as the *power* to punish and reward. I am not sure that this theory is applicable to savages exclusively . . .

Sam and Florence seem to have made a favourable impression with the authorities in Berber, despite his refusal to accept their well meant advice. The production of the Viceroy's *firman* may also have helped, for they were given every assistance during their short stay. Their heavy baggage was sent on by water to Khartoum and they bought three donkeys and the necessary baggage camels to carry their packs. By the end of the week they were ready to continue their journey with the addition of a couple of Turkish soldiers to their party, provided both as escorts and servants.

Following the course of the Nile they reached the Atbara river without difficulty about the middle of June, after a further week's travel. At this time of year the river was dry, except for occasional deep pools varying in size from a hundred yards to a mile or so in length. These pools, Sam noted, were full of life, with "huge fish, crocodiles of immense size, turtles and occasionally hippopotami . . . in close and unwished-for proximity . . ." Inevitably it was not long before Sam shot his first hippopotamus. An Arab had been seized and killed by one while working in his vegetable patch on the edge of a pool and Sam determined to avenge him. He came upon six the next morning and shot one without much difficulty. To his surprise he discovered that it made excellent soup. He noted that the local villagers were soon making short work of the carcase and he found that however much he might shoot there were always natives pleased to have the opportunity of taking any surplus to his requirements.

On the night of the 23rd of June, without any prior warning beyond a sound like distant thunder, the Atbara suddenly changed from a dry river bed to a rolling flood and their party was very nearly taken by surprise, some them only just reaching safety on the riverbank in time with Sam's trophies of the chase, the skulls of two hippopotami. Another he had shot that day was washed away. In the morning they saw "a magnificent stream, some 500 yards in width and from fifteen to twenty feet in depth", yet there was still no sign of rain anywhere in the sky. On that morning of the 24th of June Sam felt he had gained a clue as to the mystery of the Nile sources and that his work had really begun at last. He noted excitedly that "The rains were pouring in Abyssinia! *These were the sources of the Nile!*"

Continuing on their way to Cassala, some 340 miles from Berber on the edge of Abyssinia, Sam was impressed by the beauty of the wild asses he saw, so different from the common domesticated variety. After a lengthy stalk he shot a fine stallion and immediately regretted it, resolving never to shoot another. The meat, served as "rissoles", tasted like extremely tough beef.

The expedition fed daily on whatever Sam shot for them and he generally succeeded in shooting sufficient pigeons, guineafowl, hares or antelopes, or larger game to keep them well-fed. No meat was ever wasted, however much he shot, for there were always nearby villagers, or itinerant natives, who were glad of the food. If there was too much to eat at one time it was dried in the sun, or smoked over a fire, to be eaten later. The skins of antelopes were removed whole, to become useful water containers, and the fat of all animals was purified for cooking, eating, soap or candles.

Sam noted with distaste the Arab habit of eating raw the lungs, liver and kidneys of any beast they were skinning. They also had the habit of breaking the bones between rocks and sucking out the raw marrow. This he soon appreciated contributed to the prevalence of intestinal worms amongst so many of the tribes, which he encountered when acting in his role as doctor of the expedition. In his medical chest, apart from all the usual remedies, he kept a plentiful supply of "Holloway's pills", a noted purgative which he doled out in doses from one to ten at a time, depending on the effect required. On occasions he also administered a powerful mixture of tartar emetic, for he soon found out that the natives were only suitably impressed by a dose of medicine if it had an obvious and immediate effect on them, more especially if he had warned them in advance of what to expect. With a creditable record of success, he also set numerous broken limbs and treated severe wounds caused by animals, spears and bullets.

Sam was always quite amazingly adaptable and self-sufficient. When Mahomet the interpreter clumsily broke the stock of one of his rifles, he promptly mended it so that it was as good as new. He recorded with justifiable pride in his workmanship:

> The wood had broken short off in the neck of the stock. I therefore bored a hole about three inches deep up the centre of either piece, so that it was hollowed out like a marrow-bone; in one of them I inserted a piece of an iron ramrod, red-hot. I then drew the other piece over the iron in a similar manner, and gently tapped the shoulder-plate until I had driven the broken joint firmly together. I then took off from a couple of old boxes two strong brass hasps; these I let nearly into the wood on each side of the broken stock, and secured them by screws, filing off all projections so that they fitted exactly. I finished the work by stretching a piece of well-soaked crocodile's skin over the joint, which, when drawn tight, I sewed strongly together. When this dried it became as hard as horn, and very much stronger; the extreme contraction held the work together like a vice, and my rifle was perfectly restored . . .

Step by step his clothing underwent a gradual change, starting with the re-soling of a pair of Scottish brogues with leather cut from an old guncase. As he had done in Ceylon, he evolved eventually by the end of the year, through trial and error, what he considered the perfect garb for hunting in this countryside. This he described with palpable exaggeration as "an admirable dress for this, or any country". While it might have been convenient for the wilds of Abyssinia it would doubtless have caused some comment in the coverts of East Anglia. It consisted of:

> A pair of black gaiters (i.e. gaiters made like stockings to draw on at

once, and these reach the knee) made of gazelle skin tanned *with the hair on* (which throws the thorns on one side). These *tie over* a pair of short trousers made of the strong cotton cloth woven by the natives, which no thorn can tear, and the trousers fasten around the waist with a drawing string *under my shirt.* My shirt is made of the same stuff (sleeves not quite to the elbow) and I wear it outside my trousers with my belt and pouches round my waist—it has a turn down collar and no buttons, but the front ties with strings. I dyed the whole suit a rich brown with the mimosa fruit, and it matched well with the faded herbage and tree stumps. I wear mocassins which I made from the giraffe's hide, tanned. These are much better than European shoes, and having no heels they make no noise in walking over loose stones with which the country is covered—and they laugh at thorns although very light. My costume sounds rough, but it is *particularly neat* and becoming. My hunting cap is of woven dome leaf covered in gazelle skin."

In addition Sam wore a "gazelle shank-bone" suspended from his neck, through which he drank water from scum-covered rivers and pools. Although he claimed the credit for the invention of these garments, which bear a certain resemblance to those he had worn in Ceylon, there can be no doubt that Florence at least cut out and sewed them for him, if not taking an active part in their design. She, herself, wore a similar shirt and trousers made from the strong native cotton when riding. Dressed in these she was frequently mistaken for Sam's son rather than his wife by the natives they encountered in their travels.

When the expedition ran out of soap, however, Florence must surely have played her part in producing a successful substitute. Although Sam with his quite amazing versatility provided the wherewithal and the means to make it, it was almost certainly Florence whose suggestions helped him to produce this addition to their domestic ease. Sixty parts of potash to forty parts of lime were the quantities required and neither was available, although fat there was in plenty. By burning trees rich in potash and making a ley with the ashes, Sam concentrated the potash by boiling the mixture. He then turned a white ant nest into a kiln by slicing off the top of one of these cone-shaped anthills, scooping out the interior and making a draught hole in the base. This he filled up with wood and then piled about six bushels of oyster shells on top of the resultant blaze. Keeping this burning for twenty-four hours he produced a quantity of excellent lime. Finally, in a large Egyptian copper pot holding about ten gallons, he then mixed the ley of potash and the necessary amount of lime, adding finally the requisite fat. After ten hours boiling and constant stirring to prevent the concoction overflowing the pot, the mixture turned to soap. The net result was about forty pounds of "excellent" soap, which Sam formed into balls and cakes with his hands. As Sam wrote, this was soap "of a very sporting description"—"Savon à la bête féroce".

As they approached Cassala, Florence had a recurrence of her fever, but this yielded to a dose of quinine and a few day's rest in the house of a Greek merchant, who invited them to stay with him. By the 14th of July Sam was ready to leave having acquired several further camp followers. They now moved southwards towards Sofi, where Sam had heard of a German who knew the country and might be able to help him. The rainy season had now started and many of the Arab tribes were moving. They had already in their travels encountered the Bedouins, the Bishareens, Hadendowas and Hallongas and they next met the Shookeriyahs. Sheik Achmet Abou Sinn of the Shookeriyahs greatly impressed Sam, who wrote of him:

> He was the most magnificent specimen of an Arab that I have ever seen. Although upwards of eighty years of age he was as erect as a lance, and did not appear more than between fifty and sixty; he was of Herculean stature, about six feet three inches high, with immense broad shoulders and chest; a remarkably arched nose; eyes like an eagle, beneath large, shaggy, but perfectly white eyebrows; a snow-white beard of great thickness descended below the middle of his breast. He wore a large white turban, and a white cashmere abbai, or a long robe, from the throat to the ankles. As a desert patriarch he was superb, the very perfection of all that the imagination could paint if we would personify Abraham at the head of his people. This grand old Arab with the greatest politeness insisted upon our immediately accompanying him to his camp, as he could not allow us to remain in his country as strangers . . .

Sheik Abou Sinn went on to warn them that travel in the south during the rainy season now upon them became virtually impossible since the country became little more than a sea of mud. He very hospitably pressed them to stay with his tribe for the next four months, accompanying them back the way they had come, until travelling was once more feasible. He also made the offer of some good elephant hunting at which his tribesmen were noted. Despite this considerable temptation, Sam insisted that they must continue on their way to Sofi, following the Atbara, and the Sheik reluctantly gave way. He sent them off, mounted on the finest snow-white *hygeens*, or riding camels, with an escort under the command of one of his grandsons to see them safely the seventy-eight miles to Sofi.

In Sofi the Bakers met Florian, German mason, and also his friend Schmidt, a carpenter, who had left Germany with the Austrian mission for Khartoum. Finding their trades too laborious in the hot climate they had settled for a less arduous, if more hazardous, life as big-game hunters. Unfortunately Florian, in particular, was a bad shot and both were very poorly equipped with guns, although Sam was impressed by the sportsmanlike attitude they showed. During the previous season Florian had killed fifty-three hippopotami in the region of the Settite river and thus was able to give the Bakers much valuable information about the country.

With the onset of daily storm of considerable severity towards the end of July, Sam decided to set up a more permanent camp. For the princely sum of two shillings he purchased a "neat dwelling with a sound roof", of which he wrote:

> In the short space of about three hours, I found myself the proprietor of an eligible freehold residence, situated upon an eminence in park-like ground, commanding extensive and romantic views of the beautifully wooded valley of the Atbara, within a minute's walk of the neighbouring village of Sofi; perfect immunity from all poor rates, tithes, taxes and other public burdens; and not more than 2,000 miles from a church; with the advantages of a post-town at the easy distance of 70 leagues. The manor comprised the right of shooting throughout the parishes of Abyssinia and Sudan, plentifully stocked with elephants, lions, rhinoceros, giraffes, buffaloes, hippopotami, leopards and a great variety of antelopes; while the right of fishing extended through the Atbara and neighbouring rivers, which were well stocked with fish ranging from five to five hundred and fifty pounds, and also with turtles and crocodiles.
>
> The mansion comprised entrance-hall, dining room, drawing-room, lady's boudoir, library, breakfast-room, bedroom and dressing-room (with the great advantage of their combination in one circular room fourteen feet in diameter). The architecture was of an ancient style, from the original design of a pill-box surmounted by a candle-extinguisher.
>
> . . . in our arrangements there were many charms and indescribable little comforts that could only be effected by a lady's hand. Not only were our walks covered with snow-white sand and the borders ornamented with beautiful agates we had collected in the neighbourhood but the interior of our house was the perfection of neatness; the floor covered with white sand beaten firmly together to the depth of about six inches; the surface was swept and replaced with fresh material daily; the travelling bedsteads with their bright green mosquito curtains, stood on either side, affording a clear space in the centre of the circle, while exactly opposite the door stood the gun rack with as goodly an array of weapons as the heart of a sportsman could desire:—
>
> My little Fletcher double rifle No. 24

One double rifle No 10 by Tatham
Two double rifles No 10 by Reilly
One double rifle No 10 by Beattie (one of my old Ceylon tools)
One double gun No 10 by Beattie
One double gun No 10 by Purdey, belonging to Mr Oswell of South
African celebrity.
One single rifle No 8 by Manton
One single rifle No 14 by Beattie
One single rifle that carried a half-pound explosive shell by Holland
of Bond Street; this was nicknamed by the Arabs "Jenna el
Mootfah" (child of a cannon) and for the sake of brevity I called it
the "Baby"

My revolver and a brace of double-barrelled pistols hung upon the
wall, which, although the exterior of the house was straw, we had lined
with the bright coloured canvas of the tent. Suspended by loops were
little ornamental baskets worked by the Arabs, that contained a host of
useful articles, such as needles, thread, etc., and the remaining surface
was hung with hunting knives, fishing lines and a variety of
instruments belonging to the chase. A travelling table with maps and a
few books stood against the wall, and one more article completed our
furniture—an exceedingly neat toilet table, the base of which was a flat
topped portmanteau, concealed by a cunning device of chintz and
muslin; this covered with the usual arrangment of brushes, mirror,
scent bottles, etc., threw an air of civilisation over the establishment,
which was increased by the presence of an immense sponging bath,
that, being flat and circular, could be fitted underneath a bed.

Despite Florence's attempts to introduce a degree of domesticity
into their camp, it was difficult to find any servants who could
provide even a remote approach to civilised service. They had hired
an Arab boy named Bacheet in Cassala, but, though a keen gun-
bearer and brave enough, except when first faced with an elephant,
he was extremely indifferent at serving at table. In any event, despite
the fact that they expected to be held up by the rainy season for five
months, they did not stay at Sofi much more than six weeks.

Early in September Sam became exasperated at seeing game on the
other side of the Atbara, which he could not shoot. By dint of
constructing a makeshift raft he succeeded in crossing the river,
propelled by several of the hippopotamus-hunting Arabs who had no
fear of the crocodiles, and had a successful hunting expedition, killing
his first giraffes. On the 15th of September, encouraged by this
success, he had his entire party transported across the river, one at a
time, in his large sponge bath lashed to inflated skins and propelled
by the same means. He then set up camp afresh in a commanding
position named Ehetilla, on the far side of the Atbara in full view of
Sofi.

Although now in Abyssinian territory there was no-one in the vicinity and they regarded themselves as completely independent. Their party consisted of an old slave woman named Mesara, or Sarah, whom Sam had hired from the Sheik of Sofi, two arab boys and Mahomet, the dragoman. they had agreed with the Sheik that when meat was available to spare they would hoist the Union Jack and his people could come and fetch it for themselves by swimming the river and braving the crocodiles.

Apart from shooting game and exploring the nearby Settite river, Sam also fished the Atbara with spectacular results on occasions. To provide himself with live bait when required he filled a natural hole in the rock of the river bank with suitable small fish. On several occasions he caught giant Nile Perch, known as "El Baggar", weighing between sixty and eighty pounds, despite the fact that he was using only a bamboo pole with a brass ring from a gamebag at the tip as a makeshift rod. On October 4th he caught a 40lb baggar and followed this with one of 80lbs, ending the day with another fish of 20 lbs. He promptly hoisted the Union Jack and sent the largest fish across to Sofi as a present to the German Florian and his people.

At the end of October, Sam decided to move his camp some nine miles or so south-east to Wat el Negur, a village of Jalyn Arabs under a Sheik Achmet with whom he quickly became friendly. This Sheik paid tribute to the Egyptian authorities as well as to the Jalyn chieftain Mek Nimmur, known as the Leopard King, who was constantly waging a guerrilla war against the Egyptians. Being a friend of King Theodorus of Abyssinia, Mek Nimmur was always able to retreat into the mountains whenever a full-scale attack was mounted against him. Sam felt, rightly, that this was a good base from which to establish friendly relations with everyone.

At this stage Sam's intention was to examine all the main Abyssinian rivers which were tributaries of the Nile. These were the Settite, Royan, Angaab, Salaam, Rahad, Dinder and the Blue Nile. He had also intended to cross the Blue Nile in order to reach the White Nile, but in practice found that this would have interfered with his intended journey up the White Nile and dropped this plan. In November with this larger design in mind, Sam enlarged his party. He bought a powerfully built slave girl of about twenty-two, named Barrake, for £7. As was the custom her hair was heavily smeared with castor oil. Through Mahomet he did his best to explain to her that she was no longer a slave, but freed. She misinterpreted this as meaning she was to become his wife and without warning Sam found himself embraced and overwhelmed with castor-oily kisses, until finally the true situation was explained to her.

He also engaged six "Tokrooris, natives of Darfur", a tribe of Mohammedan negroes, with their camels, as a counterbalance to the predomianantly Arabic party of which his expedition consisted at that time. He noted that the Tokrooris were generally both powerful and courageous. Once he had instilled a sense of *esprit de corps* amongst them by attaching pieces of different-coloured cotton to each gun and ensuring that one man was responsible for the gun thus marked, they proved themselves excellent gun-bearers. In a short time they were vying with each other for the honour of holding the gun that killed the most game.

In the meantime Sam had made arrangements to hunt with Florian and with the famed Hamran Arabs, who hunted elephants, rhinoceros, hippopotami and crocodiles with nothing more than the sword or the spear, either mounted on horseback or on foot. While hunting, Sam also intended to explore the different rivers. He explained this to the Arabs and they assured him that they knew the country extremely well as far as Mek Nimmur's territory.

There were two separate groups of Hamran hunters. One was under the leadership of Sheik Abou Do Roussoul, "a splendid fellow, a little above six foot one . . . with well developed muscles . . . strikingly handsome". His party included "a little fellow named Jali, who was not above five feet four inches, but wonderfully muscular" and another hunter named Suleiman. Accompanying them was Sheik Abou Do's father, known by Sam as Abou Do senior, who was a hippopotamus hunter, swimming the rivers regardless of crocodiles and hunting his quarry armed only with a harpoon to which was attached a float by which the beast could be followed once successfully impaled. The other group of elephant hunters, or *aggageers*, as they were called, were the four brothers Sherrif. "The eldest was Taher Sherrif; his second brother, Roder Sherrif, was a very small active-looking man with a withered left arm . . . In spite of his maimed condition Roder Sherrif was the most celebrated hunter in the elephant hunt." Looping his horse's reins over his withered arm, he would entice the elephant to follow him, provoking it to charge, then keeping just ahead of it to give the others a chance to chop its hamstrings with their exceedingly sharp two-handed swords. This was their principal method of hunting, often successfully killing animals from elephants downwards with their swords alone.

Sam, at first, hunted with the Sheik Abou Do, who, he was forced to admit, was not all that he appeared to be. He wrote with obvious disillusionment:

> I am sorry to be obliged to confess that my ally, Abou Do, although
> a perfect Nimrod in sport, an Apollo in personal appearance, and a

gentleman in manner, was a mean, covetous, and grasping fellow, and withal, absurdly jealous.

This was an interesting confession, since by implication it is plain that Sam's conception of the perfect sportsman was a man who was in no way mean, petty, or jealous, however mighty a hunter he might be, or outwardly a gentleman. Sam was, himself, generous almost to a fault, although yielding second place to no man in the chase, if he could help it. It was only after he had hunted with Taher Sherrif and his brothers and in their company had outdistanced Abou Do, who had ruined his horse by over-riding, that he began to appreciate the man's true character. Whenever he had shot game in his company Sam had always allowed Abou Do first choice and it was then he noted the mean and grasping character beneath the handsome athletic frame of the Sheik.

There are few pursuits other than hunting which afford a chance to assess character so well and clearly, in a short time. When Abou Do's hunting companion, Jali, broke his thigh in a desperate elephant hunt, Sam immediately set it for him. With one splint from armpit to foot and another inside the thigh, he wound bandages around him from armpit to ankle. The inner bandage was left alone but the two outer bandages were soaked in gum-water. This makeshift plaster set as hard as armour and within six weeks Sam was gratified to hear that his patient was eager to return to hunt. He refused to allow him to do so, in case he damaged his leg before it was fully healed, but, significantly, he felt that he had lost his best hunter, for already he had the measure of Abou Do.

When they finally parted, after Abou Do had tried to borrow horses from Sam, having over-ridden his own, the Sheik had the temerity to hunt over ground he had been specifically asked to leave alone. Sam encountered him with a captured rhinoceros calf worth 40 dollars to Schmidt, who acted as agent for a zoo. Glancing at the calf Sam saw it was throttled as the cords securing it to the camel's back had slipped. He remarked that he would be surprised if anyone paid 40 dollars for a dead calf. Abou Do at once released the cords, but too late. Sam's Tokrooris and Abou Do attributed this to the power of Sam's "evil eye", and the former, at least, regarded it as a case of the Sheik receiving his just deserts.

Despite his abrasive parting with Sheik Abou Do, Sam was immensely impressed by the courage and agility of the Hamran elephant hunters. At the same time he was never one to be backward when it came to any form of hunting. His own activities during this period bordered sometimes on the lunatic, as he was later to admit. It was for instance only by trial and error that he discovered that forehead shots at charging African elephants were almost always quite useless, whereas in Ceylon at Indian elephants it had been his favourite shot. Despite this handicap he and Florian, in combination with the Hamran Arabs, managed to account for a considerable number of elephants. Typical was a day in December when Sam noted:

> I had been fortunate in bagging four from the herd, in addition to the single bull in the morning; total, five. Florian had killed one, and the aggageers one, total seven elephants. One had escaped that I had wounded in the shoulder and two that had been wounded by Florian.

For everything but elephants, Sam preferred his favourite little Fletcher .240. For elephants his ultimate weapon was his powerful single-barrel rifle by Holland, carrying a half-pound explosive shell. His description of using this indicated why he dreaded it;

> Bang! went the "Baby": round I spun like a weathercock, with the blood pouring from my nose as the recoil had driven the sharp top of the hammer deep into the bridge. My "Baby" not only screamed but kicked viciously. However, I knew that the elephant must be bagged as the half-pound shell had been aimed directly behind the shoulder.

Looking back on those days, Sam was later to confess that many of the risks he ran, such as entering narrow tunnels of thick thorny undergrowth, where it was impossible to do more than crawl, in pursuit of lions, were completely indefensible. On one occasion, while "strolling" by the Settite river, he shot a buffalo close by a thick covert which was known to be a haunt of lions. As darkness was falling he decided to leave the carcase until morning. When he revisited the spot, he saw distinct traces of the carcase having been hauled into the thick thorny undergrowth. He followed the trail on hands and knees, armed with a light double-barrelled .577, in pitch darkness for over seventy yards until a strong smell of raw flesh and the cracking of bones indicated that the lions were close at hand:

> . . . suddenly a dark object appeared to block the tunnel; in another moment I distinguished the head and dark mane of a noble lion on the other side of a mass which proved to be the remains of the bull buffalo; another head of a lioness arose upon the right, and at the same instant, with a tremendous roar the scene changed before I had time to fire . . . We were actually in possession, having driven the lions from their prey, simply by our cautious advance, without a shot.
>
> It required some time and trouble to cut of the head of that bull buffalo, in the narrow limits of the lion's den, but it hangs upon my walls now as a trophy. . . Upon another occasion I crept in a similar manner into one of their dark tunnels, and shot the lion within a distance of four paces. . . The Hamran Arabs persuaded me to

discontinue this kind of exploration, and my Tokrooris having taken the same view of the performance, I gave up the practice. .

It is clear that the risks he took were enough to frighten even the Hamran Arabs, whom he admired so greatly. The no less brave Tokrooris, on occasions, had to "be kicked" to restore their confidence in Sam when acting as his gun-bearers. It is easy to understand their occasional lapses when following such a man as he, who appeared to be totally devoid of fear and took unbelievable risks with total impunity and utter confidence in himself. Small wonder that his name became a by-word in the area, with tales of his feats in the field spreading far and wide. He himself described one incident thus:

> . . .a rhinoceros rose quickly from the ground and had evidently obtained our wind. I made a good shot with the No 10 rifle through the shoulder and after turning round twice . . . it fell to the ground and died. We now observed a fine young animal which was standing on the opposite side of the mother and I suggested to my famous Hamran hunters that we should call up the camels and endeavour to secure the calf with . . . ropes.

> This was quite opposed to their ideas, as the young one was sufficiently advanced to boast a pair of small horns, which the Arabs declared to be too formidable to warrant an attempt at capture.

> I thought otherwise, therefore I arranged that we should make a trial. The camels were brought and the ropes arranged. Nooses were prepared and I suggested that we should attempt to mob the young one and then secure its legs.

> My Arabs declined this plan as they rightly declared that the ground was unfavourable, owing to the number of large rocks which would prevent them getting out of harm's way should the animal charge. It was ultimately arranged that Taher Noor, my head Arab, was to lend me his sword and that I was to go first, while they would follow with the ropes and nooses, to endeavour to trip up the calf should it charge past me . . .

> The calf was about 3½ feet high . . . As I cautiously approached it, it looked much larger than when I had seen it at a distance and I began to think the Arabs were right in their conclusion. There was not much time for reflection, for the young tartar gave an angry shake of its ugly head, emitted the usual three sharp whiffs, and charged me as fast as it could gallop.

> I jumped quickly backwards by a large rock, and it passed within three feet of me, but immediately halted, instead of continuing as far as the spot where the Arabs were waiting with the ropes.

> It now turned round and seeing me, it repeated its charge in reverse, as hard as it could go. I again jumped back, but as I did so, I delivered a lightning-like downward cut with Taher-Noor's favourite sword. The young rhinoceros fell stone-dead, all in a heap!

> . . . Although only a calf, it was a large animal, and the neck was about 15 inches thick. The blade had fortunately struck exactly between two vertebrae and had slipped through the gristle as though it had been a carrot. Continuing its course it had severed the neck completely, leaving only the thick skin of the throat to which the head was still attached.
>
> This was a magnificent stroke, which delighted the sword hunters, and I should much like to hear the story as it is now told by them. . . They will assuredly have converted the calf into a full-grown rhinoceros. . .

Sam noted that there was no beast he had ever encountered which was so easily skinned as a rhinoceros. On this occasion they removed the skin, much prized for shields, from the parent beast and returned to their camp, where they met some Abyssinian hunters in search of meat. The sent them to the corpse of the rhinoceros they had just killed, which was visible owing to the hordes of vultures descending towards it. It is an indication of the speed with which the vultures could dispose of animal flesh that the Abyssinians returned within an hour to report that only the skeleton remained.

By this time, on occasions the size of the party was quite considerable, as the number of Hamran Arabs with them varied. They were also hunting in an area known to be inhabited by the hostile Basé tribe. Sam therefore ordered that the long grass round each new encampment should be cleared to avoid providing cover for any possible enemy. When this was not carried out immediately he went some distance upwind and set fire to the grass. There was an instant rush to cut a firebreak, which was only just completed in time to save the tents and gear. After that he had little further trouble on that score, and was there ws a mixture of Tokrooris, Hamran Arabs and Jaleens they never united against his authority.

They lost two members of their basic party when the freed slave girl Barrake died of acute dysentery and Mahomet, the interpreter, deserted. By this time his services as interpreter were no longer necessary as both Sam and Florence spoke passable arabic. Due to his temperamental behaviour he was really no loss. Sam wrote that "Mahomet had become simply unbearable and he was so impertinent that I was obliged to take a cane from one of the Arabs and administer a little physical advice. An evil spirit possessed the man and he bolted off with some . . . camel men".

There were also two near mutinies by the Tokrooris. On the first occasion, towards the end of December, not relishing the thought of being attacked by the Basé tribesmen, they suddenly announced their intention of leaving, on the grounds that many of them were sick and they did not wish to be a burden on the expedition. By administering three-grain doses of tartar emetic to those who claimed to be ill, Sam made sure they were and thus prevented them leaving. He then explained to them that if they did desert they would be flogged by the local governor on their return and thus talked them out of leaving. The second occasion arose on March 15th when the expedition was nearly successfully concluded after the Tokrooris learned that Sam had been invited to meet Mek Nimmur. They again announced their intention of leaving, because they were afraid that the Leopard King would steal their camels. Sam stationed himself by the camp entrance and cocking his double-barrelled rifle announced his intention of shooting the first camel to leave. After further consultation it was agreed that he would make good their loss should any camels be stolen as they feared and once again they agreed to remain with him.

In the event Sam had a very friendly meeting with Mek Nimmur and presented him with a brace of pistols by Tatham. As a rifle by Tatham had already burst when being fired, fortunately without injury to Sam, be might have been forewarned. As it was, he was disgusted to learn that the pistols had also burst on being fired. On hearing the news, Sam at once rode to Mek Nimmur's camp and presented him with a very good little single rifle by Beattie. In return Mek Nimmur sent him two camel loads of corn, fifty pounds of honey and a cow.

By this time Sam's party were very self-sufficient. He wrote:

> We . . . washed with rhinoceros soap; our lamp was trimmed with oil of lions; our butter for cooking purposes was the fat of hippopotami, while our pomade was made with the marrow of buffaloes and antelopes, scented with the blossoms of mimosa. We . . . subsisted on the produce of the rod and the rifle.

After a brief excursion into Abyssinia, combined with exploration of the Salam and Angarab rivers, Sam reluctantly returned to the Atbara once more. He decided that he had hunted enough and that it was time for serious exploration again. By April 16th he noted that "they made some stir at Gallabat" on the Abyssinian border. There he encountered a very civilised Italian merchant, Signor Angelo Bolognesi by name, also two German missionaries, who were extremely ill and equally pig-headed. Sam was always inclined to have a poor opinion of missionaries and he was not in the least impressed by these. They carried a medicine chest with them, but were afraid to use the contents because they could not distinguish one drug from another until he labelled them. One of these Germans was a blacksmith by trade and Sam noted that "Whenever I meet an exceedingly ignorant missionary he has invariably compared himself to the Apostle Paul. In half an hour I found I was conversing with St. Paul in the person of the Blacksmith."

Leaving the Italian and the missionaries Sam went on to explore the rivers Rahad and Dinder, each of which flowed northwards into the Blue Nile. From there he headed for Khartoum, where in the absence of the Consul, John Petherick, and his wife, who were away on a mission on behalf of the Royal Geographical Society to look for Speke and Grant, they found the consulate at their disposal. The journey from Berber had taken the best part of a year, almost to the day.

The Pethericks, like so many traders and others in the Sudan, collected animals to provide for the demands of zoos around the world. They had two particularly wild boars, one of which was extremely savage. Sam, who was never any sort of hand at throwing balls, or other missiles, wrote with some pride that while he was sitting on the verandah of the consulate with Florence:

> I heard a great noise from the other end of the courtyard, and I saw bricks falling from the wall, showing that the boars were once again breaking out. Before the men had time to interfere, the large boar had effected a breach, and it appeared in the courtyard. The people immediately retreated under shelter but the brute, having surveyed the scene, perceived us sitting above the flight of steps exactly opposite. Without a moment's hesitation it charged at full speed across the yard from a distance of about 60 paces. The Rakooba [on which they sat] was about 15 feet square and as we had lately arrived from Abyssinia there were numerous trophies of the chase arranged around the pavement. Among these were the horns of rhinoceros. Fortunately a long horn weighting about 10 lbs was close at hand; this I immediately seized with both hands and was just in time when the boar was half way up the steps, to hurl it with all my strength.
>
> It was a lucky shot, the heavy horn struck exactly between the eyes, in the forehead, and knocked the assailant down the steps, at the bottom of which it lay kicking convulsively, but thoroughly stunned, and unconscious. My men now rushed forward, and we secured the fore and hind legs with ropes, and dragged it to a neighbouring store, the door of which we locked . . . the effect was highly satisfactory as the objectionable boar was discovered dead when the door was cautiously opened on the following morning . . . I was rather proud of my shot on this occasion as I seldom throw a stone at an enemy without hitting a friend by mistake. Some persons are good at one sport, others at another; but throwing a stone to hit the object of aim was never my pride, as I failed in performance. The boar was within 5 feet, which is about my distance for extreme accuracy; even at that short range I should not have sufficient confidence in myself to back my own projectile at long odds. I should only have sufficient good

Close quarters

A charge of sixpences

Par force hunting

A mêlée

Caught at last

The hunter hunted

Taher Sherrif leads the hunt

The Hamran swordhunters at work

feeling to request my friend, or spectator to stand well beyond the range of my shot.

It is in such a passage that Sam's special brand of wry humour comes over so well. He was sufficiently sure of himself as a first-rate hunter and generally dead shot to admit to incompetence in those spheres where he did not excel. Nor did he ever gloss over the instances when, as everyone must do occasionally, he missed a shot in the field. Allowing for the fact that he was often shooting after a violent gallop on horseback when the quarry was travelling at speed through rough country his average of kills to shots was remarkably impressive. He could well afford to laugh at his occasional failures and misses.

It was not long after his arrival in Khartoum on the 11th of June 1862 that Sam began his preparations for further exploration. He had accomplished a surprising amount already, despite the fact that he had really only been acclimatising himself so far. In the words of Sir Roderick Murchison, President of the Royal Geographical Society, he had already "placed in a clear light the relations of the Atbara and Blue River to the main stream of the Nile, and had shown, by actual observation, that it was to these affluents the great river owed the rich sediment, which, deposited by inundations, was the source of the fertility of Egypt".

6

To The Source

In Khartoum, while preparing for the next stage of his expedition, Samuel White Baker encountered for the first time the problem that was to prove the greatest obstacle to his plans. The Sudan at this time was under Turkish government and the slave trade in the interior was organised more or less openly from Khartoum, although supposedly discouraged by the authorities. There were in fact very few living in Khartoum who were not involved in one way or another in the slave trade and, quite naturally, they actively discouraged the activities of anyone they considered might be in a position to expose them. The likelihood—indeed certainty—that any explorer of the upper reaches of the Nile would find evidence of the excesses of the slave trade was sufficient to make all concerned do their best to hamper his preparations. Sam described the methods of the slave traders as follows:

> The people for the most part engaged in the nefarious traffic of the White Nile are Syrians, Copts, Turks, Circassians and some few *Europeans* . . .There are two classes of White Nile traders, the one possessing capital, the other being penniless adventurers . . . A man without means forms an expedition and borrows money for this purpose at 100 per cent . . . He agrees to repay the lender in ivory at one half its market value. Having obtained the required sum, he hires several vessels and engages from 100 to 300 men, composed of Arabs and runaway villains from distant countries, who have found asylum from justice in the obscurity of Khartoum. He purchases a few guns and large quantities of ammunition for his men, together with a few hundred pounds of glass beads. The piratical expedition being complete he pays his men five months' wages in advance, at the rate of forty-five piastres (nine shillings) per month and agrees to give them eighty piastres per month for any period exceeding the five months advanced . . .
>
> The vessels sail about December, and on arrival at the desired locality, the party disembark and proceed into the interior, until they arrive at the village of some negro chief, with whom they establish an

intimacy. Charmed with his new friends, the power of whose weapons he acknowledges, the negro chief does not neglect the opportunity of seeking their alliance to attack a hostile neighbour . . .

At dawn, guided by their negro ally, the Arab slave traders attacked and burned the hostile village, killing the men and enslaving the women and children. They also drove off the herds of cattle and looted any ivory or iron hoes, the negroes' prized possessions, which they found in the huts. Finally they chopped off the arms of the dead to secure their copper or iron bracelets. They then traded the captured cattle for ivory with their ally. Very often they then quarrelled with their ally and plundered his village and enslaved his women and children in their turn. According to Sam:

> A good season for a party of a hundred and fifty men should produce about two hundred cantars (20,000 lbs) of ivory, valued at Khartoum at £4,000. The men being paid in slaves, the wages should be *nil*, and there should be a surplus of four or five hundred slaves for the trader's own profit—worth on average five to six pounds each.

> The boats are accordingly packed with a human cargo, and a portion of the trader's men accompany them to the Sudan, while the remainder of the party form a camp or settlement in the country they have adopted, and industriously plunder, massacre and enslave, until their master's return with boats from Khartoum in the following season, by which time they are supposed to have a cargo of slaves and ivory ready for shipment. . .

> The amiable trader returns . . . to Khartoum; hands over to his creditor sufficient ivory to liquidate the original loan of £1,000, and already a man of capital, he commences as an independent trader. . .

Even the Governor General of the Sudan, Moosa Pasha, was deliberately obstructive, and when Sam produced the Viceroy's *firman*, claimed that this jurisdiction did not extend to the White Nile. Sam described him succinctly and with loathing:

> This man was a rather exaggerated specimen of Turkish authorities in general, combining the worst of Oriental failings with the brutality of a wild animal. During his administration the Sudan became utterly ruined; governed by military force, the revenue was unequal to the expenditure and fresh taxes were levied upon the inhabitants to an extent that paralysed the entire country.

Owing to the depredations of the slave traders in the interior, the tribes were extremely hostile to any strangers, and Sam appreciated that he would have to act as if marching through an enemy territory. The trouble was that any reliable recruits for an escort were unobtainable amongst the scourings of Khartoum. A request to the British consul at Alexandria for soldiers and boats was turned down by the regent, Ismael Pasha. Fortunately, as he himself said, Sam thrived on difficulties, and furthermore, he had the big advantage of a supply of ready cash in hand in the shape of an order on the Treasury at Khartoum, with which he had had the forethought to arm himself.

He was fortunate that he encountered Johann Schmidt, the German erstwhile carpenter and friend of Florian, who arrived in Khartoum with a consignment of wild animals for an Italian zoo. From him Sam learned of the death of Florian, who had been killed by a lion after missing it with both barrels. His black servant, Richarn, a keen hunter, who had hunted with Sam, had been taken into service by Schmidt. Hearing of Sam's plans, Schmidt indicated that he would be willing to join as he felt that the voyage up the White Nile might improve the wasting disease of the lungs from which he suffered. He was accordingly engaged as Sam's "head man" and assisted greatly with the preliminary organisation of the expedition. Richarn became "Corporal" in charge of their recruits.

A further acquisition, whom both Sam and Florence were to find of immense value, was a twelve-year-old black boy name Saat, a native of "Fertit". He had been kidnapped as a child of six by Baggara Arab slave traders, but had escaped in Cairo to the Austrian mission. Taken from there to Khartoum, he had been amongst numerous black children turned out of the mission because of their general thieving and depredations, although it was accepted by all that he was entirely honest. After he had twice appealed to Florence to be taken on the strength of their party, they enquired about his background and discovered that his dismissal had been "a mistake". They thereupon promptly employed him and discovered that they had gained an unexpected paragon, fearless, truthful and loyal.

For their voyage up the Nile Sam engaged two sailing barges, or *noggurs*, and a *diahbiah*, or decked vessel with comfortable cabins, for himself, Florence and Johann Schmidt. For transport on land, Sam shipped twenty-one donkeys, four camels and four horses. Their packs, saddles, harness and pads were all made under his careful supervision, as he was well aware that any weakness or skimping in this department would result in lamed animals, useless to the expedition, and all too probably the loss of supplies on which their lives and the success or failure of the expedition might depend. Finally he secured a retinue of ninety-six followers, consisting of forty-five armed men as escort and a further forty as sailors.

Sam was nothing if not thorough in all his preparations and in a lengthy letter to his sister at home, sadly acknowledging the news of his father's death, he wrote:

> Nothing but death shall prevent me from discovering the *sources* of
> the Nile . . . I have all the requisite astronomical instruments. I learnt
> the use of them before I started; thus, when I return my maps will not
> be those of a simple wanderer, for all exact latitudes and longitudes
> shall be determined. . . In my intended journey I leave all the well-
> known elephant haunts of the White Nile untouched as I push direct
> for Gondokoro . . .

By the 18th of December, after six months of delays and vexations,
Sam and his party were ready to start, when Moosa Pasha sent an
official demanding payment of a poll-tax levied on all the inhabitants
of Khartoum. Sam promptly had the Union Jack hoisted and
informed the tax collector that he had the choice of leaving
voluntarily or of being thrown overboard. A government vessel then
crashed into one of the *noggurs* and damaged the oars. The *reis*, or
captain, of this government boat was a giant black man, who
challenged anyone to come on board and fight him, rather than
replace the oars. Sam decided that this was an occasion for his
personal intervention, ". . . so stepping quickly on board, and
brushing a few fellows on one side, I was obliged to come to a
physical explanation with the captain, which terminated in delivery of
the oars".

For the next fortnight, once finally under way and clear of
Khartoum, they had an atrocious voyage. The wretched Johann
Schmidt was dying on his feet, finally breathing his last on the 31st of
December. One of the *noggurs*, well named *The Clumsy*, kept
breaking her mast and requiring lengthy repairs. The Nile was wide
and flat with uninteresting flat banks which sloped very gradually
"like the sands at low tide in England, and quite unlike the
perpendicular banks of the Blue Nile". There was remarkably little of
interest to note, but on the 28th of December he recorded:

> Caught a curious fish [Tetrodon Physa of Geof.] that distends itself
> with air like a bladder; colour black and yellow stripes; lungs;
> apertures under fins, which open and shut by their movement, their
> motion being a semi-revolution. This fish is a close link between fish
> and turtle; the head being precisely that of the latter, having no teeth,
> but cutting jaws of hard bone of immense power. Many minutes after
> the head had been severed from the body, the jaws nipped with fury
> anything that was inserted in the mouth, nipping though thin twigs
> and thick straw like a pair of shears. . . The skin is wonderfully tough, I
> accordingly cut it into a long thong, and bound up the stock of a rifle
> that had been split from the recoil of heavy charges of powder . . .
> There is nothing so good as fish-skin—or that of the iguana, or of the
> crocodile—for lashing broken gun-stocks. Isinglass, when taken fresh

from the fish and bound round a broken stock like a plaster, will become as strong as metal when dry.

Steadily the countryside deteriorated, showing signs of the ravages of the slave traders, and the journey began to assume a very tedious monotony. On the 2nd of January he wrote of "disgusting naked savages, everlasting marshes teeming with mosquitoes" and a total lack of beauty or interest in the countryside. By the 4th of January he noted the country was "one vast and apparently interminable marsh". By January 7th they were reduced to hauling their boats along the banks against the stream with enormous effort. His one reliable "black fellow", Richarn, whom he had appointed corporal, was drunk every day and he foresaw that he would have to reduce him to the ranks.

On the 9th of January he saw a buffalo in the high grass and knocked it down with a well aimed shot. His men rushed to the spot, but the beast recovered and disappeared into the high grass. The following morning it was heard groaning not far away and some forty of his men went off armed with guns and knives in search of it. One of their number was attacked by the wounded beast and the others promptly ran away, leaving him to his fate before directing a concentrated volley at the wretched beast. Eventually, having gored the man to death, the buffalo was killed, but Sam had begun to get the measure of the cowardly ruffians he was employing as his bodyguard. At this stage he considered that he had them under control, but he appreciated that it was necessary to keep them well fed. On January 16th he wrote:

> A new dish! There is no longer mock-turtle soup—*real* turtle is *mock-hippopotamus*. I tried boiling off the fat, flesh and skin together, the result being that the skin assumed the appearance of the green fat of the turtle, but is far superior. A piece of the head thus boiled, and then soused in vinegar, with chopped onions, cayenne pepper and salt, throws brawn completely in the shade. My men have revelled in a cauldron of hippopotamus soup, I serve out grog at sunset, all ships being together. Great contentment, all appetites being satisfied. . .

Such culinary highlights were exceptional. Throughout January the boredom of the journey was only enlivened by occasional incidents, such as when one of his horses succeeded at intervals in kicking men passing him into the river, or when the black women on board quarrelled and fell amongst the water jars when fighting, breaking a number of them. Sam noted that the horses, donkeys and camels were continually biting and fighting, as "the ennui of this wretched journey appears to try the temper of both man and beast". Commenting on the frightful windings of the river and the fact that there was absolutely no game to be seen, he wrote with emphasis:

> I do not wonder at the failure of all expeditions in this wretched country . . . there is absolutely nothing living to be seen, but day after day is passed in winding slowly through the labyrinth of endless marsh, through clouds of mosquitoes.

On the 23rd of January they arrived at the Austrian mission-station of St. Croix, where he delivered a letter to the chief missionary, Herr Morlang, who had just given up his work as a total failure and had sold the establishment for £30. Sam noted:

> Herr Morlang acknowledged, with great feeling, that the mission was absolutely useless amongst such savages; that he had worked with much zeal for many years, but that the natives were utterly impracticable. They were far below the brutes, as the latter show signs of affection to those who are kind to them; while the natives, on the contrary, are utterly obtuse to all feelings of gratitude.

Towards the end of the month, as they neared Gondokoro, the character of the countryside began to change. The marshes began to give way to dry ground until eventually the banks of the river were some four feet above water level. Occasional trees began to break the monotony of the countryside and instead of the deserted regions through which they had passed they began to observe increasing numbers of natives. It was not, however, until February 2nd that they finally reached Gondokoro, which was a full twenty feet above the river level. There were also plenty of green trees to be seen and in the distance mountains rose above the horizon.

Gondokoro had once been a mission station, and the ruins of a church and a brick-built building remained beside the ravages of what had once been a garden. There was, however, no town as such. It was merely a station for the "ivory traders". In practice this meant that for two or three months in the year it was the principal centre of the slave trade in this region, but otherwise remained unoccupied except for a few natives in "miserable grass huts". At this time there were numerous encampments of slave traders awaiting the arrival of others from the interior with more ivory and slaves. Whenever Sam approached any of these camps he could hear the clink of fetters as the slaves were hastily driven into hiding. Sam recorded that one of the traders was a Copt, the father of the American Consul in Khartoum. It surprised him nonetheless when he saw a vessel "full of brigands arrive at Gondokoro with the American flag flying at the mast-head". His description of the place was plain enough:

> Gondokoro was a perfect hell. It is utterly ignored by the Egyptian

> authorities. Although well known to be a colony of cut-throats . . . The
> camps were full of slaves . . . I was the greatest stumbling block to the
> trade, and my presence at Gondokoro was considered as an unwar-
> rantable intrusion upon a locality sacred to slavery and iniquity. There
> were about six hundred of the traders' people at Gondokoro, whose
> time was passed in drinking, quarrelling and ill-treating the slaves.

Despite his efforts to assure them that he was merely interested in exploring the sources of the Nile and in learning news of Speke and Grant, Sam was regarded by them all as a spy sent by the British government. Since they spent most of their time drunk, and when drunk were prone to fire their guns off in all directions, there was a more or less constant sound of gunfire, and bullets flew all over the place. The traders did their best to discourage him, of course, and several times bullets whistled past his head or hit the dust near his feet, but, encouraged by a report that a party of traders due shortly were supposed to have news of two white men in the interior, he decided to wait until their arrival.

While he was waiting Sam investigated the habits of the local natives. He found they had developed a particularly ingenious form of poisoned arrow with barbed heads which very quickly infected any wound, causing the flesh to putrefy. He noted, however, with some satisfaction that their bows were very inelastic and since their arrows were flightless their shooting was highly inaccurate. Their range he found was not further than a hundred and ten yards.

Meanwhile the slave traders had been doing their best to suborn his followers. Sam noticed the sullen disposition of the men, but was taken by surprise when one morning they mutinied. Sam promptly knocked down the principal mutineer, but while he was holding him by the throat, preparatory to having him bound, some forty followers made a move to rescue him. The position looked extremely ugly, when Florence, who had been ill with fever, rose from her sick bed and courageously rushed amongst the milling mob, calling on the least mutinous to assist her. Sam, seizing the opportunity while their attention was distracted, ordered the drummer boy to beat the drums and at the top of his voice commanded the men to "fall in". He recorded:

> It is curious how mechanically an order is obeyed if given at the
> right moment, even in the midst of mutiny. Two-thirds of the men fell
> in, and formed in line, while the remainder retreated with the
> ringleader . . . declaring that he was badly hurt. The affair ended in my
> insisting upon all forming in line, and upon the ringleader being
> brought forward. In this critical moment Mrs Baker, with great tact
> came forward and implored me to forgive him if he kissed my hand

and begged for pardon. This compromise completely won the men, who, although a few minutes before in open mutiny, now called upon their ringleader . . . to apologise, and that all would be right . . .

Sam realised at once that he was bound to have further trouble and that his so-called escort was likely to prove more trouble in the long run than the allegedly hostile natives. However he drilled them every morning and, by buying an ox and slaughtering it to provide them with meat, succeeded in keeping them at least temporarily under control. With their appetites satisfied they assured him of their loyalty, but by this time he had realised what thoroughly untrustworthy rogues they were, merely waiting for a suitable opportunity to betray him, and he was fully alive to how little these assurances were worth. He decided to prepare himself accordingly.

On the 15th of February, after twelve seemingly interminable days at Gondokoro he heard a rattle of firearms in the distance, indicating the arrival of a party. His men at once fired off their guns, loaded with ball cartridge, and succeeded in accidentally killing one of the donkeys amidst the general excitement. At a distance of a hundred yards Sam saw two white men approaching and recognised them as Speke and Grant. He wrote of how "I recognised my old friend Speke, and with a heart beating with joy I took off my cap and gave a welcome hurrah! as I ran towards him . . ."

At first Sam thought that their arrival meant that his expedition had finished before it had truly begun, for he assumed that Speke and Grant had succeeded in completely exploring the sources of the Nile. He even went so far as to ask, or so he later claimed: "Does not one leaf of the laurel remain for me?" Despite this highly improbable remark, it transpired that there was still plenty of scope for further exploration.

Speke and Grant very generously provided him with copies of their maps and details of their entire exploration. They also indicated very generously where they had failed in entirely ascertaining the Nile's sources and where he could fill in the gaps they had left. Sam was soon cheered at the prospect of still achieving at least in part the goal he had set himself. The perils of hostile tribes, uncharted areas of unknown territory and mutinous followers, quite apart from the opposition and enmity of the slave traders, left him unaffected.

Unfortunately the Bakers had only two reliable and faithful followers amongst all their men. One was the then drunken, but honest and loyal, black man Richarn, who was much attached to both Sam and Florence. The other was the consistently truthful boy Saat, who was utterly loyal to his mistress, Florence. Neither had anything in common with the Jalyns and Dongolowas, who made up the escort, and although of entirely different race Richarn and Saat were friends. Sam obtained the promise of help from Mohammed, the *vakeel* or headman, who had come with Speke and Grant, to accompany him in return for assistance in obtaining ivory. This was, however, a complete piece of duplicity, since the man had no intention of co-operating in any way. He had indeed determined to leave before Sam's party was ready. Meanwhile the slave traders had once more been suborning his men.

One morning, after inspecting the baggage animals as usual, Sam saw that Florence looked very pale. Before he could question her she summoned their *vakeel* and accused him of conspiring with their men to mutiny and shoot Sam. The boy Saat with Richarn had overheard the entire plot and reported it to Florence. He now boldly confirmed the story. Sam immediately loaded five double-barrelled guns with buckshot, along with a rifle and a revolver, keeping on hand also a sabre "as sharp as a razor". With these readily available and backed by Saat and Richarn, both also armed, he ordered his men to line up with waterproof covers over the locks of their rifles. Only fifteen of the Jalyns paraded and Sam promptly disarmed them, discharging the men themselves with the word "mutineer" above his signature. The Dongolowas, mostly related to the *vakeel,* never appeared and Sam warned the man that he would be held responsible on their return to Khartoum.

Before Sam had recovered from this setback he heard that Mohammed's party were departing and received a message from them that if he followed them they would fire on him "as they would not allow English spies in their country". Sam then turned for help to a friendly Circassian, who promised to send him some men, but was forced to confess with shame that his men refused to obey his order to join the Bakers' party. Sam then persuaded the *vakeel,* under dire threats of punishment on his return to Khartoum, to obtain the return of some of the Dongolowa mutineers on the understanding that their past misconduct would be forgiven and forgotten. He succeeded eventually in obtaining seventeen.

The situation was not greatly improved, however, as his informants, the boy Saat and Richarn, told him that the men planned to mutiny and shoot Sam after a march of some seven days. They also behaved in a thoroughly out-of-hand manner. Typical of their behaviour was an occasion when Sam was wakened during the night by the sound of heavy breathing at the head of his bed:

> A slight pull at my sleeve showed me that my wife also noticed the object, as this was always the signal that she made if anything occurred that required vigilance. Possessing a share of *sangfroid* admirably

adapted for African travel, Mrs Baker was not a *screamer* and never
even whispered; in the moment of suspected danger, a touch on my
sleeve was considered a sufficient warning . . ."

It turned out that his "angels", as he termed them in this instance,
had been flogging the slave women with a courbatch, or
hippopotamus-hide whip, and one of the women had fled for refuge
to Sam's tent. It was only by good fortune that Sam did not shoot her
on the spot. Finding her covered with blood he rose and gave the
men concerned a taste of their own medicine, much to their
amazement, since "they were only Slave women". He saw, however,
that the sooner he could move away from the insidious influence of
Gondokoro the better. Despite knowing their plans for the future he
felt sure that once in semi-hostile territory he would be able to renew
his ascendancy over them.

He discovered very quickly through his informants that the men
had made an alliance with a *vakeel* named Mahommed Her, whose
party were also mostly Dongolowas. It was clear that they intended to
throw in their lot with this party after they had mutinied in the
interior, but Sam determined to forestall them. He started his journey
into Central Africa on the 26th of March 1863, shortly after a rival
party of slave traders, composed mostly of Jalyns, under a leader
named Ibrahim of whom Sam wrote:

> I never saw a more atrocious countenance than that exhibited by this
> man. A mixed breed, between a Turk sire and Arab mother, he had the
> good features and bad qualities of either race. The fine, sharp, high-
> arched nose and large nostril; the pointed and projecting chin; rather
> high cheekbones and prominent brow, overhanging a pair of immense
> black eyes full of expression and evil.

Thanks entirely to Florence's intervention at a crucial encounter, he
succeeded in allying himself with Ibrahim's party on the march. Sam
himself admitted freely that "Had I been alone, I should have been
too proud to have sought the friendship of the sullen leader, and the
moment on which success depended would have been lost." This
unexpected alliance was greeted with digust by his own Dongolowas,
who had planned to join Mahommed Her. When the rival party led
by Mahommed Her caught up with them, Sam's men allied themselves with them, but Ibrahim's party was the larger. As it was the
two groups quarrelled throughout the night and in the morning
Ibrahim's party started very promptly to pack up and leave.

The leader of the mutineers among Sam's men, named Bellaal,
replied very insolently to Sam's command to load the camels, clearly
intent on provoking a revolt. Sam promptly knocked the man out
with a right uppercut to the jaw and, leaving him lying on the

ground, rushed amongst the panic-stricken men with his rifle in one hand, seizing them by the throat with the other and ordering them to get on with the loading. Richarn and the *vakeel* also shouted at them to get moving and very soon Sam had them in hand again. It was not long before they overtook Ibrahim's party once more.

During this march through the Latooka country, however, three of Sam's men, including Bellaal, deserted with their rifles and ammunition to join Mahommed Her's party. With a view to impressing the remainder, Sam declared a solemn curse on the deserters, saying: "The vultures shall pick their bones!" Shortly afterwards they were killed, along with many others of Mahommed's party, when they were ambushed during a raid against a strongly held village of the Latooka tribe, and Sam's remaining men were duly impressed with the power of his "evil eye". Thereafter the superstitious Dongolowas were extremely loath to cross him in any way and his ascendancy over them was never again challenged. Ibrahim's party were also greatly impressed by this event.

Sam considered the Latookas "a fine, frank and warlike race". Their riches were reckoned in cattle, and upwards of ten thousand were to be found in each town. Their head-dress was composed of specially reinforced hair, wound round and woven with twine to form a helmet protected in front by a piece of polished copper, the whole embroidered with beads. Otherwise they were stark naked, fighting with a lance, a mace, or a sword and a special bracelet with knife blades about four inches long attached to it. They also carried shields made of buffalo, or giraffe, hide, about four feet six inches by two feet wide. They were generally about five foot eleven inches tall and "remarkably handsome", while the women were "exceedingly plain".

The combined party was based in a Latooka town called Tarrangolle. This was ruled over by two chiefs, named Commoro and Moy, with whom Sam was soon on good terms. It was not long, however, before Ibrahim returned to Gondokoro to replenish supplies of ammunition. The depleted party of some thirty-five Turks and Sam's fifteen men was not sufficient to withstand any concentrated attack by the natives. Unfortunately Sam was unable to control the ill-disciplined Turks under Ibrahim's second-in-command, Suleiman. When the Turks attacked the native women and the natives threatened to attack them, Sam took command of the situation. Aware that the natives would not distinguish between the parties he ordered Suleiman to act in concert with him and form a square ready to resist any offensive.

The drums of the tribe sounded preparations for the attack and the Turks replied with their drums. When the chieftain Commoro saw the preparations that had been made for defence, the packed forces of the natives assembled round the square began to disperse. Later, however, the Latookas admitted that had it not been for the vigilance on which Sam had insisted, they would have attacked, in which case their small combined force would almost certainly have been annihilated.

In an effort to avoid being embroiled in a similar confrontation caused by the uncontrolled behaviour of the Turks Sam decided to move his party to a separate camp outside the town. Here he had an oblong area eighty by forty yards surrounded by a thorn fence. His horses, donkeys and camels were picqueted in the corners at opposite ends. There were huts for his men and for himself and Florence. He also planted onions, cabbages and radishes. Even here, however, there was a constant stream of both natives and Turks coming for medical treatment.

Despite the fact that the natives had thousands of cattle Sam found he could obtain neither cattle nor goats. This meant that in order to keep his party supplied with meat he had to rely on what he could shoot. Fortunately there were plenty of wildfowl, both ducks and geese, as well as pigeons and doves readily available. He had no difficulty in shooting a dozen or so each morning and was thus able to feed his men and himself quite adequately. He did record with some satisfaction that it was as well he had four hundredweight of shot with him.

Sam, however, was irritated that his resolute refusal to attack neighbouring villages when invited to do so by native chieftains should be interpreted by them as due either to weakness or fear. He wrote:

> 1863, 10th April. Latooka. I wish the black sympathisers in England could see Africa's inmost heart as I do, much of their sympathy would subside. Human nature viewed in its crudest state as pictured amongst African savages is quite on a level with that of the brute and not to be compared with the noble character of the dog. There is neither gratitude, pity, love, or self-denial; no idea of duty; no religion; but covetousness, ingratitude, selfishness and cruelty. All are thieves, idle, envious, and ready to plunder and enslave their weaker neighbours.

Early in May Sam decided to visit the country of the Obbo tribe to the south-west, the direction in which he wanted to go, on the pretext of a shooting expedition. The chief of the Obbo, named Katchiba, held sway as a sorcerer, rain-maker and wizard, although rather a shambling old figure. He was estimated to have a hundred and sixteen children, and one of his sons was the headman of each village. Since his ability as a wizard was accepted by all his sons, it was also, naturally enough, accepted by his people.

Despite the fact that he found him something of a clown, Sam became very friendly with Katchiba. So much so, in fact, that when he set out for a short shooting expedition on May 7th, in the hope of bagging some elephants, he left Florence, with a guard of eight men and her faithful follower, the boy Saat, in Katchiba's care. The expedition proved something of a disaster, for although he shot a few bucks and encountered some elephants he failed to kill any of the latter and narrowly escaped with his life. There was one other side effect. Although he had never smoked in his life before, the excessive dampness of the climate persuaded him to start with an Obbo pipe and tobacco.

On his return to Tarrangolle, Sam discovered that the Turks had roused the anger of the warlike Latookas to a dangerous degree. It was not long before Ibrahim decided that for safety's sake it would be wiser to move further south-west. Accordingly on the 23rd of June, although Florence was very ill with "bilious fever", they began a five-day march into the Obbo country. By this time the rains were extremely heavy, but fortunately Florence was protected in a covered palanquin. On their arrival Sam found the area very greatly changed from the previous month, with the grass already nine feet high, but Katchiba was pleased to see him again. The climate, however, was deplorable and they were also short of food, so that both Sam and Florence were soon extremely ill with bilious fever and malaria. During their stay with the Obbos, over the next six months, Sam, in particular, suffered recurring and very debilitating bouts of malaria every week or so. Quite apart from this the tsetse flies were so bad that his horses, camels and finally his donkeys all slowly sickened and died.

It was not until January that the Asua river, which barred their way further south, had shrunk sufficiently for them to cross safely, but in the meantime Sam had gained a considerable ascendancy over both Ibrahim and the entire party. He was in much demand as a physician and by skilful use of his well supplied medicine chest his influence over them developed remarkably. He recorded that his habit of dosing them with Tartar emetic and warning them beforehand that they would vomit shortly afterwards greatly impressed them, for they admitted: "He told me I would be sick and by Allah! there was no mistake about it." This primitive treatment appears to have been quite sufficient to establish his fame as a doctor, although he did succeed in curing one man who was severely wounded by a spear in the stomach.

By this time he was regarded with awe and veneration by his men for one by one the deserters from his party had been killed in various incidents with the rival party they had joined and in each case it was attributed to the power of his "evil eye". Even Katchiba, the wizard and rain-maker, applied to him for advice. In his case Sam produced two of his powerful "steam locomotive" whistles with his fingers in his mouth, which caused Katchiba to clap his hands to his ears with an admiring smile, then glance apprehensively upwards "to see if any sudden effect had been produced". When it rained soon afterwards this was attributed entirely to his whistles.

Due to his recurrent malaria and shortage of quinine, Sam was not able to shoot nearly as much as usual during this period. On one occasion, however, feeling slightly recovered, he stayed up overnight with Richarn in a pit dug near the native cornfields waiting for elephants which were raiding them. He was armed with "The Baby" by Holland of Bond Street. With this he took a shot at the shoulder of an elephant at about twelve paces. Blinded by the flash and half deafened by the report, he could see nothing in the outer darkness, but heard a heavy fall. In the morning the elephant was found standing not far away: but within a short time it fell dead. Sam measured it as ten feet six inches at the shoulder before allowing the natives to cut it up. A few days later he shot a boar with his "little Fletcher" .240, which delighted the Obbo, but not the Mohammedans in Ibrahim's party, who considered it "unclean".

With his new-found influence over Ibrahim, Sam managed to persuade him to accompany him with a hundred men to Kamrasi's country as soon as the river Asua was fordable in January. On the 3rd of January, after swallowing the last of his quinine, he wrote in his journal: "All ready for a start tomorrow. I trust the year 1864 will bring better luck than the past, that having been the most annoying that I have ever experienced, and full of fever. I hope now to reach Kamrasi's country in a fortnight, and to obtain guides from him direct to the lake . . ."

On the first day's march Sam's riding-ox bolted and he was forced to walk the entire eighteen miles, which ordinarily he would have regarded merely as "a pleasant stroll" but in his very debilitated state he found exhausting. Florence's threw her, but Ibrahim kindly lent her another. The next day, after walking eight miles, Sam purchased a good riding-ox from Ibrahim in return for a double-barrelled gun. After some four days march they reached the river Asua. Here Sam shot a Mehedehet antelope with his favourite little Fletcher rifle. The following day he shot a water-buck. By the 13th of January they had reached Shooa, where they found supplies of food available very cheaply. At this stage Sam was deserted by his Obbo bearers, who were frightened of Kamrasi, and the Turks began to be dubious of advancing further. Fortunately Sam was able to convince Ibrahim that it was in his interests to go on and guaranteed him a large quantity of ivory (10,000 lbs). With the change of country and climate his health was greatly recovered and Sam now took entire command of the expedition, even correcting their guides by the use of Speke's map. He wrote:

> I thanked Speke and Grant at that moment, and upon many other occasions, for the map they had so generously given me! It has been my greatest satisfaction to have completed their great discovery and to bear testimony to the correctness of their map and general observations.

Finally they reached the Karuma Falls on the edge of Kamrasi's country. Here they managed to persuade the people that he was "Speke's brother" come to visit them. Sam, dressed in a tweed suit something like that worn by Speke, and looking as "imposing as Nelson in Trafalgar Square", stood on the opposite side of the falls, showing himself to them before being accepted. Thereafter Sam had considerable difficulty in obtaining an audience with Kamrasi.

The delays and frustrations of the African traveller now piled on him. Both he and Florence were ill with fever. By January 30th it was arranged that he should march to Kamrasi's capital, from whence he was promised a guide to the lake. In the first week of February Florence was very ill and Sam was so weak he could not ride an ox even when held in place. By February 10th, however, Sam was recovered enough to meet Kamrasi at last. They met on an island where Sam gave the king numerous presents. Ibrahim became his blood brother and allied himself to Kamrasi. It was finally agreed that Kamrasi would provide guides and an escort to take Sam and his party to the lake. On February 21st Ibrahim and his men departed to continue their slave-trading activities, leaving Sam with his small party of thirteen men to go on to the Lake. The slave-traders, however agreed to link up with them on their return journey.

For several wearisome interviews Kamrasi begged for various items as presents and Sam was fobbed off with promises of transport to the lake. He wrote wearily that "It is the rapacity of the chiefs of the various tribes that renders African exploration so difficult. Each tribe wishes to monopolise your entire stock."

In late February the day finally arrived when Kamrasi was unable to find any further excuse for preventing Sam from journeying to the lake. He tried once more to beg the gift of his watch, though Sam had many times pointed out that it was entirely necessary for him to have it. Nor would Sam allow him to have his favourite little Fletcher .240.

The start with Kamrasi's escort

The storm on the Lake

Hauling the steamer through the Sudd

A hippopotamus attacks at night

The square is formed

The charge of "The Forty"

Newly-released female slaves kiss their liberator

The charge of the lioness

Finally Sam pointed out that they must go. He wrote:

> I now requested Kamrasi to allow us to take leave, as we had not an
> hour to lose. In the coolest manner he replied: "I will send you to the
> lake and to Shooa, as I have promised; but, *you must leave your wife
> with me.*"

Sam promptly drew his revolver and pointing it at Kamrasi
announced that surrounded by his followers as he was this would be
the end of him. Florence herself rose in indignation and delivered a
furious speech in Arabic, not a word of which he understood, with "a
countenance almost as amiable as the head of Medusa". Kamrasi was
utterly astounded by this reaction and calmly replied:

> "Don't be angry! I had no intention of offending you . . . I will give
> you a wife if you want one, and I thought you might have no objection
> to give me yours; it is my custom to give my visitors pretty wives, and
> I thought you might exchange. Don't make a fuss about it; if you don't
> like it, there's an end of it; I will never mention it again."

Sam accepted this apology with unbending British severity and
demanded that they started on their journey. Kamrasi then ordered
some porters to carry their loads, and with a very icy farewell Sam
and Florence started on their way accompanied by their greatly
reduced party. For the first few days, however, until Sam dismissed
them, they had a very noisy escort of Kamrasi's people also following
them.

Two days after they had started Florence was struck down by a
severe attack of heatstroke, when crossing a marsh, and for several
days Sam thought she was dying. The illness lasted a week, during
which they carried her on a litter and survived on occasional guinea
fowl, which Sam managed to shoot. He spent most of the nights by
her side doing his best to nurse her back to health, but she was
delirious and in convulsions. His men even reached the stage of
digging her grave, and Sam finally slept from sheer exhaustion. When
he woke it was to find that she had survived the crisis and was once
again sleeping soundly. After two days' rest they continued their
journey with Florence on a litter, still weak, but recovering. Finally,
on the 14th March they reached their goal. In his journal Sam
chronicled their success thus:

> At about 12, the long sought lake suddenly presented itself—the
> long sought Lut an N'zige! far as the eye could reach to the south west
> and west, the boundless sheet of water lay like a mirror; while to the
> north west it was bounded by a high range of mountains . . . Went to
> the water's edge directly, drank a long draught, thanked God most
> sincerely for having guided me, when all hope of success was lost, to
> this much wished for end. I christened the lake the Albert *N'yanza.*

In his book, *The Albert N'yanza*, which he wrote on his return, based on his journal, Sam wrote more fulsomely that "The waves were rolling upon a white pebbly beach. I rushed into the lake and thirsty with heat and fatigue, with a heart full of gratitude, I drank deeply from the sources of the Nile."

By reaching Lake N'yanza Sam had achieved the main object of his expedition and the problem of the true sources of the Nile appeared to be solved satisfactorily. The subject, however, remained open to question for a further decade after his return. Livingstone, for instance, until his death held firmly to the view that the ultimate sources were much further to the south. It was not until 1875 that Stanley finally circumnavigated Lake N'yanza and the area was not accurately surveyed until 1901 by Colonel C. Delmé-Radcliffe.

7

The Return Home

Although they had finally achieved their object, both Sam and Florence were extremely debilitated from the continual attacks of malaria and the other tropical ailments which had assailed them in the past few months. Florence, in particular, was undoubtedly still badly affected by the recent attack of heatstroke, which had so nearly resulted in her death. The rest of the party were in little better state. They were all exhausted and incapable of any really sustained effort.

Within a quarter of a mile of the point at which they reached the lake there was a fishing village named Vacovia. Here Sam established his party and purchased a bullock to provide a feast "in honour of the discovery". He then attempted to obtain boats to explore the lake and the river Somerset, which had been marked in Speke's map, but not visited. Aware of the need for haste, since the boats would leave Gondokoro in April, Sam nevertheless persisted in completing this self-imposed task, but it was a full eight days before the necessary means of transport arrived.

While they waited for the boats the entire party was prostrated with malaria, due to the change of climate on the lake shore. Eventually they obtained two hollowed-out trees. One of these Sam roofed over with a framework of ox-hide over bent wands, forming a protective arch against sun and rain, which was to prove very necessary. With four native paddlers in each boat they finally set off on their journey.

Despite large numbers of hippopotami, which provided very tempting targets, Sam refused to shoot, since he knew that the boatmen would insist on stopping to obtain the flesh, thus delaying them for a full day. As it was, the men deserted at the first opportunity, though fortunately Sam had retained their paddles. Rigging a rudder and mounting a sail made from a Scots plaid, Sam continued indomitably on his way, but the second boat was left hopelessly behind. At this stage they fell in with friendly natives, who came to their rescue, sending a party to the aid of the second canoe.

Then they encountered a storm and only just managed to beach their boat on the shore in time to prevent its being swamped. Their second boat, which they had given up for lost, also managed to reach the shore successfully, but the following day they were held up by "a heavy sea" and did not get under way until the afternoon.

Although they passed within thirty yards of a large elephant bathing in the lake, with little more than his head showing, Sam resisted the temptation to shoot, again because of the delay it would have caused. Not long afterwards, however, he decided to see whether his "little Fletcher" was still working, despite the damp to which it had been exposed, by shooting a crocodile. He killed it neatly and his men promptly removed some choice morsels from the body, much to the disgust of the natives, who regarded it as totally uneatable. Sam himself noted:

> I have eaten almost everything; but although I have tasted crocodile, I could never succeed in swallowing it; the combined flavour of bad fish, rotten flesh and musk, is the *carte de diner* offered to the epicure.

Despite the sporting temptation of herds of elephants on the shore, they continued their journey and after a fortnight arrived at Magungo, a village at the north-east end of the lake. Once again stricken with malaria, they forced their way on up the river Somerset. Here they found the large falls, which they named the Murchison Falls, after Sir Roderick Murchison, President of the Royal Geographical Society. Finally they reached the island of Patooan, where the tsetse fly killed all their riding oxen and they were unable to find porters. Had they been fit Sam might have abandoned everything but their arms and ammunition and marched directly to Gondokoro, but they were scarcely able to walk a quarter of a mile without fainting. They were ferried across the river, however, to a deserted village named Shooa Moru. Worn out with fever and fatigue, they remained there for nearly two months, barely able to survive and leading a miserable existence. Aware that by this time they were too late to reach Gondokoro for the boats, even had they been able to make the journey, they had nearly given up hope. In fact they had been deliberately abandoned there by the orders of the native chieftain, Kamrasi.

At last Sam's party was guided to Kamrasi's camp at Kisoona, where ten of Ibrahim's men remained. There Sam met again the man he had been introduced to previously as Kamrasi, who now confessed that he was merely a younger brother, named N'Gambi. Sam, however, was presented with a cow and calf by Kamrasi from which he obtained much needed milk and butter. With these the chieftain Kamrasi sent a message requesting the gift in return of his

Fletcher rifle, his compass and his watch. Sam refused to part with any of these on the grounds that they were essential equipment, but sent him some powder, caps and "a few trifles".

In the end a meeting with Kamrasi was arranged and for the occasion Sam dressed in the full regalia of a Scottish Highlander, "sporran and Glengarry bonnet . . . with plaid and kilt of Athole tartan". Apparently he had been keeping this startling outfit in reserve amongst his depleted baggage throughout his entire journey for just such an occasion. The effect was immensely successful and Kamrasi promptly demanded the clothes "as proof of friendship", along with his watch, compass and the Fletcher rifle, but all were in turn refused. Sam carried this off by maintaining that Kamrasi could not possibly be the great king he claimed to be if he had to keep begging for things, but must merely be another imposter, like his brother N'Gambi.

There followed a period of rest at Kisoona, where Sam built a strongly fenced hut and fattened quickly on the milk and cheese from the cow Kamrasi had given them. They also received an ox a month and "a quantity of flour". Nevertheless Sam's attacks of malaria still left him very weak, until he started a series of vapour baths with castor oil leaves in hot water, which produced an intense heat. This apparently he found a great relief.

Meanwhile Kamrasi kept attempting to get Sam to attack his neighbours, Fowooka and Rionga, but Sam resolutely refused to be involved in native warfare. However, when a rival slave trader started to invade Kamrasi's territory with Fowooka, Sam hoisted the Union Jack and after a parley convinced the man that it would be wiser to withdraw his forces than attack British territory. Sam also insisted on the slaver explaining the reasons for his retreat in front of Kamrasi's brother, N'Gambi, with the result that Kamrasi was most impressed.

The Turks, under Eddrees, Ibrahim's lieutenant, then attacked Fowooka with Kamrasi's forces and were notably victorious. It was not long, though, before they fell out with each other and Sam was able to act as mediator, agreeable to both sides, rapidly gaining a complete ascendancy over them. He had at the same time no illusions about Kamrasi's methods of ruling his kingdom, occasionally meditating allying himself with his opponents and ending his dictatorship of terror. There are modern parallels with Sam's description of his rule:

> To be suspected of rebellion was to die. A bodyguard of about 500 men who were allowed to pillage the country at discretion secured the power of the king, as with this organised force always at hand he could pounce upon the suspected and extinguish them at once . . .

Sam himself, as ever, was not content with half measures. He found that the natives in the huts surrounding his often went to bed in drunken slumber with their pipes still alight, with the result that their dwellings went up in flames. Afraid for the safety of his gunpowder supplies, without which he would have been defenceless, he took firm action. He wrote that ". . . after a conflagration in my neighbourhood, I insisted upon removing all huts within a circuit of thirty yards from my dwelling; the natives demurring, I at once ordered my men to pull down the houses, and thereby relieved myself from drunken and dangerous neighbours."

Early in September the natives of Uganda, the M'Was, invaded Kamrasi's territory with a large army. Sam immediately sent word to Ibrahim at Shooa (quite distinct from Shooa Moru) requesting him to come to their relief at once with a hundred men. Showing his customary cowardice in the face of danger, Kamrasi fled for safety to the Karuma Falls, leaving Sam and his party without porters in the hope that they would be forced to act as an involuntary rearguard. Sam, however, withdrew his party successfully to a deserted village.

In due course, in the latter part of September, Ibrahim arrived with the relief force requested and the M'Was retreated in front of them. Sam received mail some two years old and basked in the luxury of reading *Punch* and similar journals with details of Speke and Grant's triumph in finding the sources of the Nile. Ibrahim found a vast store of ivory awaiting him, much of it amassed through Sam's interventions, and was amazed at his good fortune. As for Kamrasi, he seized several enemy villages and plundered the cattle and women, so that all were in their own way entirely satisfied.

While Ibrahim was conducting operations against Kamrasi's enemies, Sam constructed a still to produce potato whisky. Richarn, Sam's faithful aide-de-camp, was frequently found asleep with the still out and everything cold. Despite this, the still worked well and Sam wrote:

> I found an extraordinary change in my health from the time that I commenced drinking the potato-whisky. Every day I drank hot toddy. I became strong, and from that time to the present day my fever left me, occurring only once or twice during the first six months, and then quitting me entirely.

The idea was promptly copied both by the Turks and by the natives. They each developed similar stills to produce crude spirits. Kamrasi in particular decided that this was an excellent innovation, to the extent of planting acres of roots specifically for this purpose. Neither had Sam's medicinal motives in mind.

In November, at last, Ibrahim set off for Shooa, accompanied by

Sam and his small party. Ibrahim had acquired such an enormous quantity of ivory from Kamrasi that he needed seven hundred porters to carry it. The entire party numbered well over a thousand. When Sam shot a hartebeest weighing some 500 lbs with his favourite Fletcher .240, it vanished in a few moments after Sam had taken all he needed from the carcase.

Sam was forced to spend several months at Shooa before the boats were due at Gondokoro. During this period he filled his time "rambling" and shooting varied game, from crocodiles to antelopes, waterbuck and hartebeest. He also acquired various botanical specimens, including two varieties of cotton indigenous to the country, which he later presented to the Royal Botanical Gardens at Kew.

It was February of 1865 before Sam and Florence finally left Shooa for Gondokoro. They had good riding oxen, but very little baggage of their own, although Ibrahim had nearly £10,000 worth of ivory. They followed the course of the Nile on the same route previously taken by Speke and Grant, first crossing the nearly dried-up bed of the Asua river, before marching through the territory of the hostile Bari tribe. Sam wrote caustically when they were attacked that "The rattle of musketry and the wild appearance of the naked vermilion-coloured savages, as they leapt along the craggy ridge twanging their bows at us with evil but ineffectual intent, was a charming picture of African life and manners."

There were no casualties amongst his party and only a few amongst the natives, for the native bows were most inferior and, as Sam noted, both the trader's men and his party were "shooters, but not hitters". Eventually they reached Gondokoro, only to find that there were no boats, letters or supplies awaiting them as they had for a long time been given up as dead in Khartoum. Furthermore the Egyptian authorities had decreed that slaving must cease and had sent a regiment, along with several steamers, which had already seized various parties of slaves, to enforce the order. Apart from this plague had broken out in Khartoum and 15,000 people had died of it. Instead of attacking Baker as responsible for this setback to their trade, the slavers were completely cowed and acknowledged that he had foretold it.

Sam engaged a *diahbiah* which had been sent for ivory that could no longer be delivered at Gondokoro in these circumstances. Numbers on board the craft had died from the plague during the journey from Khartoum. He had it thoroughly scrubbed with boiling water and sand, then fumigated with several pounds of tobacco burnt in the cabin. With the plague rife in Gondokoro Sam was glad to get away down the Nile as soon as possible. By the end of March they were well on their way, Sam taking the opportunity to write to England and look back over the past three years.

The voyage was not entirely without incident. At one point they halted to stalk a herd of several thousand antelope of a species he had not previously encountered. He bagged five, leaving all bar one for nearby natives. Then they encountered a natural dam of floating vegetation and weeds, three quarters of a mile wide, which they managed to navigate successfully through a channel which had been cut in it, although forced to unload their boat to get through. Then, when all their troubles appeared to be over, the plague broke out on board. The boy Saat, their faithful follower throughout all their tribulations, was amongst the last to die; a death which greatly affected both Sam and Florence.

On 5th of May 1865 they arrived at Khartoum, half an hour after sunset, to find that here too they had long been given up as dead. It was here for the first time that Sam learned of the sad death of Speke, who had been killed in a shooting accident, caused by pulling a loaded gun towards him by the barrels, when crossing an obstacle. Since he had been challenged on the authenticity of his claims to have found the true sources of the Nile by his old fellow explorer and adversary, Sir Richard Burton, and was about to speak in his own defence at the time of his death, this tragedy had cast doubts in some minds on his success. Sam was at once eager to vindicate him to the full.

Owing to the fact that he could obtain neither camels nor boats Sam was forced to stay in Khartoum for two months, despite the fact that the plague was raging. Suffering the effects of boils and dust storms, Sam and Florence survived this further hiatus. Sam even had the satisfaction of encountering his old adversary, Mahommed Her, the slave trader who had encouraged his men to mutiny in the early stages of his journey. Sam had him charged, tried and bastinadoed, or flogged on the bare feet. After 150 lashes he had him pardoned.

On the 30th of June, when the Nile had risen sufficiently to allow the passage of the Cataracts, Sam and his party left for Berber. Their *diahbiah* stuck on a sandbank broadside on in the Cataracts and nearly sank, but Sam managed to rally the terrified crew, saving the boat by clearing a narrow channel in the sand. They then let the current take them clear of the rocks beyond.

There seems little doubt that at this stage Sam became un-characteristically dispirited and as well as having a heavy cold he most clearly had intimations of mortality. After reaching Fashoda in April he entered in his diary:

> Sunday, 16th of April. Bad cold, evening hot and sultry in Fashoda, government camp. Fever is dangerous here and life is so uncertain that I have given Florence B. Finnian two cheques for £300 and £200 on the Bank of Egypt, Cairo Branch. This is in addition to money left her by my will made in Khartoum previous to my departure . . . I have made this arrangement as one is utterly helpless should the fever attack one and I should be incapable of action in business matters and she would be in great trouble in Egypt and Khartoum in case of my death.

It is notable that this is the sole mention of Florence by name in his diaries, since elsewhere she is referred to solely by her initials with no reference to her sex. Sam was subsequently to make up for this by his fulsome references to the part she had played in the books he wrote after his expeditions, but this fits in with his explanation that had they both died he had no wish for mention of her in his diaries to be the first occasion that his children learned of their relationship and that it had always been his intention to introduce her to them personally. Now that they were nearly home he was intent on making provision for her should anything happen to him at this stage.

At Berber there was a slight delay while they procured camels. His party by this time consisted of himself and Florence; Richarn, who had married a six-foot Dinka girl named Zeneb; also a servant named Schmet, engaged at Khartoum, and a Swiss missionary. Sam decided to take the route east to Souakim where he hoped to get a steamer up the Red Sea, rather than try to cross the Korosko desert during the hottest month of the year.

Arriving at a solitary tree in the desert they found its shade occupied by a band of Hadendowa Arabs. Apart from refusing to move over to make room as was the desert custom, they attacked Sam's party with drawn swords. Although armed only with a sunshade Sam parried the leader's cutlass blow with his seemingly harmless weapon and thrust the point into the man's throat with sufficient force to send him sprawling on the ground. Left with no other weapon after parrying a second blow he was reduced to using his fists, with which he knocked down three or four more of the gang. Fortunately he was beneath the tree and since the Arabs did not understand the use of the point, but only slashed, he was saved by the overhanging boughs. Very quickly Sam and Richarn disarmed the few Arabs left who were capable of resisting. Zeneb, the muscular Dinka girl, knocked down one who was about to attack Richarn, and Florence kept another at bay with a discarded cutlass. Very soon they were all disarmed, lined up and about to be thrashed, when an elderly white-haired Arab in Sam's party begged that they should be forgiven. This Sam duly agreed to do, on condition that they should only receive their weapons back after the last well on the route.

The journey from Berber to Souakim, a distance of about 275 miles, took them twenty-five days. There the thermometer stood at 115° or more and they were forced to wait a full fortnight for a ship. Fortunately the governor, Djiaffer Pasha, proved extremely friendly. He had been an Admiral in the Egyptian Navy and had visited Europe. As a result he had a high regard for the concept of "the English gentleman", which he did his best to emulate. He provided them with a comfortable house and entertained them lavishly.

Even so, at the end of the fortnight, Sam and Florence took themselves thankfully on board an old troop transport steamer and after a further five days reached Suez. Here they found the pleasures of "Allsop's Pale Ale" on draught and beds which had *sheets and pillowcases!*" They went on swiftly to Cairo, where there were letters from England awaiting Sam at the British Consulate. The first he opened was from the Royal Geographical Society informing him that he had been awarded their Victoria Gold Medal at a time when they still did not know whether he was alive or dead. Others were of a more private and personal nature from his family and friends, delighted to learn that he was alive after all, seemingly returned from the dead.

Leaving his loyal servant Richarn in service at Sheppard's Hotel, with the best reference he could provide, Sam and Florence took ship for England with all possible speed. The simple life of the explorer with his "wife" beside him, camping in the wilds, generally the only white people for hundreds of miles, and living off his rifle, was now behind them. The return to civilisation posed problems which had been shelved for seven years, ever since Sam had first met Florence in 1858.

Very shortly after their arrival in England, on November 4th 1865, Sam and Florence were married quietly in the fashionable St. James' Church in Piccadilly. Sam's brother James and his wife Louisa were the witnesses. Whether making good a vow he had made in 1858 on first meeting her, or merely acknowledging the undoubted debt he owed her, Sam was not the man to shirk the issue.

As a temporary expedient Sam had taken a London house, while he introduced his new wife to his family and friends, especially to his four daughters, to whom he was almost a stranger after seven years' separation. Fortunately the girls, not much younger than their new step-mother, and Florence, took to each other at once. There was, understandably, a somewhat restrained, even sour, reaction from Sam's sister Min, who had been acting as a mother to his children and now saw her position of authority unexpectedly usurped, but the Baker family, as a whole, always ready to back their own, welcomed her into their midst loyally. Even so the transition must have been an abrupt one, making a remarkable impact on the young Hungarian girl, still only twenty-four and accustomed for the past five years to hardship and danger. It says much for her remarkable poise and control that she fitted instantly into place amongst fashionable London society.

On November 13th, just nine days after his marriage, Sam was invited to give the inaugural Autumn address to the Royal Geographical Society at Burlington House and was introduced by Sir Roderick Murchison, the President. *The Times* for November 14th contained a vivid account of the evening, quoting Sir Roderick's introduction:

> . . . Let me call your attention to one or two salient points in the conduct of this man who is now happily among us, and who, by his devotion to geographical science has worked out, entirely at his own cost, this grand addition to our previous knowledge. (cheers) Mr. Samuel Baker was no sooner acquainted with the perilous and exhausted condition in which Speke and Grant were supposed to emerge from Equitorial Africa . . . than at his own cost, he fitted out an expedition and carrying adequate supplies, was the first to relieve them of their wants. (cheers) It was for this noble conduct, as well as for the gallant and determined manner in which, undaunted by all the dangers through which Speke and Grant had struggled, he resolved to go forward into the country of King Kamrasi, there to work out that important portion of the course of the Nile, which was left undetermined, that we awarded him our Victoria Medal . . . I have here to announce, and with a pleasure and gratification that will, I know, be shared by everyone in this assembly, that in all his arduous and perilous travels our medallist was accompanied by Mrs Baker (cheers) to whom, as he himself has told me, much of his success is due, and who, by her conduct, has shown what a courageous wife can do in duty to her husband.

Sam, always a good public speaker, then gave his account of the journey, holding his audience gripped throughout. Acknowledging fully his debt to Speke and Grant, he amply confirmed their discovery of the sources of the Nile. He ended with a flourish:

> And there is one whom I must thank and whom I am truly glad to thank in your presence, one who though young and tender has the heart of a lion, and without whose devotion and courage I would not be alive to address you tonight. Mr. President, my Lords, Ladies and Gentlemen, allow me to present my wife.

Sam then strode into the wings, bowed and returned with

Florence, immaculately coiffeured and gowned in the height of fashion, young and lovely, on his arm. The audience rose to their feet as one and applauded her wildly. Sam and his young wife had taken London by storm and from then on they were the toast of fashionable society with every door open to them.

Ever an individualist, Sam cared little for public opinion, paying heed only to the views of his family and a few close friends, but had he wished to have his wife of nine days publicly accepted by all he could not have managed the affair better. With the ready acceptance of double standards which typified the Victorian era, no-one dreamed of investigating matters too closely. There may have been a few wild stories going the rounds of the clubs, though none likely to be as wild as the truth, but on the whole people saw a beautiful and devoted wife and merely considered Sam a lucky fellow, as indeed he was.

Although lionised by London society neither Sam nor Florence was fond of the fashionable life of the metropolis. However they each had plenty of other distractions to keep them fully occupied. Getting to know the Baker clan, in particular her own newly acquired family of four step-daughters, was Florence's immediate concern, as well as improving her English, especially her writing. Picking up old friendships with those such as Lord Wharncliffe, with whom he had hunted in Ceylon, and the Duke of Athol, on whose Scottish estates he had stalked, and many others, kept Sam busy, as well as completing the book on his explorations that he had begun on the voyage back from Egypt to England. Quite apart from all of this, they were also trying to find themselves a house in the country where they could make a permanent home.

Fast writer that he was, Sam must have put in some hard work to finish the book before the end of January. Thereafter there was proof-reading with corrections to be made to the galleys, then the page proofs to be read again and corrected and the index to be checked and all the multifarious work of authorship, which must have kept him busy until well into June. The book itself, entitled *The Albert N'yanza, Great Basin of the Nile and Explorations of the Nile Sources*, was dedicated by permission to "The Queen" and was published in July by MacMillan. Perhaps his most important, if not his best, book, it was an instant success. (New editions: 1867; 1869: Reprinted 1872, 1873, 1874, 1877, 1879, 1883, 1885, 1888, 1892, 1962, 1974.)

Mr. W.E. Gladstone, then a powerful political figure, although not Prime Minister, wrote an enthusiastic letter to his friend Sir Roderick Murchison on July 23rd after reading the book. He suggested:

> Could we not have some Testimonial, by subscription to her, or to him and to her? Baker has done us very great honour in a distant and

barbarous land; he has made another great discovery; the lives dearest to him have been imperilled; and he has achieved his work without costing the State a shilling . . . if it be worth while, consult with higher authorities. I know not whether the State can confer some mark of honour; but that need not clash with my suggestion . . .

It is clear that Gladstone's reaction to Sam's book was by no means an isolated one, for, although his suggestion came to nothing, soon afterwards the Earl of Derby wrote to Sam as follows:

> Downing Street; 15th August 1866
> I am commanded by the Queen to express to you Her sense of the services rendered to Geographical Science by your laborious researches in Africa; and to add, that Her Majesty will have pleasure in testifying Her appreciation of those services by conferring on you the Honour of Knighthood, should it be agreeable to you to accept it.

Sam was agreeable to becoming Sir Samuel White Baker, and already by this time he and the newly created Lady Baker had begun to settle down with their family in a newly rented house, Hedenham Hall, near Bungay in Norfolk. He wrote to his sister in early August:

> Here we are, settled at last, in a queer old place with a hall that is now adorned with all my African spoils. There are no greenhouses, nor even melon-frames, as the place is pre-Adamite. The garden is that of Eden; but man has spoiled Eden by the erection of a pump. No spade or rake appears to have interfered with the arrangements of Nature. The old house stands in a park of very rich grass, with very beautiful oaks and sweet-chestnuts many centuries old, beneath which the children are happily cutting-about on their pony, as happy as possible. We have our cows, pigs, turkeys, ducks and fowls; and the art of wandering having taught us the habit of quickly settling-down in a new camp, we are as much at home as though we had lived here since the day the old oaks were planted.

It is plain from this letter that Sam and Florence were supremely happy in their rustic idyll, but even in this Eden there was a snake. Captain James Grant, Speke's faithful companion, had returned to the Indian Army and was serving in the Punjab. A son of the manse, aged 39 and newly married, he was filled with jealousy at the glowing reviews of Sam's book which appeared in the papers. When he learned that Sam had been awarded a knighthood and he had merely received a Companionship of the Bath, while Speke had received no posthumous mention or honour, his spleen was fully roused. Before even having read Sam's book, which gave full measure of praise to Speke and Grant, he wrote to everyone of influence whom he knew, including Sir Roderick Murchison, Lord Camden and Blackwood, the Edinburgh publisher, as well as to Sam himself, proclaiming himself "disgusted". The letter to Blackwood reads at times as if Grant was almost unhinged. It would be unfair to quote it in full since, apart from the fact that it covers some eight pages of nearly illegible scrawl, he almost certainly regretted it later, for his subsequent relations with Sam appear to have been cordial enough. Indeed it is very much to Sam's credit that in all the almost inevitable wrangling regarding the value of the various discoveries made by them and subsequent explorers, he remained on good terms with all.

Grant undermined his own case to start with by admitting that Speke had suggested he should explore the Albert N'yanza when they were at Kamrasi's, warning him that unless he made a discovery he would not be acknowledged on their return. Kamrasi, predicatably refused to allow him to go, so that in the end they never saw the lake and relied on native reports of it. In such circumstances he could scarcely complain when Sam's efforts proved their assumptions correct.

Nevertheless he accused Sam of having snatched the discovery "from those who were so generous to him", of improving "his tale by introducing this lady's name" while abusing them "for never having publicly mentioned her"; of diverting "the attention of the public from our lake to his" and, most absurd of all, being "knighted in a few weeks after his return". This, he considered, "a *transaction* or rather job which I should be very sorry to have had a part in". As he had earlier claimed that Sam introduced Florence to them as his "chere amie" and went on to quote secondhand gossip as to her origins as a barmaid in a continental inn at which Sam had stayed, but also indicated that Sam had stated his intention to marry her, it is impossible to attach any weight to anything in his letter. It was that of a man eaten up with jealousy and rancour.

It is true that Sam in his book carefully avoided any mention of Florence at his meeting with Speke and Grant. It is almost certain that he had asked Speke not to mention her presence, except possibly to his brothers, since he wanted to introduce her to his family himself, and Grant as good as admits this was the case. It is also likely that he told Speke of his intention to marry her on his return, although Grant twisted this to appear as if Speke had suggested this to Sam and the latter had meekly agreed. Such behaviour is so highly un-characteristic of Sam's forthright approach to life that the accusation is laughable.

Despite Grant's letters, Florence and Sam were invited to country house week-ends all over the country. Lord and Lady Wharncliffe, Sam's old friends, Lord Derby, the Duke of St. Albans, the Duke and Duchess of Sutherland and numerous others invited them to stay. Indeed they had far more invitations than they could cope with and often preferred to stay at home at Hedenham Hall.

In February of 1867, while staying with the Wharncliffes, Sam asked Lady Wharncliffe to present Florence at Court. He was not prepared for the hurtful reply that this was not considered possible. The rumours about Florence, whether spread by Grant or others, had reached the ears of the widow at Windsor. Predictably Sam was both hurt and furious. On the 4th of March he wrote to Wharncliffe:

> My dear Wharncliffe,
>
> I was very miserable when I left you, and am still—more especially on Lady Wharcliffe's account, as I am so deeply distressed that *she* should have to have any annoyance and heartburning for her kind intention of presenting my wife. Had I had the slightest suspicion of the consequences of asking her, you know I should have been the last to have done so.
>
> I cannot understand the laws of marriage, nor do I attach the least importance to the various forms that each country separately adopts as custom—
>
> If a Scotch marriage is valid (and we know it is) even in England, and where the simple fact of registration, before a magistrate, in *London* is itself valid—what form shall be adopted when one party is Roman Catholic and the other Protestant, and in a wild country like Hungary or Turkey?!—this was our case until my wife became a Protestant—but the vows entered into were never more faithfully kept, or more devotedly acted upon through years of danger and trial than by us, and the very moment we entered England we were married according to the forms of our Church so that no custom of the country should be infringed . . . Never was marriage more sacredly kept than it has been from the moment we first exchanged those vows. What care I for Kings or Princes!
>
> For years I have been happy without the world, when we have been together with a poor hut or shady tree for home, thus with her I can be happy again and lay the world down at will with satisfaction that my course has not been worldly-wise—To her I have done my duty, and for her would I sacrifice position, wealth, life—everything.
>
> Forgive me, my dear Wharncliffe, for writing all this, but I know your sincere friendship and you know mine to you.
>
> Ever yours, Samuel W. Baker.

At this time the fate of Livingstone, believed to have died or been murdered while exploring alone in Africa, was very much on people's minds and in an unusually sombre frame of mind Sam wrote on this subject to his friend Sir Roderick Murchison on the 8th of March:

> I would rather die thus than be slowly poisoned by a doctor; and the hard soil of Africa is a more fitting couch for the last gasp of an African explorer than the down-pillow of a civilised home. Livingstone's fate seems to have cast a gloom over African travels; and the papers appear to taunt African travellers with running quixotic risks. If England is

becoming so cowardly and so soft, that travel shall cease in dangerous countries because some fall victims to it, then it is time to roll up the English flag and to admit the decline of the English spirit. In all humility, I can only say that I am ready.

Apart from these two brief explosions neither Sam, nor Florence, allowed the royal rebuff to worry them unduly. Sam was soon busy completing the accounts of their travels in Abyssinia during 1861 and 1862. This was published in the Autumn of 1867 by Macmillan entitled *The Nile Tributaries of Abyssinia, and the Sword Hunters of the Hamran Arabs* and again achieved considerable success, with new editions in 1867; 1868; 1871 and reprints in 1872; 1880; 1883; 1886; 1894. A more racy, lighter book than the two-volume *Albert N'yanza*, it reflected the first pleasurable year of wandering before he and Florence settled down to the rigours of serious exploration. It was perhaps the best book he ever wrote on Africa, lively, humorous and highly readable.

When King Theodosius (or Theodore) of Abyssinia fell foul of the British government in the same year, through imprisoning certain British subjects, Sam was certain that with his intimate knowledge of the country he could supply a better answer than mounting a full-scale expedition to release them at a cost of several million pounds. On 29th October 1867 he wrote to his friend Lord Wharncliffe outlining his plan:

> I am trying to persuade the Government to send a small expedition of 1,000 men via Suakim to Abyssinia, through my old friend Meg Nimmur's country; and to endeavour to release the captives by this means; as he is a great friend of Theodore's. Should he fail, the force of 1,000 British troops . . . would be in the heart of Theodore's country in a few days, and would, in my opinion, settle the affair long before Napier's column could commence the march from the coast of Massawa.

It was, of course, much too simple a plan for any government official to accept. Every obstacle and objection was raised against the advice of almost the only man in England who knew the country. In the end Sir Robert Napier's expedition left Bombay and landed at Annesley Bay in January of 1868. The prisoners were released and King Theodore committed suicide, but the total cost was in the region of nine million pounds.

Meanwhile Edith, Sam's eldest daughter, had become engaged to Mr. Robert Marshall, the rector of Hedenham, a good-looking, well set-up young man, who was to remain in the same living for the next forty years. The marriage took place in the Autumn of 1867 and was extremely well attended. Sam found it necessary to add a large conservatory onto the hall to accommodate all the guests.

No doubt that Christmas at Hedenham was a particularly close family affair. Perhaps it was this that inspired Sam to write his next book, his first venture into fiction—an adventure book for boys, entitled *Cast Up by the Sea*. The background included smuggling and the Napoleonic Wars, Press Gangs, and, of course, almost inevitably, the slave trade in Africa. It was not particularly outstanding, although fully up to the standard of the times and for a first attempt at fiction it was good. He admitted that he enjoyed writing it, although his family considered it something of a come-down compared with his previous books. It provided further evidence, if that was required, that had he wished he could have made his living by writing. His was undoubtedly a gifted pen and on the whole he wrote as he lived, directly and without artifice. Furthermore, like his previous books, this sold well with a new edition in 1869 and reprints following in 1870; 1872; 1873; 1874; 1876; 1879; 1884; 1890 and 1931.

From mid-September until mid-October of 1868 Sam and Florence were guests of the Duke and Duchess of Sutherland at Dunrobin where they became friendly with the Prince and Princess of Wales. In the meantime Edith had given birth to a son and Florence wrote to her step-daughter as follows:

> My Dearest Edith,
> I shall indeed be so delighted to be godmother to your darling child, for I feel towards you all quite the love of your real mother and I only hope the other dear children will love me when they grow up as much as you have done, and be so good, dear Edith.
> I cannot tell you how I long to see my little grandson, I have put his dear hair in my locket, where I shall always keep it.
> It is very annoying that we cannot manage to be (together) but it can't be helped. Papa returned yesterday; he had been away deer stalking since Monday: Altogether he shot six stags.
> We shall have a very gay party the week after next, as there will be two balls given for the Prince of Wales. It is so very kind of the Duchess to insist upon our staying so long. We shall have been here for nearly a whole month by the time we leave.
> Give my love to dear Robert and a kiss to the darling grandson, Dearest Edith,
> Your ever affectionate, Florence Baker.

On September 27th, a few days after his arrival at Dunrobin, the Prince of Wales was writing a revealing letter to his mother:

> My dear Mama,
> . . . Sir W. Knollys wrote to me that you had heard that Sir Samuel and Lady Baker were here, and that you wished us to know that she had been on intimate terms with her husband before she married. I had also heard the report; and spoke to the Duke about it, and he

assures me that he and the Duchess had made enquiries into the matter and they had no doubt that there was *no* foundation for the story, and the Duchess is very particular about the ladies she asks and would certainly not have asked Lady Baker to meet Alix unless she felt certain that she was quite a fit person to know.

She is one of the quietest most ladylike persons one could see, and perfectly devoted and wrapt up in her husband, and I think it is very hard on both that this story should be believed, which must be most distressing for him, and very dreadful for her—and his name will always be known in history as a great discoverer. . .

I remain, your dutiful and affectionate son, Bertie.

In late January 1869 the Prince and Princess Alexandra of Wales went to Cairo on a private visit to the Khedive of Egypt, Ismail Pasha. Their intention was to take a sightseeing trip up the Nile as far as the Second Cataract, exploring the countryside and shooting some crocodiles and other animals on the way. Despite Queen Victoria's protests, the guide chosen by the Prince was Sam. The Duke and Duchess of Sutherland were also included in the party, but on this one occasion Florence remained behind. With his knowledge of the country and of Arabic, Sam arranged for steamers to be fitted out to take the royal party up the Nile. The Prince of Wales wrote to his mother on February 9th:

> We find Sir Samuel Baker very agreeable, and with so much to tell me about the country, which no one knows better than he does—that I cannot say how glad I am to have him to accompany me here.

At a grand Masked Ball, which followed a banquet given by de Lesseps, the French constructor of the Suez Canal due to be opened that Autumn, Ismail Pasha approached the Prince of Wales with a tentative proposal for suppressing the slave trade on the White Nile. He enquired whether the Prince thought Sir Samuel White Baker would be prepared to take on such a monumental task. The Prince promptly took Baker aside and revealed the proposition. Sam was enthusiastic. Before he had left the ball the decision was taken. Baker returned home to Florence with a contract for four years at a salary of £10,000 a year and apparently unlimited powers. Willy nilly he was committed.

8

Suppressing the Slave Trade : First Stage

In addition to his salary of £10,000 a year, Sam was made a Pasha, the first Briton to be thus honoured, and he was also appointed Governor General of the Equatorial Nile Basin. With this high-sounding title went absolute authority over "all the countries belonging to the Nile Basin south of Gondokoro". To enforce his authority he was to have a force of 1,645 men, including infantry, irregular cavalry and artillery. His contract as Governor General was to run from April 1869 for four years.

Since suppressing the slave trade in the Nile Basin inevitably entailed the annexation of a very large area, there were plenty to suggest, after the event, that Sam was merely being used by the Khedive to increase his Egyptian Empire. It was said that Ishmail had no real desire to suppress the slave trade on which at that time the Egyptian economy virtually depended. Both Sam and his successor, Gordon, however, were convinced of the Khedive's sincerity. With his characteristic simplicity of purpose, Sam wrote to his old friend Lord Wharncliffe:

> The main objects of the enterprise, are, after crushing the Slave Trade:
> 1. To annex to the Egyptian Empire the Equatorial Nile Basin.
> 2. To establish a powerful government throughout all these tribes now warring with each other.
> 3. To introduce the cultivation of cotton on an extensive scale, so that the natives shall have a valuable production to exchange for Manchester goods, etc.
> 4. To open to navigation the two great Lakes of the Nile.
> 5. To establish a chain of trading stations throughout the country to be annexed. . .
>
> The natural productions are ivory, native flax, beeswax and cotton, but I take seeds of the finest quality of the latter from Egypt. Every tribe will be compelled to cultivate a certain amount of corn and cotton in proportion to the population. No wars will be permitted. Each chief will be held responsible for the acts of his tribe. Tribute will be exacted

> on labour to be performed in opening our roads on the same principle
> as the road-tax in Ceylon.
>   To carry out this plan I have absolute power, conferred by the
> Khedive.

He stated firmly: "The success of an expedition depends mainly on the organisation." By this time he knew, better than most, the requirements of such an expedition in Central Africa. Even so the list of supplies that he bought personally at a cost of around £9,000 was daunting by any standards. It included Manchester goods, calico, blankets, scarlet flannel, serge, scarves and numerous similar merchandise, coloured prints, tin spoons, cheap watches and the like, as well as many other items from musical boxes to magic lanterns and magnetic batteries to provide electric shocks, all the product of his past experience of African travel.

Sam also brought stores sufficient for four years for his European party of some fifteen persons, including himself and Florence, his nephew, Lt. Julian Baker, on leave from the Royal Navy as his aide-de-camp at a salary of £500 a year from the Khedive, Mr. Edwin Higginbotham, chief civil engineer, Dr. Joseph Gedge and sundry shipwrights and specialists. It was the task of the engineers to assemble the two twin-screw steamers, the paddle steamer and two steel lifeboats, which he proposed to transport in sections to the White Nile. The purpose of these vessels was to facilitate transport along the line of stations that he intended to set up in the interior.

Knowing the hazards and difficulties of travel in the area, Sam arranged for his expedition to approach the starting point at Khartoum in three different parties, each taking separate routes, by which means he hoped to ease the pressure on the transport available, particularly camels. Six steamers, fifteen sloops and fifteen *diahbiahs* were ordered to leave Cairo in June to ascend the 1st and 2nd Cataracts during the period of high water, taking with them the merchandise. Owing to deliberate procrastination and delaying tactics of the Egyptian authorities, opposed to the expedition, they were held back until the 29th of August, by which time the steamers were too late to get through the Cataracts until the following season. Sam was thus deprived of their use until then.

He was not prepared to risk the valuable sections of the dismantled steamers on the dangerous route via the Cataracts. These were to be disembarked at Korosko to be transported by camel across the desert to Khartoum under the command of Mr. Higginbotham. The heavier pieces were to be towed on gun-carriages drawn by two camels, the rest carried slung on poles between camels.

Sam himself brought up the rear with his party, starting early in

December and travelling from Souakim to Berber. He made the journey from Suez within thirty-two days including delays on the way. He was shocked to see the desolation throughout what had previously been a well cultivated region, caused entirely by over-high taxation.

The arrival of Sam and his expedition in Khartoum was not popular, even with the Governor-General Djiaffer Pasha, who had been so kind to him on his arrival at Souakim on his previous journey of exploration and whom he considered a personal friend. Although Sam had ordered twenty-five vessels to be ready to take his expedition on to the next stage at Gondokoro, none were ready. To make matters worse Djiaffer Pasha had just prepared and sent off eleven vessels with troops to form a settlement on the frontier under the command of a notorious slave trader named Kutchuk Ali. Sam noted grimly that, "I at once perceived that not only was my expedition unpopular, but that it would be seriously opposed by all parties".

His 1,645 troops, consisting of two regiments, one black Sudanese, many of whom were experienced in battle, and one Egyptian, mostly composed of convicted felons, with 250 irregular cavalry and two batteries of artillery, had been awaiting him in the company of the slave traders of Khartoum and had already become disaffected. On the other hand his merchandise had arrived and he learned that Mr. Higginbotham was successfully crossing the four hundred miles of scorching Nubian desert with a train of 1,000 camels carrying the heavy machinery.

Within a month Sam had gathered together a fleet of thirty-three vessels, as well as two steamers. He had reviewed his troops and promptly dispensed with the 250 irregular cavalry, who proved to be "*very* irregular". He also selected forty-six men from the two regiments under his command as a special bodyguard and armed them with breech-loading Snider rifles. This élite force he put under the command of Lt. Colonel Abd-el-Kader, who proved a first-rate choice, sneeringly named by his compatriots "The Englishman" because of his loyalty.

On the 8th of February 1870, eleven months after the start of his contract, having lost a precious month in Khartoum at a time when the level of the rivers was falling, Sam and his expedition left for Gondokoro, a further 1,450 miles to the south, leaving Mr. Higginbotham, who by then had already reached Berber, to follow on behind them. After 103 hours' steaming they reached the government station of Fashoda in the Shilluk country, garrisoned by an Egyptian regiment. The handsome old governor, Ali Bey, assured Sam that he was following the Khedive's instructions and preventing any slaving vessels from passing his station.

By the 18th of February Sam's expedition had reached the point where the Sobat river joined the White Nile, some 648 miles from Khartoum. From here on the White Nile was completely blocked with an accumulation of floating vegetation which had formed an impenetrable mass, known as the Sudd. Their guides claimed there was a route through the Bahr Giraffe, a tributary of the White Nile, but from this point on their progress gradually slowed until it became a struggle to advance at all and the water level dropped daily, increasing the odds against them.

For Sam the tedium of the journey was at first occasionally enlivened by the shooting. Whenever they halted to cut wood for the steamers there was good wildfowl shooting. He and Julian also shot numerous francolin (a type of partridge), which were very good eating. One afternoon he killed a hippopotamus, two crocodiles and two pelicans with a rifle. As they entered the Bahr Giraffe he bagged twenty-two duck with a right and a left from a ten-bore gun. His favourite rifle, which seldom left his side, like the .240 on his previous expedition, was named "The Dutchman", a double-barrelled breechloader, made by Holland of Bond Street and accurate up to 300 yards.

From the river Sobat to Gondokoro Sam estimated they had to cover some 750 miles and by the end of February they were reduced to cutting channels through the matted vegetation. About this time he recorded passing a camp of slave traders belonging to Kutchuk Ali, the man employed by the Governor General to lead his expedition. There was plenty of evidence that they had been plundering the countryside, but Sam continued to press southwards.

Throughout March their difficulties multiplied. The river was completely blocked and between March 7th and March 21st they only advanced some twelve miles, digging six miles of canal through stinking black mud. Their guides had lost the river completely and the troops sickened in the eternal mud and unhealthy conditions. The Egyptians in particular were very badly affected.

On the 17th of March Sam saw a hippopotamus in a patch of open water and secided to shoot it, as meat was badly required for his troops. He was rowed out in a small dinghy to where it had been seen and when it rose to the surface again he shot it at a range of some thirty yards with his Reilly No. 8 breechloader, using an explosive shell he had invented. He noted:

> This shell was composed of iron covered with lead. The interior was a cast-iron bottle. . . the neck formed a nipple to receive a percussion

> cap. The entire bottle was concealed by a leaden coating which was
> cast in a mould to fit a No.8 or two-ounce rifle. The iron bottle
> contained three drachms of the strongest gunpowder and a simple cap
> pressed down on the nipple prepared the shell for service.
>
> On examination of the head of the hippopotamus, I found that the
> shell . . . had traversed the skull and had apparently exploded in the
> brain, as it had entirely carried away the massive bone that formed the
> back of the skull . . . I was quite satisfied with my explosive shell.

Unfortunately as the month progressed it became increasingly obvious that they would be unable to break through to Gondokoro. By the end of the month six soldiers had died and 150 were sick. By April 2nd even Sam was forced to admit that further progress in these conditions was impossible and he wrote that he "was obliged to with a heavy heart, to give the order to turn back." Predictably the soldiers were delighted, imagining that they were about to return to Khartoum, but of course to Sam any sort of retreat was anathema. On April 3rd, while he waited to allow all the rest of the fleet to get well ahead, he saw an antelope standing sentry on an ant-hill "about a mile and a quarter distant". He wrote:

> There is no change so delightful as a little sport if you are in low
> spirits; thus, taking the rifle, I rowed up the river for about half a mile
> in a small boat, and then landing, I obtained the right wind . . . I was
> shooting with a very accurate express rifle, a No. 70-bore of Purdey's .
> . . . It was of course necessary to keep several tall ant-hills in a line
> with that upon which the antelope was standing, and to stoop so low
> that I could only see the horns of the animal upon the sky-line. In
> some places it was necessary to crawl upon the ground . . . The sun
> was very hot, and I found crawling so great a distance a laborious
> operation . . . At length I arrived at the base of the last ant-hill from
> which I must take my shot . . . the antelope was standing unconsciously
> about 170 yards . . . from me . . . Almost·as I touched the trigger, the
> antelope sank suddenly upon its knees . . . It was a very beautiful animal,
> a fine bull . . . that would have weighed thirty stone when gralloched.

For the next ten days their progress was slow and on the 13th of April Sam recorded that he and Julian walked along the banks, already three feet higher, armed with both rifles and shotguns. He wrote of "a very curious bag during the afternoon, that in England or Scotland would have been difficult to carry home; we shot and secured two hippopotami, one crocodile, twenty-two geese and twenty ducks."

That evening they passed Kutchuk Ali's station, and Sam warned the *vakeel*, or agent, against sending slaves to Khartoum, explaining the principles of the suppression of the slave trade. The *vakeel* appeared to think that as he was employed by the commander of the government expedition he could not possibly be affected. To Sam this was further proof of the insincerity of the Egyptian authorities, which no doubt made him more determined than ever to put it to the test.

Thereafter they made better speed and on April 19th reached the White Nile, where, seeing natives running in all directions, Sam discovered that the governor of Fashoda, Ali Bey, was making a *razzia*, or slaving attack, on the Shilluk tribe. Sam promptly anchored for the night in a bend which concealed his fleet and at dawn of April 20th steamed down on the governor's encampment to find that he had 155 slaves there and in his boats. When the governor challenged Sam's authority over him he was requested to put his refusal to free the slaves "in writing". Sam then departed, but warned Ali Bey that he intended to remain in that area.

The following day to his great delight Sam was joined by Mr. Higginbotham and eleven vessels with the English shipwrights and Dr. Gedge. On the 22nd he returned to Ali Bey's camp with European witnesses and insisted on the unconditional release of the slaves. Finding himself in a difficult position the governor agreed, and Sam personally explained to the slaves that they now had their freedom. Although satisfied that he had done all he could and sending a full report of his actions to the Khedive, Sam was well aware that the exposure of the governor would not increase his popularity amongst the Egyptian officials, who were opposed to his mission virtually to a man. In particular he appreciated that his friend Djiaffer Pasha was inevitably implicated in the general laxity of government, if no worse, since Ali Bey was his immediate subordinate.

On the 23rd Sam chose a site by the river for an encampment with some fine mimosa trees providing shade, and by May 1st the camp, named Tewfikeeyah, after the Khedive's eldest son, Tewfik Pasha, was well advanced. With a quayside five hundred yards long at which the entire fleet could lie, the camp was neatly laid out with straight rows of wooden huts, drains dug to the water's edge and gardens planted with melons, pumpkins, cabbages, tomatoes, cauliflowers, beetroot, parsley, lettuces and celery. There was soon a workshop with lathes at work building small boats, while a smithy nearby was producing bill-hooks for cutting the vegetation of the Sudd when they renewed their attack on it later in the year.

Sam and Florence lived aboard the *diahbiah*, which they had made into a very comfortable floating home, with his special bodyguard nearby. As usual Florence gathered round her a retinue of young servants and helpers. Her domestic arrangements were much more efficient than on their previous expedition and the boys were neatly dressed in different uniforms for various occasions. These were "very becoming", consisting of fez, scarlet flannel suits, or white with red facings, or dark blue trimmed with red, or brown cotton for "rough wear". Sam and Florence themselves wore somewhat different clothes from those on their previous expedition. Sam did not wear uniform except on very formal occasions. Mostly he wore a "Norfolk shirt", a type of bush shirt, and cotton trousers. Florence generally wore a dress with a hat and anti-fly veil. In letters home to her step-daughters she made occasional requests for such items as "corset whalebones". Gone were the days when she and Sam were dressed alike in somewhat outlandish, if utilitarian, garb.

As ever, Sam took occasional "strolls" and on one of these he stalked and shot the first and only ostrich he ever killed. Fired by his success he carved an ostrich head from a piece of wood, using glass from the neck of a wine bottle for eyes. This he proposed to mount on a pole and with ostrich plumes in his cap intended to use it as a stalking device, one of the age-old methods of hunting. Unfortunately the onset of heavy rains prevented him ever trying out this idea.

While at Tewfikeeyah, Sam took particular care to drill his bodyguard, "The Forty Thieves", as they were called amongst the English party. Initially they may have richly deserved the title, although always known only as "The Forty" in the main camp. By degrees, however, Sam got rid of the thieves among them and succeeded in instilling a code of honour until it was considered a disgrace to "The Forty" that a theft should be committed by any of them. They wore a special uniform of a red shirt over their Zouave trousers and Sam never allowed them to work at general head-quarters but kept them as his personal escort. At Tewfikeeyah he was most particular in training them to shoot accurately with their Snider breech-loaders and although the Egyptians were better shots than the Sudanese he much preferred the latter. By degrees he drafted all the Egyptians except four and filled their places with carefully selected Sudanese, mostly from the crack grenadier company of the regiment.

In August Sam made a thorough exploration of the Sudd, looking for a route through the series of lakes from the White Nile. After a prolonged exploration he concluded there was no way through at that time. He decided that when they came to move south he would have to take the Bahr Giraffe route once more, but determined to start on December 1st when the river was in full flood.

On September 21st Sam returned to Khartoum to ensure that his arrangements were being properly executed. He had sent Mr. Higginbotham on ahead to speed matters up, taking with him Dr.

Gedge, who was clearly dying. Until Sam's arrival Mr. Higginbotham had been in despair, for only seven boats had been provided, although thirty had been ordered. This meant that the camels necessary to carry the sections of steamer beyond Gondokoro could not be transported. Once again Sam encountered the deliberate procrastination of the Egyptian authorities, in this instance in the person of his friend Djiaffer Pasha.

Furthermore Sam discovered from Mr. Higginbotham that Sheik Agad, the principal slave trader of the White Nile, had entered into a contract with the government, approved by Djiaffer Pasha, for the exclusive right of trading over ninety thousand square miles covering the very territory it was intended to annex. Although it required the exercise of some diplomacy, Sam insisted on modifying the terms of this contract. Arguing his case in the public divan, Sheik Agad maintained that if Sam established a government in the countries which had been independent this would upset his trade. Ostensibly, of course, his trade was ivory, not slaves, but eventually it was agreed that his contract would terminate on April 9th 1872, thus allowing Sam a year to finish his task before his contract ended in April 1873.

It was on this occasion that Sam first met Sheik Agad's son-in-law, Abou Saood, of whom, with the benefit of hindsight, Sam wrote:

> I did not admire the personal appearance of Abou Saood. A judge of physiognomy would have objected to the downcast look of humility, the *un*certain squint of one eye, the furtive expression of countenance, added to the ultra-holiness of his ejaculations when called upon for an answer, and the pious cant of his protestations against all wrong doings.

A forthright man himself, Sam preferred an outright scoundrel and swashbuckling rogue rather than the Uriah Heep type of fawning snake represented by Abou Saood. For instance Sam admitted that he was "much attached to Djiaffer Pasha in his unofficial capacity" and the worst he could say of him otherwise was that he "was not sufficiently vigilant or severe with the sub-officials throughout the vast territory which he governed". This may have been true, or it may have been that Djiaffer Pasha was playing a double game. It is a human trait to dislike admitting that a friend may be double dealing, and Sam was very human.

On a higher level than Djiaffer Pasha, whether or not the Khedive was playing a double game is also open to question. On the face of it, with hindsight, it is easy to feel that he must have been doing so, since he was aware that the economy of his entire country depended to a large extent on the slave trade, while equally he was aware that the European governments deplored it. It certainly cannot have been easy for the Khedive to show the support for Sam and his successor, Gordon, that he undoubtedly did. On the other hand the rewards if they succeeded in their mission were quite considerable and could readily be balanced against the corresponding loss of revenue resulting from the curtailment of the slave trade. On the face of it, at the very least, he was hedging his bets, and probably much the same could be said of Djiaffer Pasha, who could remain friendly with the Christian Pasha on a private basis while hindering him by every means short of open opposition.

On December 1st, as planned, Sam's advance guard set off from Tewfikeeyah. By December 11th, when Sam himself brought up the rear, the entire camp had been dismantled and everything was under way to Gondokoro. Both Mr. Higginbotham and Lt. Colonel Abd-el-Kader were ill with fever, so the bulk of the organisation fell on Sam and his nephew Julian. On the 17th of December Sam learned that one of his vessels varrying invaluable sections of steamer had sunk. He immediately turned back and by organising several other vessels to assist he succeeded in raising the sunken boat with the all-important sections. The entire operation, however, kept him fully occupied until December 27th.

By January 15th he had overtaken his second-in-command, Raouf Bey, who had taken twenty-six days to reach the point from Tewfikeeyah, which the previous year had been reached in twenty-two days from Khartoum. The men were soon engaged in re-cutting the old canals, making only a matter of several hundred yards' progress each day. Sam was constantly disconcerted to find that the depth of the Bahr Giraffe was little over three and a half to four feet, knowing that within a month or so it would be dry.

By January 28th they had reached the point where they had turned back the previous year. By February 6th, the date on which they had started from Khartoum the previous year, they were well on their way. Sam now appreciated that their previous attempt was "inconceivable madness had anyone known the character of the river". He assured his men, however, that this time there was to be no retreat and that if necessary they would spend the season high and dry. From February 11th to March 9th he urged them on relentlessly, exhorting and encouraging them, forcing them to dig through the seemingly endless Sudd and at one point for six hundred yards through stiff clay. At another difficult stage he unloaded the vessels, hauled them forward, then built a road on the dried up surface over which they transported the cargo in waggons and re-loaded it.

Unaffected apparently by fever or illness, Sam reconnoitred daily ahead of his fleet in a small boat manned by some of his favourite

"Forty Thieves". Foremost among these was a corporal named Monsoor, of whom he wrote:

> This man was a Copt [Christian descendant of the true Egyptians];
> he was rather short, but exceedingly powerful; he swam and dived like
> an otter, and never seemed to feel fatigue. He was always in good
> health, very courageous, and he accompanied me like my own shadow;
> he seemed to watch over me as a mother would regard an only child.

Eventually, after labouring for two months and just as it seemed that the entire fleet must be stranded, Sam, reconnoitring some sixteen miles ahead of them in a small boat, reached the open waters of the White Nile. On opening a channel for his fleet the water ran out, leaving them high and dry behind. He had, however, foreseen this possibility and, ever resourceful, raised the water level by damming the river behind the boats. In this way the fleet was soon able to float clear and by March 19th they were all safely in the White Nile. Sam recorded laconically:

> After the usual voyage upon the White Nile during which we . . .
> had excellent sport in antelope shooting when the steamer stopped at
> forests to cut fuel, we arrived opposite the old mission station at
> Gondokoro on April 15th, 1871.

In a letter to her step-daughter Edith, Florence described the scene as they found it:

> What a change has taken place in this spot! Formerly there were
> numerous neat little villages scattered over the country each surround-
> ed by a tall hedge of euphorbia. Now there is not a dwelling. All have
> been destroyed—The slave traders have set every tribe against its
> neighbour and the result is desolation. . .

The warlike and savage Baris under their leader Sheik Alloron had allied themselves with the slave traders and raided their powerful neighbours the Loquia. On the slave traders' departure the Loquia had attacked the Baris and driven them out of their land, forcing them to take refuge with their prized cattle on islands in the river. Their old villages and park-like land remained deserted, although daily the Baris swam across from their islands to graze their cattle on their old land.

While attempting to reach a friendly understanding with the Baris, for the first few weeks Sam was primarily concerned with establishing a new station at Gondokoro, which he was resolved to make his permanent headquarters, re-naming it Ismailia after the Khedive Ismail Pasha. The main station was laid out on the high ground above the river, commanding all approaches. Sam and Florence remained aboard their *diahbiah*, as they had done at their previous camp. "The Forty" were camped nearby on a small knoll by the riverside, some fifty yards from the vessel. As before, gardens were at once established beside the lines of huts and a variety of vegetables were grown.

On May 26th Sam held an official parade and ceremony of annexation to which Sheik Alloron and the local headmen were all invited. The troops in their best uniforms paraded with fixed bayonets before an eighty foot flagpole, forming three sides of a square in front of it. The fourth side was occupied by the artillery with ten guns. The official proclamation of annexation was read out and a royal salute fired as the Ottoman flag was hoisted at the top of the flag pole. The troops were then marched past and indulged in some mock combat, firing around 10,000 blanks, before finally being dismissed.

Despite this show of strength the Baris continued to be completely intransigent and unhelpful. Sam countered at first by impounding their cattle when they were brought across the river, only returning them in return for promises of services which were never fulfilled. It was not long before more cattle were impounded and the situation deteriorated into open warfare when the Baris tried to seize them back by force of arms.

Sam did not waste time, but decided to teach the Baris a lesson by invading one of their islands, only to find it deserted, although he captured some more cattle. He was then attacked by the Baris of Gondokoro and those of the neighbouring Belinian tribe. He promptly counter-attacked the Belinian Baris and drove off some of their cattle.

On June 9th he learned that Abou Saood had arrived in eight boats with 500 men and some 1,400 cattle, which he had stolen on his way from the natives of Shir. When he presented himself on the 10th, he was ordered to camp on the other side of the river as Sam did not wish to have his men undermining the discipline of his troops. Through his telescope on the 11th Sam observed the Baris of Gondokoro flocking to greet the slave traders as old friends and fraternising with them. On the 12th, accompanied by Lt. Colonel Abd-el-Kader, Monsoor and Julian Baker, with four soldiers, he crossed the river in a dinghy and entered the slave traders' camp, observing the flight of numerous Baris as he approached. He promptly put the soldiers on guard over the cattle and sent Abou Saood the following letter:

> Ismailia June 12th 1871;
> To Abou Saood, vakeel of the firm of Agad & Co.
> Sir,

> You arrived here on the 10th inst. with a large number of cattle stolen by you and your people.
>
> You knowing that the Baris were at war with the government, have nevertheless been in daily and friendly communication with them.
>
> The Baris of this country are rendered hostile to all honest government by the conduct of your people, who, by stealing slaves and cattle from the interior, and delivering them here, have utterly destroyed all hope of improvement in a people naturally savage but now rendered by your acts thieves of the worst description.
>
> It is impossible that I can permit the continuance of such acts.
>
> i therefore give you due notice that at the expiration of your contract you will withdraw all your people from the district under my command. At the same time I declare the forfeiture to the government of the cattle you have forcibly captured under the eyes of my authority.
>
> Samuel W. Baker.

Sam himself subsequently appreciated that he made a bad mistake at this point. He wrote:

> The only error that I can acknowledge throughout the expedition was my present lenience. I should at once have placed Abou Saood in irons, and have sent him to Khartoum, instead of leaving him at large to carry on his intrigues against the government.

Although Sam had made his feelings regarding Abou Saood plain, the latter remained very friendly with Colonel Raouf Bey. They had originally become friendly while the regiments awaited Sam's arrival in Khartoum and now they dined together regularly in Colonel Raouf Bey's quarters. Quite deliberately Abou Saood used the friendship to sow dissension throughout the camp.

Subjected, as he had been, to constant procrastination and at times outright opposition from the authorities, Sam had already achieved a considerable amount. His admission regarding Abou Saood, however, was, if anything, an understatement. Had he given the man a summary trial and had him hung it would have been merely what he deserved. It might have caused considerable dissension, but considering how much trouble was to result from the man's activities, long after Sam had left, it is not too much to say that had he been eliminated at this stage the whole history of the area might have been altered. He was more than just a constant thorn in Sam's flesh. He was literally an evil influence and a blight on the country.

9

Suppressing the Slave Trade : 2nd Stage

The attacks from the Baris continued throughout June and July, while Sam's troops were engaged in building the station at Ismailia. Sam responded by placing guards in front of the camps and the cattle, and they were usually alert enough to capture the advance scouts of the main bodies attacking at night. Meanwhile Abou Saood continued to supply the natives with ammunition.

On July 21st the Baris allied themselves with their powerful neighbours the Loquia and attacked the main camp in considerable force. The 1,200 troops in the main camp repulsed the attack simply with sustained musketry fire, but did not use the artillery. When Sam enquired the reason for not using the artillery Colonel Raouf Bey replied that he *"had forgotten its existence"*. Sam later learned that the reason his smaller camp had not been attacked was that the natives feared "The Forty" more than all the rest of his troops together; also that camp contained only a few milch cows, whereas the main bulk of the cattle were in the main camp.

At this stage in his expedition Sam was considerably handicapped by being utterly unable to rely on his troops from Colonel Raouf Bey downwards, with the shining exception of "The Forty". Soon after arriving at Gondokoro he learned that his officers had acted against his direct orders and during the journey from Khartoum had secretly purchased 126 slaves, which now meant 126 more mouths to feed. To have ordered their immediate freedom would have caused a mutiny. When one small Abyssinian boy of eleven, named Amarn, slipped past the senties, still bleeding from the ill-treatment he had received from his master, a Captain in the Egyptian regiment, and claimed his freedom from Sam and Florence he was immediately freed and taken into their service. Sam noted, however, that this action was very unpopular, as was his order that no women or children should be captured when fighting the Baris.

Sam recorded that the troops often behaved disgracefully. Both officers and men when attacking a village vied with each other in looting and pillaging. On such occasions men separated from each other were often killed by the natives. Whenever Sam saw any looting he at once had the culprits seized and flogged on the spot. Gradually the discipline improved, but naturally there was a lot of discontent, particularly amongst the officers.

Before starting an organised campaign against the Baris, Sam fortified the new camp at Ismailia with a ditch and rampart, mounting ten guns behind it. He also fortified his own small encampment in much the same way. Thereafter, confident that his base was well protected, he began operations against the Bari in earnest, setting off on August 30th with a force of 450 men to attack the Belinian Baris.

At first they found it difficult to counter the guerrilla warfare of the Baris, who stalked up to the edge of the camp and killed any stragglers. Finally Sam evolved a counter technique, using much the same methods. He ordered his "Forty", together with fifty selected men from the regiments, to lie in ambush along the river bed by which the Baris generally approached. By dawn they were covering an area of some eight miles in parties of two or three. This plan worked very well. Eventually the Baris were afraid to come near them.

In the meantime Sam had been endeavouring to gather sufficient corn to keep his troops fed for twelve months, but a mere 670 bushels had been gathered, enough for only two months. Had it not been for the Sudd all would have been comparatively simple as Sam had planned a monthly mail service by steamer between Khartoum and Gondokoro. At the time of his previous visit that would have been perfectly feasible but with the Sudd making the course of the river utterly unpredictable they were more or less cut off from civilisation. The expedition had to be self-sufficient, which was not to the liking of the troops.

Despite the final discomfiture of the Belinian Baris the discontent which had been simmering amongst the officers burst into open resentment on the 12th of October. Under the aegis of Colonel Raouf Bey, inspired directly by Abou Saood, the officers, excepting those of "The Forty", produced a round robin letter of complaint proposing that owing to shortage of corn the expedition should now withdraw to Khartoum. In his journal Sam fulminated: "By God! not a man shall go back, except by my orders! no matter whether they mutiny or not. I shall forward the officers' letters to the Khedive." Without even answering the letters he gave orders to cross the river at 2 a.m. and advanced against the Baris of Regiaf, who despite his efforts to negotiate, threatened to attack them. Here they found so much corn that there was no difficulty in stocking up with supplies for the next twelve months. All that was necessary was to fill the vessels they had towed upstream with them and let the current take them back to their fort at Ismailia.

Sam sent Raouf Bey back to Ismailia on the 18th of October with strict instructions to send the sick and incapable back to Khartoum, but on no account to send anyone other than invalids. On the 3rd of November the boats were sent back to Ismailia heavily laden with corn. On the same day Raouf Bey sent 1,100 people, including soldiers, sailors, invalids, women and children back to Khartoum, reducing the strength of the entire expedition to 552 officers and men. As Sam at once appreciated, it was thought that with such a reduced force he would be compelled to stay at Ismailia until his term of office expired in April 1873, but they underestimated their man.

On the 10th of November Sam explored the final cataracts of the White Nile. These lay some six miles south of Regiaf. On the way he encountered another powerful Bari tribe, led by Sheik Bedden who appeared friendly. Sam did his best to cement this friendship, making him gifts of a blue shirt, a fez, some beads and a bugle, with which he was much pleased.

Although they were in a highly populated area Sam was surprised to see a herd of eleven bull elephants approaching the river. Using his elephant gun, "The Baby", loaded with twelve drachms of powder and his Reilly No. 8, he had a magnificent opportunity of bagging them all as they mounted the river bank in single file broadside on to him, but his servant had made a mistake and brought the wrong bag of ammunition so that he only killed the first two. In one of his fascinating digressions, which make such interesting reading, he noted that elephants float when shot, while hippopotami sink, the difference being due to the larger cavity of the elephant carcase.

Sam secured the heads of the elephants as trophies and presented the Bedden Baris with the carcases. The hostile Baris watched the scene enviously from the hills above as the Bedden Baris removed the flesh. Finally they could bear it no longer and to Sam's surprise they sued for peace. Although he had offered them cattle worth far more than the elephants in return for the corn he had taken, they now professed friendship in return for permission to help themselves from the elephant carcases. Sam held a meeting of some twenty headmen, giving them presents, and they agreed to provide porters to take his baggage into the interior. On the 18th of November, with all the Baris at peace, Sam turned back for Ismailia. There he gave the English engineers orders to divide up the No. 3 steamer into suitable pieces for transport on carts above the rapids. Raouf Bey with 340

men was to be left at Ismailia and with the remaining men Sam
intended to set off south into the interior.

Although aware of the danger of advancing southwards with
such a small force as 212 officers and men, Sam was determined to
take the risk rather than remain tamely in Ismailia without accomplishing the task he had planned. He had written to the Khedive that
if his work was not finished successfully he would continue as
required and the Khedive had written to him suggesting that he
extend his contract a year and ensure that Ismailia was secure before
advancing further south. Sam, however, did not receive the Khedive's
letter and started south in ignorance of it on January 22nd of 1872.

By the 27th of January his small force had reached the cataracts. He
had with him 2,500 cattle, and 1,800 sheep as well as the sections of
the No. 3 steamer on board the boats. He was accompanied by the
English engineers who were to assemble the sections once the Baris
had carried them the further sixty miles to Labore.

As Sam had half expected, the Baris, including the Bedden Baris, all
refused to honour their promises to act as porters. Sam then ordered
his troops to haul the carts with the sections of steamer but they
mutinied at a task they considered beneath them. Only "The Forty"
loyally declared that they would draw the carts or anything Sam
wanted, but he wisely ordered the English engineers to return to
Ismailia with the steamer parts and told them to assemble the No. 2
steamer there. This steamer with twin screws instead of paddles
would be able to navigate the narrows of the Bahr Giraffe and
establish ready communication with Khartoum.

It was the end of February, after recruiting 396 natives from the
friendly Madi tribe as porters, before the expedition started on their
journey to Fatiko. By March 2nd they had reached the plain and from
there could see the White Nile flowing from the Albert N'yanza. Sam
estimated that it only required 120 miles of railway at this point to
open up the whole of Central Africa. He reflected bitterly that had he
had the camels, which in previous years could have easily been
transported by the White Nile, he could have taken the No. 3 steamer
to the Albert N'yanza. Throughout the area all the villages were
deserted and desolate due to the activities of the slave traders, but
game abounded. On one occasion Sam and Julian shot five antelopes
within two hours so that the troops were well supplied with meat.

On the 6th of March they approached Fatiko, some 85 miles from
Labore and 165 from Ismailia. Here Sam ordered his men to put on
their best red uniforms. As well as the 212 soldiers, the numerous
porters along with 1,078 cattle and 194 sheep, appeared from a
distance a much stronger force than they were. Sam watched the

effect of their advance on the slave traders' camp with the aid of his powerful telescope. He soon saw large numbers of slaves being driven away amid considerable confusion.

Then two men came forward and on learning that it was indeed the Pasha one went back to inform Abou Saood, who was at the station. The other came forward somewhat hesitantly and turned out to be their old Nile dragoman, Mahomet, who had been with them on their first expedition. He was emotionally overcome at seeing them again, for he had joined the slave traders and having fallen on hard times was no longer the boastful character he had been when they first knew him. In due course he proved a mine of useful information about the slave traders' intentions.

Abou Saood greeted them with his "usual humble appearance" but Sam refused to accept the huts he had prepared for them and chose his own place to camp, where he had camped on his previous visit. He then sent messages to all Abou Saood's men that his contract was ending within a few days, on April 10th, and that they must make arrangements to leave the country, or become respectable subjects of the Khedive. He offered them the chance of becoming irregular government troops at the same rate of pay as the regulars and many of them agreed to this.

Abou Saood's *vakeel* at Fatiko, named Ali Hussein, was noted for his vicious propensities, but his principal *vakeel* was a very black man named Mohammed Wat-el-Mek, whom Sam had previously met and, knowing him to be very influential and courageous, if drunken, wished to employ. Abou Saood, however, took care to prevent any meeting and on Sam's arrival at Fatiko sent Wat-el-Mek to Fabbo, twenty-two miles to the west, to keep him out of the way. The stations at Fatiko, Fabbo, Faloro and Farrageia were full of slaves, but Sam made a point of not visiting them for he appreciated that if at this stage he tried to enforce their release he would not only meet with armed resistance, but would be faced with the insoluble problem of finding food for them and returning them to their homes, often far distant and often destroyed. Sam was no fool and he realised that his "absolute power" had to be tempered with discretion.

Fatiko was a district of the Shooli country, ruled by the Sheik Rot Jarma, who had never visited the slave traders. Before Sam left, however, Rot Jarma presented himself and announced his wish to render his allegiance to the government. Sam agreed to leave Major Abdullah with 100 men and the bulk of the heavy baggage and ammunition at Fatiko to represent the government, in return for which Rot Jarma was to supply corn and render the same obedience to him that he would to Sam himself.

On the 18th of March Sam set off with the remainder of his force to Unyoro to visit King Kabba Rega, who with the backing of the slave traders had succeeded his father King Kamrasi, now dead for two years. On the 23rd of March he reached the slave traders' station at Foweera on the banks of the Victoria Nile, where two *vakeels* of Abou Saood were in charge, Suleiman and Eddrees, both of whom he had known during his previous journey. Here he also met Sheik Quonga, whom he had known as one of King Kamrasi's favourite advisers. Sam now found himself surrounded by treachery and intrigue on the part of both the natives and slave traders, inspired in the background by Abou Saood. Soon after their arrival Sheik Lokara, Kabba Rega's principal warrior, arrived with a large force and requested help to attack King Rionga, both neighbour and cousin of Kabba Rega. As he had so often with Kamrasi, Sam refused the request and forbade Suleiman to ally himself with Lokara either.

On March 28th Sam enlisted Suleiman, Eddrees and sixty-five men as irregulars for twelve months' service. Despite promises to provide food the natives were slow to bring sufficient quantities and Sam's cattle were dying from the change of herbage. In addition Kabba Rega was very slow about making arrangements for Sam to visit him at his capital Masindi. It was April 11th before Sam could make all the necessary arrangements and at the last moment Suleiman made an excuse for staying behind.

After two days' march Sam's porters suddenly deserted his force, leaving them stranded. In the meantime Suleiman had beheaded a native, whom Sam had pardoned, for releasing some slaves. He had then gone on to prepare an attack with the Kabba Rega forces on Rionga. Fortunately Sam sent Colonel Abd-el-Kader and thirty men back with a message to Suleiman to provide three hundred porters. He found him in conference with the sheiks and on his arrival the slave traders, thinking their plot was discovered, fled. The Colonel, however, led the sheiks back to Sam as captives and they revealed the whole story. Sam sent a Captain and fifty men to bring Suleiman and Eddrees back as prisoners. He then held a public trial in front of the sheiks and had them flogged, staging trial and punishment theatrically by the light of blue flares.

It was April 25th before Sam's force reached Masindi and the 26th before he met Kabba Rega at his divan with the officers and troops in their best uniforms and the band playing. Sam returned those slaves he had found in Suleiman's camp who were from Unyoro. He exhibited Suleiman and Eddrees in the Sheba, or slaver's method of securing prisoners with a forked stick round their necks. He expounded all the advantages of accepting the security of the Khedive's government.

He found Kabba Rega a neat, well groomed young man of about twenty, but soon discovered that he was very like his father, "cowardly, cruel, cunning and treacherous to the last degree". He thought him "an undignified lout". His regular habit was to suck cider through a hollow bone and thus get disgustingly drunk every night, rising at 2 p.m. to attend his public divan.

Sam built himself a grandly styled "government house", being a simple room twenty-eight feet long by fourteen feet wide and twenty feet high, with overhanging eaves and entered by a porch. Attached by a covered walk was his own private residence twenty-four feet long by thirteen feet wide. The walls were hung with scarlet blankets. The floor was covered with mats, while on opposite walls were two large oval gilt-framed mirrors. At one end was a nearly life-size colour print of the Princess of Wales. Large sporting prints and colour pictures of beautiful women, life-size, also hung on the walls. Two stretchers covered with Persian carpets served as sofas, or beds by night. The tables were square metal boxes covered with blue cloths. Various gawdy trinkets were laid on the tables, of little value, but intended as gifts if admired. This "became the wonder of Central Africa".

The large gilt mirrors had been specially brought from England as presents for Kamrasi and M'tese of Uganda. Sam knew full well that if news of this treasure awaiting him reached the latter he would at once "open a communication". In the meantime Kabba Rega built himself another divan within fifty yards of Sam's, ostensibly so that he could easily communicate with him, but clearly so that he could watch everything he did.

On the 28th of May, shortly before the ceremony of annexation he had planned, Sam released the twenty-five slave traders who had been taken prisoner with Suleiman, enlisting them as irregular troops once more, thus removing the necessity of guarding them. This resulted that night in a carefully planned sudden demonstration of drum-beating and horn-blowing from the town of Masindi, intended to intimidate the government forces. Sam promptly replied by ordering the band to play as loudly as possible in response, pretending to accept the noise as a compliment. It was not, however, a very reassuring portent and he ordered the sentries to keep a sharp look out.

The next day some of Rot Jarma's men appeared to tell him that Abou Saood had ridiculed the authority of Major Abdullah. To prove he was powerless he had attacked Rot Jarma's tribe and taken cattle and slaves, although himself losing some men. Sam decided at once it was necessary to have Abou Saood arrested. He resolved to send

Major Abdullah orders to this effect along with Suleiman under escort.

On the 14th of May Sam took formal possession of Unyoro in the name of the Khedive. The troops were lined up. As Sam put it: ". . . the irregulars (late slave hunters) formed in line with that charming irregularity which is generally met with in such rude levies". The flag was hoisted on a tall flagpole at the east end of government house. The usual salutes were fired and after a short address the ceremony was concluded.

Soon afterwards there was further trouble with Kabba Rega. He had taken guns from Suleiman's men on the orders of Colonel Abd-el-Kader. Despite numerous witnesses he maintained he had never had them. Finally on the 21st of May Sam had to threaten to leave Unyoro, which would have left Kabba Rega open to attack by Rionga on one side and M'tese in the south. With ill grace the guns were then returned.

On the 23rd of May Suleiman was sent off with an escort of thirty-six men, including eleven regulars and twenty-five irregulars, leaving Sam with a force of only 108 men. With the escort went instructions to Major Abdullah to arrest Abou Saood and an offer to Wat-el-Mek to command an irregular force of 400 men, which he was given power to raise from the slave traders whose employment had ended.

Matters now went swiftly from bad to worse. When the troops were being drilled on the morning of the 31st of May in the open space of some two acres behind Kabba Rega's divan, as was customary, the war drum suddenly sounded. In a very short time several thousand armed natives gathered threateningly round the troops who were promptly formed into a square with their bayonets pointing outwards. Sam then advanced unarmed towards three chiefs he saw standing in the crowd. He affected to treat the matter as a joke, laughing loudly, and asking if they wanted to dance when the band struck up, or whether his men should start the dance. He then ordered a mock bayonet charge which cleared the square around them effectively.

Meanwhile Florence, with her usual presence of mind at their station some three hundred yards away, had armed every available man. She had also placed rockets ready to fire into the town if she heard the sound of rifle fire. Every available gun was loaded and laid out ready to fire, with spare ammunition to hand. Small wonder that Sam referred to her as his "good little officer".

Although there were absolutely no grounds for Kabba Rega's hostility, it was obviously wise to take precautions and on the 2nd of June Sam started building a fort with ditch and palisade. Ostensibly this was to store his gunpowder and ammunition safely since several nearby native huts had burned down and the long grass grew close to the station, although as usual Sam had cleared the immediate area around it for vegetables. On the 3rd Sam received emissaries from the M'tese of Uganda and gave them gifts, pressing them at the same time to look after Livingstone if he should appear in their area, for at that time his long absence was causing concern.

By the 7th of June supplies of food for the troops had run out and several times Sam sent Monsoor or others to request fresh provisions. Finally they received seven jars of cider along with two sacks of flour. The cider turned out to be poisoned, but Sam promptly dosed the troops with tartar emetic which resulted in them vomitting it out of their system, leaving them weak but alive. The guards were immediately doubled and the sick men taken to the fort. At 5 a.m. Sam visited them and found them all well but weak and sent them back to the station. He then sent Monsoor and another man to request a chief to come and examine the cider. While Sam and Florence strolled out as was his morning custom with a bugler and sergeant in attendance they suddenly heard a chorus of savage yells followed sharply by two shots. Sam instantly ordered the bugler to sound the alert and sent Florence to fetch his rifle while he turned back to the station. At the same instant they were fired on by sharpshooters stationed in ambush in the long grass close by and the sergeant close behind him was killed.

The troops quickly formed in open order round the station and returned a steady fire into the long grass. While they provided covering fire the native huts on either flank were set alight with flares. Sam then led a sortie driving the natives through the town and setting the huts alight as they went. Meanwhile a steady fire was kept up on the long grass where numbers of the enemy were concealed. Within an hour and a quarter Masindi was reduced to ashes and the enemy had fled, but much to Sam and Florence's distress the faithful Monsoor had been killed along with three others.

Although the battle of Masindi established the superiority of Sam's forces and taught Kabba Rega a lesson it was obvious that matters had come to a head. In spite of the victory their position was virtually untenable. Vastly outnumbered, without the benefit of supplies, they could not stay at Masindi indefinitely. Kabba Rega had proved himself intractable and intransigent. Further negotiations were obviously bound to be as fruitless as those that had preceded them. The time had come to move.

For the next few days there were attempts at parleys, and messengers from Kabba Rega, delivering two cows as presents, put the blame for the attack on one of the lesser chiefs. Sam then sent an interpreter and another man unarmed to Kabba Rega with a musical box as a present. They did not return and on the 13th his force was attacked again, but this time Sam retaliated by setting the neighbouring villages on fire and scattering their assailants.

Sam decided to march for Foweera on the Victoria Nile, which was close to Rionga's stronghold, for he intended to set him up in the place of Kabba Rega. Fortunately Florence, unknown to anyone, had prudently been holding six chests of flour in reserve which now provided sufficient vital food supplies for the journey. On the 14th of June everything not strictly necessary was burnt, all the buildings were set on fire, and they started their march. After ten miles they were attacked and lost one man. Then they cut down some plantain trees and formed a camp for the night.

The following day they abandoned their cattle which were proving troublesome to drive and Sam reviewed their loads again, burning everything which was not essential. This included, amongst other items, a case of brandy and Julian Baker's naval uniform and cocked hat. Then they continued their march despite frequent attacks by natives hidden in the long grass. Fortunately they were not attacked at night and thus gained some rest. For the next five days they continued under almost constant attack and although their casualties were remarkably few they inevitably suffered some, and all had narrow escapes. On the 19th of June Florence was greatly upset when one of her favourite boys was killed immediately behind her, transfixed by two spears, but that evening they reached Kisoona, only some 21 miles from their objective, Foweera. Here they rested for three days as Florence was suffering greatly from fatigue.

On the 23rd they marched sixteen miles and only one man was wounded. Finally on the 24th they reached Foweera to find it burned. From the period when the fighting had begun on the 8th of June up to the 24th they had only lost ten men killed and eleven wounded, including the assassinations of his messengers. His party now consisted of 97 soldiers, 5 natives, 3 sailors, 51 women, boys and servants, with 3 Europeans, making a total of 158.

On the 1st of July they received a messenger from Rionga to whom Sam explained that he now wished him as an ally against Kabba Rega, provided he would agree to act as the Khedive's representative. Within a few days Rionga had presented them with meat and corn. On the 16th of July they started down the Victoria Nile to visit him in canoes they had constructed from hollow logs with outriggers. Even at its narrowest the river here was some three hundred yards wide. Sam still did not wish to advertise their presence by unnecessary shooting, otherwise at one point he might have made an epic bag. He wrote later:

> . . . We were paddling with six rowers along this desolate river . . . when we observed a small island . . . The bare gray granite shelved gradually towards the water and exposed a clear surface of about sixty feet; upon this were large rounded masses resembling boulders of rock . . . when within about twenty yards the great boulders of granite began to move! I could not believe my eyes; great masses commenced to unfold, and in a few seconds resolved themselves into vast forms each as thick as the body of a hippotamus and of enormous length. these two antideluvian monsters glided slowly and fearlessly along the gently sloping granite, and when half beneath the water they exposed a breadth of back which was the most extraordinary sight I have ever seen in my long experience of crocodiles. . .

Having restrained himself from shooting the monstrous crocodiles, Sam reached the rendezvous appointed by Rionga, where he set up camp. On the 18th of July they met and Sam found him to be "a handsome man of about fifty with exceedingly good manners". He did, however, insist on an exchange of blood with Sam as he maintained the natives would then know he would always be true to the Pasha and vice versa. Julian Baker and Colonel Abd-el-Kader had to go through a similar ceremony with his minister and his son. A knife incision produced a few drops of blood which were then sucked by the other in what Sam termed "rather a disgusting performance, but at the same time absolutely necessary for the success of the expedition. I had now really secured a trustworthy man who would act as my vakeel."

Sam then left Colonel Abd-el-Kader and 65 men in a powerful stockade by the river's edge to support Rionga, while he continued with his "Forty" to Fatiko. On the 27th of July they set off on the 79-mile journey and on the second day met messengers from Major Abdullah. Reports had been received that Sam and his men had been killed by Kabba Rega, and Abou Saood was threatening to attack Major Abdullah and take the ammunition. By August 1st Sam's force was within ten miles of Fatiko and he held a meeting of the local sheiks. They informed him that Wat-el-Mek, in command of Abou Saood's men, wanted to join the government forces, but had been misled by Abou Saood. Abou Saood had withdrawn to Fabbo but had commanded Ali Hussein and Wat-el-Mek to attack Major Abdullah.

The following day Sam halted his men a mile and a half from Fatiko where they changed into their best red uniforms and then marched down to Major Abdullah with the bugles sounding the assembly. He at once drew his men up in their red uniforms to greet "The Forty" and Sam. No-one, however, came from Abou Saood's camp, which was only ninety yards away. They drew up their men in a show of force, but did not come forward—a deliberate insult. Sam was about to send Major Abdullah to summon them when they opened fire on his forces. In a few minutes seven men had been hit. The slave traders were retiring behind huts to reload in safety then coming out to fire and Sam saw that a charge was the only way to deal with them. At the head of his "Forty" he led a charge with fixed bayonets. Wat-el-Mek in a distinctive yellow suit fired a shot at Sam, who returned the fire. A bullet from "The Dutchman" struck Wat-el-Mek's right hand destroying his rifle and removing his middle finger. He was then made prisoner.

Sam, Julian Baker and "The Forty" followed the slave traders for nearly four miles, killing a considerable number, including the infamous Ali Hussein. Wat-el-Mek thought that Sam had shot his finger away intentionally and regarded it as divine intervention. There was no difficulty in making him swear allegiance on the Koran and he became a very useful addition to the government irregular forces, for he knew the native mind well. In his journal Sam wrote:

> August 5, 1872. I ought to hang Abou Saood, but much diplomacy is necessary. The rebels in their three stations, Fabbo, Faloro and Farragenia number about 600 exclusive of armed Baris. I have with me 146 men including officers. . .

Sam knew that to raise the natives would entail the death of all the slave traders and the consequent arming of the natives with their rifles, which might well then be used against him. He therefore sent messengers ordering Abou Saood to come to him at Fatiko, promising him a safe return to Fabbo if he did so, "without which written assurance I might as well have summoned the man in the moon". His messengers were fired upon, but on the 7th of August Abou Saood appeared. He lied strenuously, denying any complicity or blame for anything and trying to blame Wat-el-Mek. Sam finally let him go in disgust and he left for Fabbo. He then went on to Ismailia, where his friend Raouf Bey, to Sam's annoyance, allowed him to go to Khartoum although he had no pass to do so. He then went on to Cairo and spread a false report of Sam and Florence's death, as well as protesting at Sam's treatment of him.

After the final departure of Abou Saood, Sam was able to consolidate his success with little active opposition and get down to the pacification of the interior. Some of the slave traders left at Fabbo threatened to be troublesome, but Wat-el-Mek, backed by Sam, soon put them to flight without a shot being fired. Amongst those remaining was Suleiman, who had been sent from Masindi to Major Abdullah at Fatiko in the charge of Mahomet the dragoman. The party had been attacked by natives, but before freeing him Mahomet made him swear to surrender himself afterwards to Major Abdullah. He had duly done so and had been released on parole, taking up the post of *vakeel* at Fabbo. He now threw himself on Sam's mercy and he took the wise course of forgiving the man, scroundrel though he was, and enlisted him in the government service, which he thereafter served honourably. As Sam remarked, without "immoral characters" he would have had a "skeleton" force.

From the end of August Sam concentrated on building a strong fort at Fatiko. The base was the rock which commanded the surrounding country upon which he built a fire-proof magazine and store. Around this were 455 yards of ditch and rampart. As ever he planted seeds and laid out gardens. On the 25th of November he sent Wat-el-Mek with eighty irregulars and twenty regular troops to Ismailia with instructions to Raouf Bey to send 200 men under Lt. Colonel Tayib Agha and a herd of cattle as they were running short of meat.

Soon after Wat-el-Mek had left, a force of 3,000 cannibal natives from Makkarika approached the Nile under the command of a *vakeel* sent by Abou Saood to transport the ivory left at Fabbo. Sam informed the *vakeel* that anyone crossing the Nile would be shot. The *vakeel* withdrew for instructions, and smallpox providentially broke out amongst the Makkarika, who lost heart and withdrew to their own country. Meanwhile Rionga, with the aid of a force of irregulars sent to his assistance, when Colonel Abd-el-Kader's force had been withdrawn, had defeated Kabba Rega's men. Unyoro had also been invaded from the south by M'tese, who was furious to learn that because of Kabba Rega's treachery at Masindi the presents destined for him had been destroyed.

By December 25th the fort at Fatiko was completed to Sam's satisfaction and he had nothing to do but await the arrival of the reinforcements from Ismailia. Since it was the season for hunting he naturally required little encouragement to join the natives of Shooli in their sport. He was interested to find that various families had manorial rights, which descended by inheritance, over large areas of uninhabited ground between Fatiko and Unyoro. Although unaware of the fact, he described their manner of hunting as very similar to that employed by the Saxons in Britain.

Their hunting was conducted with nets, each man having a net about twelve yards long and eleven feet deep with meshes about six inches square. Areas, or manors, contiguous to each other were selected when it was decided where to hunt. On the chosen day several thousand natives armed with spears assembled with very little noise. A line of about a mile and a half would be netted on the edge of an area that had been burned. The long grass to windward would then be fired, causing the animals to run towards the nets. Both behind and in front of each net a native armed with a spear would be hidden behind a screen of grass tied together at the top. The owner of each section of netting was entitled to any animal caught in it, but the owner of the ground was given a leg from each animal caught in his area.

The guns were stationed on the flanks and it was difficult shooting as there were so many people about. On the day he described, Sam's bag was five antelopes, Julian had three and Colonel Abd-el-Kader had one and shot a native in the leg. Sam noted, "from that day the natives gave Abd-el-Kader a wide berth".

On another day Sam saw a lioness advancing towards the ant-hill behind which he was concealed. He rolled her over with a shot from "The Dutchman" in the chest, but she recovered and advanced on his gunbearers, whereupon he gave her the second barrel, which appeared to make no difference. He then stepped forward and as she swerved away at his sudden appearance shot her in the hindquarters with a load of buckshot. She was then wounded in the paw by Abd-el-Kader and lay up in the long grass. Sam fired at the yellow mass they could just see from about twenty yards range. She then charged again and Sam fired a second barrel, but neither this, nor Julian Baker's light rifle stopped her until Sam rolled her over again with a twelve bore loaded with ball at point blank range. She then retreated to the grass once more and Sam stalked her to within twelve yards, finally killing her with a shot in the neck. The bag that day was "one lioness and seven antelopes *all* of which were to be eaten".

The women of Fatiko were disturbed to learn that Sam had nearly been killed and sent word "that the Pasha must not be allowed to go out hunting as he might possibly be killed by a lion or buffalo . . . Would not the slave hunters immediately return . . . and destroy us?" Sam's comment was that since they were stark naked this could hardly be termed "petticoat government" but might be regarded as "a distinct assertion of women's rights".

On the 15th of January 1873 Sam received envoys from M'tese, the king of Uganda. He had sent an army into Unyoro which was to be placed at Sam's disposal and requested Sam to visit him. His people were still looking for Livingstone, and Sam wrote a letter to be given to the explorer if he was found. He also sent some gifts and a representative to M'tese, but explained that he no longer had any need of the army, as his forces, though small, were in command of the situation.

Finally on the 8th of March Lt. Colonel Tayib Agha arrived with his relief force, but Raouf Bey had not supplied any cattle. Tayib Agha had quarrelled with Wat-el-Mek and angered the Baris, who attacked him, forcing him to retreat despite his force of 280 men. Sam determined at once to leave Major Abdullah in command as Tayib Agha had proved so incompetent. Leaving a strict list of orders for running the fort, Sam departed for Ismailia on March 20th.

His party reached Ismailia, without encountering any form of trouble on the way, on the 1st of April, the day on which his contract officially expired. The first news he received, to his sorrow, was that Mr. Higginbotham had died the previous day. The fort he found in a filthy state, although the gardens had been well maintained. He learned that the reinforcements sent from Khartoum had merely been slaves sold to the government, many from the White Nile, who on their return as supposedly trained soldiers had promptly deserted. The Baris of Belinian had sheltered them and when attacked by Raouf Bey had inflicted numerous casualties on his forces. The 108-ton twin-screw steamer, however, was assembled and lying at anchor. Sam inspected this steamer and then sent for Sheik Alloron, now faithful to the government. He ordered him to visit the Belinian Baris and bring back the deserters under threat of a visit from "The Forty". Two deserters were brought back and after trial by court martial were shot. Following this severe example there was no further trouble from the troops.

On the 26th of May, after preparing everything for his departure and taking leave of his "gallant Forty Thieves" in an emotional scene, Sam and Florence left on their *diahbiah*, towed behind the new steamer. On his way through the channels of the Bahr Giraffe, which had considerably deepened due to the current, they overtook three slave ships, and the *vakeel* in charge told Sam that during his absence in the south several had passed Fashoda. On the 19th of June they reached Fashoda, which now had a new governor. He assured Sam that no slave ships would pass without being arrested.

Sam then went to Khartoum, but stopped five miles short of the town and sent a messenger ahead to the new governor, Ismail Yagoob Pasha, whom he had known for eight years since his first expedition. He requested him to "telegraph *instantly* to Cairo to arrest Abou Saood". Otherwise Sam knew that it was likely he would be warned of Sam's approach and might go into hiding. Soon afterwards he had a visit from the governor and a lengthy talk with him. The next day he received an official welcome to Khartoum and a few days later was pleased to see the slave traders from the slave ships he had passed brought ashore in irons. From Khartoum he wrote several letters home including one to the Prince of Wales:

> Khartoum, 1st July, 1873.
> His Royal Highness, The Prince of Wales.
> Sir, I have the honour to announce the arrival here on the 29th of June of the European party, and ourselves, from Ismailia, all well after an easy voyage.
> My labour expended in cutting canals during the first voyage through the Bahr Giràffe had had a grand result. The rush of water has cleared away the sandy shallows and the channels are permanent.
> I left all officers and troops in good health and spirits, and no trace of original ill-feeling remains.
> The troops prefer Central Africa to Khartoum.
> I have met with a good reception in the Sudan and the expedition that commenced with evil auspices has, thank God, closed satisfactorily in every branch.
> I trust your Royal Highness will be satisfied that although I have been unable for the want of transport animals to convey a steamer to the Lake, I have at least paved the way to future success and the expedition has now taken firm root in the soil.
> We are now on our way home and I look forward with impatience to the first duty of waiting upon your Royal Highness on my arrival in England.
> Lady Baker joins me in presenting our humble respects to her Royal Highness, the Princess of Wales.
> Your Royal Highness's
> Obedient Servant,
> Samuel Baker.

Florence's reaction was a little different. In her diary she wrote after a small domestic upset, when two of the boys had stolen some of Julian's wine.

> I am quite heartbroken sometimes, to see that kindness is wasted . . . I have always taken a great deal of trouble with my people to teach them all that is good, but they will not learn. I shall be very glad never to see a black face again.

In effect Sam had laid a firm foundation on which his successor was able to build successfully with hardly any of the difficulties he had to face, beyond the eternal apathy and procrastination of the authorities. The succession of well garrisoned bases along the route of the Nile made it easy to transport the steamer to Lake N'yanza and ultimately gain at least a measure of control over the slave trade as well as facilitating the cultivation of cotton. Sam and his party had achieved a near miracle given the conditions they encountered and it is doubtful if anyone with less strength of character or physique could have begun to achieve as much. There is little doubt, however, that Florence's words echoed the sentiments of most of the party.

They did not stay long in Khartoum and took the route via Berber and Souakim to Cairo, arriving there on August 24th. On the 25th Sam had an audience with the Khedive when he received the Imperial Order of Osmanie, 2nd class. Julian received the order of Medjidie, 3rd class, in recognition of his services. The Khedive also promised to have a special tribunal brought together to judge witnesses.

After six weeks in Cairo, Sam and Florence started home with Julian. Accompanying them was the Abyssinian boy Amarn, who was to become a permanent member of their staff in England. Behind him Sam left an abiding memory, which was summed up years afterwards by the natives of Unyoro, who were quoted as saying:

> We don't care for Gordon or Emin. Baker is our man! When he fought, he was always in the front; when he fired he never missed; if we did not obey orders he shook us; then our teeth dropped out.

10

Around the World

On their arrival in England in September 1873 Sam and Florence found themselves popular heroes, lauded on all sides. Perhaps typically, however, Julian found that during his absence the Admiralty had not extended his leave and for a while it even seemed that he might be forced to resign from the Navy. After a question had been raised in Parliament, however, he was reinstated and instead complimented on his gallantry during the expedition.

Sam and Florence moved at first to Brighton, for both of them were immediately affected by the abrupt change of climate and for a while were quite seriously ill, having to refuse numerous invitations to stay because of their ill-health. By December they had begun to recover. On the 8th of December Sam once again addressed a crowded meeting of the Royal Geographical Society. Sir Bartle Frere likened the occasion "to the return of some sea king or Crusader". At the end of Sam's speech the Prince of Wales congratulated him personally.

Amongst numerous other engagements, Sam only managed a very brief meeting with his successor, Colonel Charles Gordon, better known at the time as "Chinese" Gordon, after his successful service in China. He was a man of entirely different mould from Sam, although both had the gift of command over native troops. From the first, however, it was an attraction of opposites, the visionary and mystic attitude of Gordon as opposed to the practical and direct methods of Sam.

This meeting in January 1874 was sufficient to form the basis of a lasting friendship between the two men, although this at first was strained by Gordon's action soon after taking office in employing Abou Saood. This led to a pained postscript to the book which Sam, inevitably, wrote from his journals during the Spring. It only took him sixty-four days of actual writing, or as he put it "scribbling", to produce the two-volume work entitled *Ismailia, or A Narrative of the Expedition to Central Africa for the Suppression of the Slave Trade*, which was published in the Autumn of 1874 and provided an account of his four years' work.

Even by Sam's usual speedy writing standards this was too fast. Although, like all his work, extremely readable, it suffered somewhat from the speed at which it was written and he was later to admit, in a letter to Gordon, that he "was foolishly careless" when writing it. Although it sold two editions in 1874 and a third in 1878 and was reprinted in 1886 and 1890 it did not enjoy quite the same popularity as some of his earlier works.

Not long after his brief meeting with Gordon, Sam addressed the Mayor and Corporation of Brighton at a public banquet given in his honour. Some of the more indiscreet remarks he made then were later used against him by the Anti-Slavery Society, who by a perverted form of reasoning regarded him as "a man of wrath" rather than a deliverer. Speaking with his tongue perhaps slightly in his cheek, he said; "Our mission is said to be to civilise Africa; then I say let us call it by the simple word—improve. I have endeavoured to improve Africa in some little degree, and the first thing that must be done in endeavouring to improve a savage country is to annex it . . ."

During the Spring a gradual campaign was mounted against Sam's work in Central Africa by certain sections of "humanitarian" opinion. In the Summer a particularly virulent correspondence was conducted in *The Times*, in which the principal protagonists were on the one hand McWilliam, the engineer, who accused Sam of the unnecessary slaughter of large numbers of natives, and Julian Baker on the other. It was probably in part because of this that Sam wrote the book *Ismailia* as fast as he did.

By the Spring, having wintered in Brighton and recovered their health, Sam and Florence moved to Seymour Street in London, spending much of the Summer there or at Hedenham Hall with their grandchildren. Part of the time was also spent in house hunting, for once again they required to find a permanent home in England. By November they felt sure they had found the ideal place at last, at Sandford Orleigh, near Newton Abbott in Devonshire. Built of granite and Bath stone on the foundations of an older house, it commanded fine views across the river Teign. Here both Sam and Florence settled down at once to create a background which suited them ideally. As ever they enjoyed the planting and planning of the garden, with sweeping lawns and delightfully wooded stretches, in particular an avenue of cypresses leading to a thatched "Palaver House" built like a divan in Central Africa. Inside the house, the hall and billiard room were hung with heads and trophies of the chase from all round the world.

A house of this size, of course, required a considerable staff, including butler, housekeeper, cook, kitchen and serving maids and outdoor staff such as coachman, grooms and gardeners. Included among the Sandford Orleigh staff was the Abyssinian boy Amarn, who was to remain a devoted member of the household for the rest of his life. Perhaps as a result of her experience during their various expeditions, or perhaps from a natural aptitude, Florence was always excellent at handling staff and there are many reports of how well her household was run.

With their customary skill in settling down in new surroundings, it was not long before they were comfortably established in Devon. No doubt the villagers and townspeople of Newton Abbott were pleased to have such a renowned figure living in their midst. Nor would it have been long before the customary exchange of visits with their neighbours had integrated them into the local society of the countryside.

In June of 1875, however, there was an unfortunate incident involving Sam's younger brother Valentine. By this time a full Colonel on the staff at Aldershot, he had just spent a year on half-pay in the Near East, appraising the political situation in Turkey and Russia as a result of which he accurately forecast the coming confrontation between them. He was confidently expected to have brilliant career in front of him. It was thus astounding to his family and to the general public when the news broke that he was to appear in court on a triple charge of assault with intent to ravish, indecent assault and common assault.

The facts were simple enough. Valentine entered the Waterloo train at Liphook on the hot afternoon of June 17th. There was no corridor and the only other occupant of the carriage was a twenty-two-year-old girl, Miss Dickinson, of eminent respectability with one brother a barrister and another an army officer. Soon afterwards while travelling at forty miles an hour, the train driver, glancing back, saw a female figure clinging to an open carriage door. He immediately applied the brakes. Miss Dickinson, in a very emotional state then accused Valentine of attacking her. She was removed to another carriage in the care of a clergyman and the train completed its journey to Waterloo, where there was an enquiry. Valentine, expostulating that Miss Dickinson had simply misunderstood him, gave his name and address. Shortly afterwards he appeared before the magistrates and was committed for trial.

Fate seemed to conspire to prevent him receiving a fair trial. It was a very hot June and July and the Press could find little else of interest. If ever anyone was pre-judged by the Press and public opinion beforehand it was the unfortunate Valentine. The trial took place on August Bank Holiday Monday at Croydon and the public interest was so intense that the court room was besieged. There was such a large crowd outside that at times it was hard to hear the proceedings. The judge, Mr. Justice Brett, was known to be exceptionally severe, particularly on sexual offenders, and from the beginning it was obvious that he was hostile to Valentine. The jury, composed mostly of small shopkeepers from Croydon, were hardly the men in those days of rigid class distinctions to comprehend Valentine's notions of honour. In these circumstances it is understandable that his counsel anticipated an adjournment to a more suitable time and place, so that a fair trial might be expected, but the judge refused to agree to the suggestion and the trial went on in these highly unsuitable conditions.

In essentials it was simply a question of whether Miss Dickinson or Valentine was lying. They each agreed on a harmless opening conversation about the weather and the countryside. Then Miss Dickinson described Valentine putting an arm round her waist and making amorous advances with glaring eyes. This she claimed so frightened her that, finding the communication cord would not work, she opened the carriage door and stood on the running board. Valentine on his part simply denied the charge completely, claiming that she appeared to have misunderstood some remark he made and took fright, whereupon he tried to coax her back into the carriage.

The fact that his shirt was protruding through his fly buttons when the train stopped was brought out in evidence and seems to have made a considerable impression on some minds. On the other hand a moment's consideration will make it plain that anyone attempting rape between stations on the southern line must be out of his mind and Valentine explained this adequately enough by claiming that it happened when he tried to pull her back into the carriage. The truth was that while expert at handling men, he was clearly at a loss when dealing with a hysterical young female and who can blame him? Even had he misread the situation and concluded that a young girl unaccompanied was no better than she should be and offered to kiss her, this was hardly a serious assault, yet that was all that was alleged. In any other age it is likely that the case would never have arisen, but this was the height of the Victorian period. To the disbelief and disgust of his family and friends Valentine was found guilty of the lesser two counts, fined £500 and condemned to a year in prison.

Naturally Sam and Florence gave what comfort and support they could to Valentine's wife and daughter. The stigma of gaol was very real in the Victorian era and the fall from high rank to convict must have been hard to bear. Sam was very close to Valentine and for all his relations these must have been difficult times, but the Bakers were not given to whining.

Sam, of course, had his correspondence with Gordon to keep him occupied. Throughout Gordon's term of office, until December 1878, they were very much in the position of Colonial Governor and unofficial Colonial Office. Gordon, who at first thought Sam had been too severe with the natives was later to acknowledge:

> I am convinced that, but for Baker's energy in dealing with the slave traders and their friends along the river, and the fear he inspired among the natives, I should have encountered the most active opposition.

Typical perhaps of Sam's letters to Gordon was that from Sandford Orleigh dated 18th September 1875, soon after the start of his brother's prison sentence.

> . . . I admire your patience and perseverance amazingly. You will, I am sure, by this time have experienced that terrible strain upon the nervous system, caused by the constant and annoying delays in Africa, when your spirit is craving to advance. It is this perpetual fretting that saps both health and strength.
>
> If you can establish your line of vessels above each Cataract to the navigable river beyond Jebel Kuku (west of the Asua junction) you will certainly have achieved an immense success. I cannot tell you how thankful I am that you are my successor; as I was always afraid that no-one would take the same enthusiastic interest in the work which I have felt. When a steamer shall be on the Albert N'yanza there will be a grand development; and if your health remains I feel quite confident of your ultimate success . . .

Typical perhaps of Gordon's to Baker was his dated 1st October 1875 from Labore.

> . . . next rainy season I hope to get the *Khedive* and 'No 9' steamers into the Lake. The *Khedive* is now at Mugi. I have quelled the three tribes on this, the left, bank; and I wait till the grass is dry enough to burn, to quell the Mugi by a combined move on all sides. I have gone through much trouble; and can now appreciate the worries you had with one-tenth of my means . . . I can now see how you were thwarted; and on my return, D.V., if I ever return, I will state my opinion publicly about your mission, so far as I can judge it . . . I feel so beaten down by my worries in the opening of this route, that I have lost spirit . . . it is *hopeless, hopeless* ever to do anything with these people.

Occupied with their garden and settling into their new house, Sam and Florence no doubt found plenty to keep them busy during 1875 and 1876. Valentine's release from prison in 1876 was welcomed within the circle of family and friends. Fortunately both he and Sam had influential friends in Turkey and now that the war with Russia that he had foretold was imminent the Turks were quick to seize the opportunity to employ one of the finest military men in Britain when he was so fortunately available. With the outbreak of war in 1877 he was offered the post of Major-General and the rank of Pasha. At the battle of Taskhessan a war-correspondent watching wrote:

> Eight squadrons of Turkish regular cavalry came out from behind a low hill on the Turkish right. They were led by a man on a fine grey Arab, the grandest horseman I have ever seen. They came round the hill at a trot, then broke into a gallop and came swooping down on the left flank of the Russians, tearing through them like an express train through a flock of sheep.
>
> I could not help watching the man on the grey Arab and I saw his sabre go sweeping up and down and all round like lightning flashes. He made a lane through the ranks of the Russian Infantry in whatever direction he went. Some bodies of Russian cavalry came out to meet him and they came into contact in a large field of high maize.
>
> But there was no holding back Baker and his Turks, and the Russian cavalry was soon tearing back as hard as they could go, to get under the shelter of their guns. The Turkish cavalry followed them hard, like tigers who had once tasted blood and longed for more. I saw a shell explode within a few yards of the Pasha; his horse fell and down he came. That was the end of the grey Arab, but not of his master, for Baker was up in a moment on the charger of a common trooper, in the middle of his men, hacking like a very Hercules. The old Artillery Officer, who was standing quite close to me laid down his field glasses and said:
>
> "I swear by the Prophet that the Infidel who commands our cavalry fights with the courage of ten thousand tigers."
>
> "And yet," said a younger Artillery Officer, "Allah has smitten the English with such mad blindness that they allow a man like him to leave their Army."

It was not only Sam and Florence and the Baker family who were cheered by reports such as this of Valentine's exploits. There had been a considerable revulsion of feeling at the time at his very savage sentence, and the courageous manner in which he accepted all that came to him brought him considerable popular support. He was already well on his way to becoming a popular hero and this epic rearguard action at Taskhessan, which lasted ten hours against vastly superior Russian forces, saving the Turkish army and becoming regarded as a model of its kind, brought him widespread acclaim and support.

In 1878 on the 1st September , Gordon, the bachelor, was writing to Baker pressing him to come out to visit him and discard plans which he was making to visit Cyprus. Gordon wrote from "Khartoum":

> How I wish you were here in my place with all my worries and

> bored to death! . . . The screw steamer *Khedive* has been completed and is on the Lake Albert. It took 3 17/30 months . . . Now we have two steamers on the Lake. If you could come out how glad I would be to see you! . . .
>
> You will be well received by H.H., if you went to Cairo. I think he would be quite glad to have you here instead of me; and pray do not think I should be in the least degree vexed . . .
>
> Come up and see the south end of Lake Albert. You could get up here from Suez in 19 days. From here you could go to Lado in 15 days in the *Ismailia,* your own boat (such a picture she is). From Lado to Dufli—by steamer to Kirri and by elephant to Dufli—in eight days. And then up and round Lake and back to Dufli in ten days at the outside . . . Come up and write another book . . . Telegraph to me that you will come; start at once; Cyprus will keep.

Sam replied to Gordon in a letter date 16th October, 1878:

> Your letter of 1st September arrived yesterday . . . I should like immensely to come and see all the great changes you have made and to have a look at the Albert N'yanza; and both Lady Baker and I thank you for your kind invitation. I should not hesitate for an instant, personally; but she is, I know, afraid that, if once I should get into the old groove, my visit would be prolonged; and she rather dreads a return to savagery. Nevertheless I shall not give up hope; and, *Inshallah!* I may yet be able to manage it.

It is clear from this exchange that Sam the old adventurer at the age of fifty-seven had finally, at least to some degree, been curbed by marriage. He had in a weak moment promised not to go out to Africa again without Florence. She was well aware that she had to allow her husband some scope for his adventurous instinct, but equally she knew that, if they returned to Africa, sooner or later the law of averages would operate and one of those poisoned arrows, spears or bullets would put an end to her happiness.

Sam's next letter to Gordon was from Cairo, dated 16th December 1878, and read in part, along with some sound advice on dealing with the slave trade:

> We are here for a few days waiting for a good opportunity for Cyprus . . . I should have much liked to run up and see you at Khartoum; but Lady Baker has had so many years of the Sudan, and, after all she has endured there, it would be selfish of me to persuade her. Thus I regret that we cannot meet . . .It was very kind of you my dear General Gordon, to invite Lady Baker (with myself and Julian) to come and see you; and she begs me to thank you much; but she hopes some day to see you in our own home in England, instead of in Central Africa.

Florence obviously had no intention of ever again returning to

Central Africa if she could avoid it and Sam had planned this expedition with her to Cyprus following the controversial Treaty between Great Britain and Turkey on the 4th of June 1878, by which Cyprus became a British base. At that time few Britons knew anything about Cyprus and there was considerable question as to whether it was worth the trouble likely to be involved. Sam had decided to combine the opportunity for a holiday in the sun, the first they had had since their return from Central Africa, with writing a book about the island, which was eventually entitled simply *Cyprus as I saw it in 1879*. In his Introduction he wrote: "At first sight the political situation appeared vague, but I determined to examine the physical geography of Cyprus and to form my own opinion of its capabilities."

Having heard harrowing descriptions in England of the lack of accommodation and the unhealthiness of the island, Sam had bought a gipsy caravan in which he proposed to live with Florence while touring the countryside. This along with a four-wheeled van to carry all their luggage and supplies, he had shipped out ahead of them to Larnaca. With them they brought their essential luggage along with Amarn, their faithful Abyssinian attendant, and three spaniels over which Sam intended to shoot.

Compared with an expedition living under canvas, Sam considered that the caravan was perfect luxury. He wrote of it:

> This van was furnished with a permanent bed; shelves or wardrobe beneath; a chest of drawers; table to fall against the wall when not in use, lockers for glass and crockery, stove and chimney, and in fact it resembled a ship's cabin, nine feet six inches long, by five feet four inches wide . . . Although the space was limited, the furniture was so carefully arranged that we had plenty of room to move about. The fall-slab table was usually down and was only required for writing; the chest of drawers was American walnut; a good solid and well-seasoned wood . . . This good American chest was only three feet two inches high, therefore it formed a convenient toilette table beneath a window, which curtained with muslin and crimson cloth, had an exceedingly snug appearance; and a cushioned seat upon either side upon the lid of a locker combined comfort with convenience. We had a tiny little movable camp-table that could be adjusted in two minutes, and would dine two persons . . . The bed was athwart-ship at the far end beneath the stern window, but at such a height from the floor that several broad shelves beneath contained gun-cases, ammunition, clothes, boots, tins of preserved provisions, and in fact everything that, although necessary, was to be kept out of sight.

They arrived at Larnaca on the 4th of January 1879 and found that contrary to reports in England there was a pleasant new hotel named

Craddock's "which was scrupulously clean". They very quickly found, however, that their caravan required alteration to face the conditions in Cyprus. The axle trees were strengthened and a bullock pole replaced the shafts since oxen were the only reliable draught animals. The van was likewise modified. They thus had to engage oxen and drivers. In addition they had to hire mules for their own personal transport. Finally they hired a Greek cook named Christo and a young man named Georgi who could speak Turkish, Arabic and Greek, as well as a smattering of French.

Sam soon found that one of the snags of camping in Cyprus was that there was no fuel available, which meant that they had to carry charcoal for fires. He also soon found that, as every Cypriot was armed with a gun, game was extremely scarce and wild. Nevertheless Sam usually managed to shoot something, even if occasionally reduced to shooting larks "for want of larger birds" for breakfast.

Sam found the Cypriot women "generally short and thickset" and that their houses were "extremely filthy and swarm with vermin". He soon noted an undercurrent of dissension between Turks and Greeks on the island since under Turkish rule the Greeks felt that they could not expect justice. On the other hand Sam noted that in all his varied experience of travel he had "never met with such kind and courteous people as the inhabitants of Cyprus". Throughout their whole journey they only encountered one unfriendly Cypriot.

As was always his custom, Sam took every opportunity to enjoy the chance of a "stroll" with his dogs and a gun. Despite the scarcity of game he shot snipe, duck, red-legged partridges and hares, but few woodcock. The hares he considered delicious due to the aromatic food on which they fed. His highest praise, however, was accorded to the francolin, "considerably larger than the common partridge, but not quite so heavy as the red-legged birds of Cyprus, although when flying it seems superior". He regarded it as a matter for regret that they had not been introduced in England.

They stayed at Government House in Lefkosia for a week with Sir Garnet and Lady Wolseley and then continued on their journey. Touring the island they passed on to Famagousta, the only harbour available for large vessels. He pointed out that while many people of experience would have preferred Crete, which already had a good harbour in Suda Bay and a better climate than Cyprus, now they had occupied the island it was essential "to do something". Famagousta he pointed out could be turned into a first-class port for "a very moderate outlay". He also made the point that without Famagousta the island "would be worthless as a naval station; with it as a first-class harbour and arsenal we should dominate the eastern portion of the Mediterranean . . . and keep open . . . our route to India".

They went on to Kyrenia, which they found quite the most pleasing part of the island. Sam did not like the Cyprus wines grown there, but saw there were prospects for wine-growing as one of the leading industries of the future, although he felt the wines could never become popular with the "upper classes in England". On the other hand he admitted that when the only method of transporting them was in a goatskin on the back of a mule no wine could be expected to taste its best.

They visited Limassol, which he saw as the future commercial centre of the island. Finally they spent three peaceful months in the Troodos mountains at the monastery of Trooditissa. Here Sam attempted without success to shoot a *moufflon* and settled down to writing his book. In a postcript dated the 22nd of August, when the manuscript had already gone to the publishers, he commented that he had found the monastery filthy and the monks dirty, but he had instituted order out of chaos. Their gardens now bloomed, the monastery was clean and the monks themselves well washed. He now found it a charming "calm and cool asylum". Although undoubtedly the poorest book he wrote, it sold well and was reprinted the following year.

At the end of August Sam and Florence began the first stage of what was to be a leisurely world tour lasting for over three years. From Cyprus they went via Beirut intending to travel through the Euphrates valley to India, but, hearing there had been a severe famine in the interior, they turned back to Damascus and Jerusalem, taking ship from Port Said to Madras. From there they crossed India by rail to Bombay stopping en route at Poona. In February 1880 they went on to visit the Gaikwar of Baroda who entertained them royally with falconry, shooting and coursing with cheetahs for black-buck on the plains. Sam found this extremely interesting, describing the method of stalking behind carts to within some 90 yards of the buck when the cheetah, which was hooded like a falcon, was unmasked and shown its prey:

> Springing, with the lightness of a cat, from the high platform of the cart, the tall, long-legged cheetah appeared to be at full-stride almost immediately; . . . there was no bounding in the cheetah's action; but the extreme lightness of its body, compared to the length and power of limb and the great length of tail, produced an effect between the swinging gallop of a monkey and the long, steady stretch of a greyhound at full speed.

Although the black-buck is one of the fastest antelopes, the cheetah gained on it in the first 200 yards. The black-buck tried doubling back in vain. After 400 yards at full speed the cheetah was within ten or twelve paces of the buck. Sam continued:

> . . . the cheetah appeared to fire-up like a rocket as he neared his prey . . . Suddenly there shot up a heavy cloud in the midst of which we discerned two wrestling figures . . . When we galloped to the spot, we found the noble buck upon its back and the cheetah . . . fixing its relentless grip upon the throat of its prize. The race was over.

From Baroda they returned to Bombay and started for Allahabad and Delhi in Central India. From thence they moved to the Northern Province for some tiger hunting. At the end of April Sam wrote to his old crony Lord Wharncliffe from Jabalpur that in the past week he had bagged two tigers after a month's hunting in the intense heat, shooting from an elephant. Of the first tiger he wrote that he "was met with a splendid charge. My new .577 double rifle . . . is a beautiful weapon and closed his account on the spot". Of the other he wrote more fully:

> I got a shot at about 80 yards, as the tigress, having passed directly under the elephants hind-quarters when it turned, dashed across the ravine and went off at full-speed on the other side up a lawn-like slope of grass. The shot was one of those pretty accidents that are remembered with pleasure for a lifetime; the bullet struck the back of her neck . . . You can imagine the pretty somersault she made, going at full-speed, like a rabbit! She never moved a muscle afterwards.

After Jabalpur they moved to Calcutta and so to Hong-Kong, then on to Canton and Shanghai, visiting the interior of China in a leisurely sight-seeing tour. They then crossed to Nagasaki and spent some eight months touring Japan, which they found "fascinating". Sam found himself collecting porcelain and bronzes and was surprised how much money he spent in the process. He also acquired a full set of Samurai armour and numerous Japanese swords and weapons.

While in Japan for such a lengthy period Sam naturally spent some time hunting, but with little success, since game was scarce "owing to the dense population". He noted two types of pheasant and the Japanese deer, a type of Sambur, which he described as like a fallow but not palmated and with only four points to each antler. He also examined the Japanese fresh-water salmon, which he thought should be introduced to Britain.

Another matter which very much exercised his mind were the Russian policies and attitudes in the Near and Far East. On the 8th of March he wrote to Lord Wharncliffe from Yokohama:

> The Russians are very strongly represented in the Japan seas; and I think they mean to establish themselves in the Korea, having no port

further south than Vladivostok, which is frozen, like the Baltic, for several months in the winter. I think we should not offer any objection to their move; but we should make a counter-move, by asking Japan for the right of settlement in the island of Tsu-Shima, where there is a lovely harbour, situated between Tsu-Shima and Nagasaki . . .

Next they crossed the Pacific to the west coast of the United States. In California they visited San Francisco, which had then been established for little more than forty years. From there they followed the example set by Lord Lonsdale eighteen months previously and set off on a hunting expedition into the Big Horn range of the Rocky Mountains. They set out from San Francisco on the Union Pacific Railway as far as Rock Creek, about 240 miles inland and 7,000 feet above sea level. From there they rode by coach 90 miles across the prairie to Fort Fetterman. They stopped at two stations on the way to change horses, and Sam found them dirty and full of bugs, Thereafter he and Florence always made a point of sleeping out in the open.

On arriving at Fort Fetterman they presented letters of introduction to the commandant, Colonel Gentry, and to Major and Mrs. Powell, with whom they spent the night. The station here was even dirtier than the previous ones and had just been the scene of a quarrel between two card players one of whom had shot the other dead. The Colonel had held an inquest and buried the dead man that same morning.

The next day they rode 22 miles in an American buggy to the ranch of the Frewen brothers, facetiously known as Castle Frewen because the log building had an upper storey. Here they were well entertained by Mrs Moreton Frewen and the two Frewen brothers, who had 8,000 cattle on their ranch. From there the next day they rode a further 25 miles to the ranch of a Mr. and Mrs. Peters, a young couple who shared with an English partner, Mr. Alston. Their log cabin was still not completed, but they had a private telephone line to the Frewens' ranch. At this point they were 237 miles from Rock Creek, and the Big Horn range lay before them.

They camped in two simple canvas tents at about 10,000 feet up the mountains. There were only four men in the party, Jem Bourne, the principal guide, his assistant Texas Bill, "who was a splendid young fellow", Gaylord, who looked after the horses, and a German cook called Henry. Sam and Florence made the numbers up to six, which meant that they could not "consume the flesh of the animals killed". Sam wrote:

> I cannot shoot to waste; therefore upon many occasions I declined to take the shots, and thus lost numerous opportunities of collecting splendid heads; this destroyed much of the pleasure which I had

anticipated. There were no Indians, as they were confined to their
reservations; therefore it was almost criminal to destroy wantonly a
number of splendid beasts, which would rot upon the ground and be
absolutely wasted. Several parties of Englishman had not been as
merciful . . .

Sam was amazed to find that his men did not "exist upon the
produce of the rifle as I had done so frequently . . . they required
coffee, sugar, an immense supply of bacon, an oven for baking
bread, flour, baking powder, preserved apples (dried), ditto peaches,
ditto blackberries together with the necessaries of pepper, salt, etc."
When it came to hunting, however, he was delighted to find that
although the American buffalo, or bison, had been shot to the point of
extermination on the plains, there were still plenty in the hills.
Having shot one fine specimen he thereafter contented himself with
stalking them whenever possible and after taking aim merely
touching the trigger with the rifle at half-cock so that it could not fire.
His hunter commented sourly: "If you came all the way from the Old
Country to shoot, and you won't shoot when you've got the chance,
you'd have done better to stop at home."

Sam soon found that Jem Bourne was a tiresome grumbler, jealous
of the others and not even knowledgeable about the country in which
he was supposed to be the guide. When he shot bears on ground
Sam had told him to keep in reserve it was too much. Without loss of
temper, Sam quietly gave him a note to deliver at the Frewens' ranch
telling him to remain there until told to return, "and Jem Bourne
ceased to be a member of our party". On the other hand when Texas
Bill managed to hunt down and shoot a bear on horseback in almost
total darkness using a long-barrelled frontier .450 revolver, Sam
regarded this with admiration as "an unprecedented triumph in
shikar". On his return to London he immediately ordered a similar
revolver from Messrs. Colt and Co.

Sam shot both bears and wapiti, as well as black-tail deer, getting
some fine shooting and throughly enjoying his sport. He also enjoyed
the company of two skin-hunters, a very large man of Swedish
parentage known as Big Bill and a small wiry man of Scots extraction
known as Little Bob, who were camped near to them. On more than
one occasion he went hunting with them and admired the amazing
dexterity with which Little Bob could skin a beast, almost as fast as a
man undressing from his overcoat downwards.

After some three weeks, having started their expedition in mid-
August because the flies were impossible before the 15th of the
month, they had a fall of snow on the 6th of September and on the
8th decided to return. Hardly had they arrived at the Peters's ranch

when they learned of the unexpected approach of a party of nine including some "British lords and ladies!" This was something of a shock to the Peters, who were scarcely geared to provide any large-scale hospitality and barely had the wherewithal to provide a presentable dinner. Sam and his party rallied round, however, and while the ranching partners caught some fish in the creek Sam went hunting for ducks. Fortunately he was able to shoot eight widgeon which more or less saved the day, and the dinner party on a plank table covered with a table cloth proved a considerable success to be remembered with pleasure on their return to England and the comfortable atmosphere of Sandford Orleigh.

11

The Latter Years

Sam and Florence returned from their world tour early in 1882 and once again settled down comfortably to their routine in Sandford Orleigh. There was first, of course, the excitement of unpacking the collections of porcelain and bronzes from Japan and setting them out to best advantage. The suit of Samurai fighting armour and other Japanese weaponry also had to find a space on the walls. Quite apart from this there were the bear and tiger skins and mounted heads to be displayed. Pride of place went to the mighty head of the American bison Sam had shot. This was hung in the main hall after it had been "stuffed and set up, as though alive, by that great artist Mr. Rowland Ward, who declared it to be the finest he had seen".

Apart from adding to their possessions, their world tour had one other effect. From then on they decided that the English winters were too severe for their liking and they began a routine of leaving each year for five months for warmer climes. The winter months would generally find them in Egypt or India.

This in no way meant that Sam relaxed his interest in eastern matters, but rather that it was intensified. For in the interval, while he had been in Cyprus and travelling around the world, events in his old theatre of interest, Egypt and the Sudan, had changed dramatically. The Khedive Ismail's government had finally tottered into bankruptcy in 1879 to be replaced by a Dual Control of the principal debtors, the French and English governments. Their first step had been the replacement of the Khedive Ismail by his son Tewfik, at which stage Gordon had left Egypt, as he then thought for ever, for both he and Sam remained stubbornly loyal to Ismail's intentions.

After France had handed over control to Britain alone in 1881, the Gladstone government fumbled and mismanaged matters in an unbelievable fashion. Such policies as they had were never adhered to and were as unstable as the public opinion they were intended to conciliate. The entire British intervention in Egypt at this period is

best characterised by the phrase "order, counter-order, disorder".
This is underlined in a letter from Lord Morley, then the Under
Secretary of State for War in Gladstone's government, who wrote to
Sam on June 1st 1882:

> I know little of the course of the negotiations which led to the
> Egyptian mess . . . I cannot but join in your regrets that prompt action
> was not taken sooner . . . For the time one's fears are chiefly for the
> safety of the Canal and the fresh water supply . . . I am writing in
> rather mutinous terms of the Government . . . they no doubt have had
> a very difficult game to play, and their hands were tied in a great
> measure by the Joint Control system . . . and consequent French
> susceptibilities.

In 1881 there was a popular uprising in Egypt, led by a Colonel in
the Egyptian army named Ahmed Arabi, with the slogan "Egypt for
the Egyptians." After the killing of a number of Europeans in
Alexandria in May 1882, the British and French fleets bombarded the
forts protecting the port. Britain followed this unilaterally by sending
in troops under Sir Garnet Wolseley, who suppressed the revolt at
the battle of Tel-el-Kebir in September 1882.

Meanwhile in the Sudan matters had also gone from bad to worse
and it is interesting to note how many familiar names recur. Gordon
had been succeeded as Governor General by Sam's old commander,
Raouf Pasha, who proved himself as incompetent as ever. As his aide-
de-camp he employed none other than his old friend Abou Saood. In
1881, when an obscure fanatic named Mohammed Ahmed living on
an island in the White Nile 150 miles above Khartoum proclaimed
himself the Mahdi, or Mohammedan Redeemer, and summoned his
followers to rise against the government, Abou Saood was sent to
bring him into Khartoum. Finding him surrounded by followers
armed with swords, Abou Saood returned to Raouf Pasha. He was
sent again with 300 troops but despite every opportunity to capture
or kill the Mahdi he allowed his men to be ambushed and massacred
while he remained on board the boat that had brought them. From
this point the rebellion developed rapid momentum and by mid-1882
Raouf Pasha was replaced by Sam's old friend, commander of "The
Forty Thieves", Abd-el-Kader. By this time it was already too late, the
damage had been done and the Sudan was in open rebellion.

In the year 1882 Valentine Baker was offered the post of
Commander-in-Chief of the Egyptian army and resigned his Turkish
command in order to accept. On his arrival, however, the authorities
changed their mind under pressure from Britain and he was offered
instead the post of Commander of the Egyptian gendarmerie and
police. This was a semi-military mixed force used chiefly to enforce
civil obedience in lieu of troops.

For the winter of 1882 to 1883 Sam and Florence went to Egypt where they took a *diahbiah* named *Osprey* on the Nile. It was a family party, for they had taken Sam's daughters Agnes and Ethel with them and, of course, they saw a lot of Valentine and his wife and daughter, Hermione. They were greatly saddened, however, by the news of the death of Sam's brother John, his old hunting companion in Ceylon. He had returned to England for an operation, which was not successful, and had gone back to their old estate of Newera Eliya, by then re-named Mahagastotte, to die. Sam wrote to his sister-in-law recalling their old happy times and advising on Julian's future.

During these months Sam completed the manuscript of a book to be published later that year entitled *True Tales for my Grandsons*, which was a collection of short stories based on facts that he had learned during his travels. It did not have the success of his other books, being only reprinted once, in 1891. It was, of course, a rather slight work, as the title indicates, but like almost everything he wrote it is highly readable.

While in Egypt he also conducted a correspondence with Lord Dufferin, who had been sent there as High Commissioner to report to the situation. He dispatched a copy of his report with a covering letter to Sam, who replied:

> Dahabia *Osprey* (on the Nile) 27th April 1883:
>
> . . . In your 'Conclusion' (page 83) there is a passage which attracts my keenest sympathy and awakens my regret:
>
> "Had I been commissioned to place affairs in Egypt on the footing of an Indian subject-State the outlook would have been different, The masterful hand of a Resident would have quickly bent everything to his will . . . I feel confident that . . . the final scene of the drama will be that in which 'the masterful hand of a (British) Resident' will represent the authority of England, and 'bend everything to his will'. . ."

In May 1883 Sir Evelyn Baring, later Lord Cromer, was appointed British Resident in Egypt. He was the necessary "strong man", but his appointment came too late to save the Sudan. Events had already gone too far, for by this time Colonel William Hicks had been sent to Khartoum with nine European officers and a force of 10,000 troops, very largely untrained. Sam was to write later:

> General Valentine Baker represented the only authority for Sudan military operations, although he was no longer Commander-in-Chief in Egypt . . . General Hicks started from Cairo under the command of General Baker with the . . . most positive instructions, the result of a plan of operations determined upon in conjunction with myself, as I knew the frontiers upon the Blue and the White Niles for the proposed strategy.

Hicks and his troops marched via Suakim to Khartoum and carried out the first part of the plan successfully in conjunction with the Governor General Abd-el-Kader. Then the Egyptian ministry ordered Hicks, in direct contravention of Valentine and Sam's plan, to advance on the rebellious Mahdi's forces. The result was that they were caught early in November at Kashgil near El Obeid and utterly annihilated.

By the 30th of November Lord Dufferin was writing to Sam admitting that his judgment had been incorrect and Sam's more accurate. This did not stop the Egyptians putting pressure on Valentine to raise a force to quell the rebels at Suakim. Only his high sense of duty made him attempt what he knew to be an almost hopeless task with a hastily conscripted army lacking any will to fight.

At Sandford Orleigh Sam postponed the intended date of his departure for Egypt as he anxiously watched events and tried to influence the government in Britain to take action. On the 4th of January he received a letter from Gordon in Brussels proposing that Sam and Valentine should take on the task of civil and military governors. Then on the 8th of January Gordon wrote from Southampton that he intended to accept Sam's invitation to visit Sandford Orleigh, but as he only had fourteen days in England could only spend one night and would telegraph due warning. Robin Baily, Sam's nephew, wrote of the meeting subsequently:

> From the accounts of Aunt Florence and Ethel I have the most vivid picture of the visit. Sam was on the platform at Newton Abbot to meet the train and as there was plenty of time before tea he took Gordon on a two hours drive. Gordon lost no time in coming to the point. The government he said were thinking of sending him back to Khartum to evacuate the Egyptian garrisons. He did not want to go as he had been asked by King Leopold to go to the Congo and he had been authorised to invite Sam to go instead. Gordon was magnetic and compelling. By the time they arrived at Sandford Orleigh Sam had got so far as to make practical suggestions about the mission, including that his own brother Valentine should accompany him with a force of Turks. During tea this "insubstantial pageant faded away". (*Sic.*) Florence had a suspicion what was in the wind and no sooner had Sam begun to open the subject than she uttered these words calmly and with no play of expression, no movement of hands:
>
> "Sam, you promised me you would never go back to the Sudan without me. I do not go. So you do not go."
>
> This was final. Sam did not attempt to re-open the subject. Gordon was angry with Florence and showed it. Sam led him away and it is recorded he said:
>
> "My dear Gordon, you see how I am placed—how can I leave all this?"

> Though Gordon was his usual courteous self at dinner the atmosphere was never again relaxed and everyone was relieved when he returned to London by the first train in the morning.

Robin Baily went on to speculate on what would have happened if Sam had gone to Khartoum instead of Gordon. He had none of Gordon's magnetism, but although over sixty "gave the impression of a tower of strength, of immovable will power, of common sense." He also spoke good colloquial Arabic while Gordon had to rely on interpreters.

On the 16th of January in a letter to *The Times* Sam wrote: "If General Gordon were in command in the Sudan, he would solve the difficulty." On January 20th Gordon sent a postcard to Sam from Bologna: ". . . I came to London on the 18th of January at 6 a.m. Nothing was decided until 4 p.m.; and at 8 p.m. I was off; so I had no time to write; and I hope you will excuse it. *Under no circumstances* will the Government guarantee the future. The only thing now is to get the Sudan to settle down." In a second postcard of the same date he wrote: "I hope to be back in four months . . . I hope we may meet; and that you are all well. Any hints will be thankfully received." Even at this stage Gordon was apparently still relying on Sam's experience and sound advice.

On February 3rd, aware that he would be in action the next day, Valentine wrote to his wife that "he hoped for success, as far as the utterly worthless character of the troops permitted; but that the proclamation (by the British Government) of the abandonment of the Sudan had naturally won all the wavering and even the friendly tribes over to the Mahdi". As he was told, it was case of that or "have our throats cut". On February 4th, as he had feared, his troops were decisively defeated at Suakim despite his determined leadership. Valentine himself, with considerable skill, extricated little more than a thousand men from a force of 3,500.

Meanwhile Sam and Florence had reached Cairo and were once again on a *diahbiah* on the Nile, this time named *Hermione*, after Valentine's daughter. Here they received a telegram from Gordon in Khartoum dated 26th February; "By your letter, 26th January, you are at Cairo. Hope all well. Sorry Suakim business. Tell your brother, heads or tails up here! but will trust." Another dated 29th soon followed: "Thanks; we are all right up here for present. You and Lady Baker would enjoy the excitement. It is a question of weeks (?) but hope to pull through."

Meanwhile, wounded though he was, Valentine and the remains of his gendarmerie joined the forces under General Graham being assembled at Suakim. Amongst these by a freak of fate was his own old regiment the 10th Royal Hussars, of which he had been a most popular colonel. They greeted him with great enthusiasm and in return he had pleasure in presenting them with the horses of his gendarmerie, for they had none with them. He was with them on the 29th of February when the 10th and 19th Hussars with two brigades of infantry and the Naval brigade thrashed the Mahdi's forces at the battle of El Teb.

From their *diahbiah* on the Nile Sam and Florence anxiously watched all these events and did their best to stir the government to take more positive action to relieve Gordon. On starting back home through Cairo in the middle of April Sam received the award of the Grand Cordon of the Medjidie from the Khedive. Before leaving Cairo, however, he received a somewhat desperate cable from Gordon suggesting he might consider the possibility of starting an appeal to raise money for the relief of Khartoum "as you think fit". In May an appeal was started in England probably initiated by Sam, but it only had the indirect effect of forcing the Government to appreciate their responsibilities.

One event in June must have gladdened Sam's heart. On June 27th the Prince of Wales inspected the 10th Royal Hussars, the Prince of Wales's Own, and presented medals to officers and men. Amongst the old officers of the regiment present as honoured guests was Valentine, who was thus completely vindicated in the eyes of the public.

There was little enough to cheer Sam during the rest of the year. In May and August Lord Wolseley consulted Sam from the War Office on the subject of the navigation of the Nile and the best type of boats for a relief force. Meanwhile the situation in Khartoum steadily deteriorated. It was early in November before Lord Wolseley reached Dongola. Amongst those accompanying him was Commander Julian Baker. Meanwhile Gordon was writing to Sam:

> Khartoum; 5th November 1884
>
> . . . Remember the Expedition (under Wolseley) comes up for *"relief of garrisons"*, which I failed to accomplish; it does not come up for *me*! Are you coming out to Cairo this year? I shall not return to England; I cannot stand it; but shall go to Brussels . . .

On December 12th Lord Wolseley was writing to Sam:

> Events on the Upper Nile are marching quickly, and what the end is, or how we are to get out of the false position the folly of Gladstone has forced us into, is more than anyone can say.

Khartoum fell on the 26th of January and Gordon was killed. On the 28th Sir Charles Wilson and his relieving force arrived too late. On hearing the news Sam is quoted as saying in disgust: "I shall never publish another remark concerning Egypt. Now that poor Gordon is sacrificed I . . . remain a passive spectator of the misery and shame that have been the result of British interference." From then on whenever he heard Gladstone referred to as the Grand Old Man he would thunder: "G.O.M.? M.O.G. you mean—the Murderer of Gordon."

Unable to face the thought of visiting Egypt that year Sam and Florence visited India instead. By late March they were at Mymensing on the Bramahputra river, where the numerous islands were at one time famed for their population of tigers, although by then already greatly reduced in numbers. Sam was shooting with the Rajah of Suchi Khan, who had a number of hunting elephants which were his especial pride. Compared with the heavy animals Sam had been loaned by Mr. G.P. Sanderson, the superintendant of Kheddas, they were like hunters compared to carthorses. The best hunting elephants glided rather than swayed so that it was possible to stand in the howdah and shoot without holding on with one hand, furthermore they would withstand the charge of a tiger and show no fear.

The first day, in extremely hot weather, they marched and counter-marched without much effect and Sam could only compliment the Rajah on his patience rather than his science. On the second day it was much the same and he noted:

> It was 2 p.m., hot work for ladies—my wife was in the howdah behind me. I confess that I am not fond of the fair sex when shooting, as I think they are out of place, but I had taken Lady Baker on this occasion as she hoped to see a tiger.

She was not disappointed, for soon afterwards Sam took control of the operations and they drove systematically. Soon they saw a tiger in front of them, which would have been a perfect shot had the elephant not misbehaved through fright and made a shot impossible. They continued the beat and the tiger was seen for an instant by the Rajah, who fired a shot and wounded it in the stomach. A further beat with the elephants resulted in Sam finally managing to kill it with a clean shot between the shoulders. Thereafter Florence dutifully stayed in the camp.

On the 1st of April Sam went on the Rohumari to meet Mr. Sanderson, who brought more elephants with him. On the first day Sam shot two leopards with a twelve-bore shotgun loaded with S.S.G. (i.e. buck-shot). This had the advantage that it was possible to hold it with one hand while holding on the howdah with the other. Mr. Sanderson then killed a tiger, but that evening fell ill with malaria and Sam had to continue hunting alone. On one occasion he killed a tiger, which was about to leap on his mahout, with a blast from his shotgun at a range of about two feet, straight into its open jaws, blowing the lower jaw to pulp, taking out all the upper teeth and entering the brain. He kept the remains of the skull as a curio.

Within a few months of his return from India, despite his threat never to publish another word about Egypt, he began a campaign for the re-conquest of the Sudan, which he continued for the rest of his life. He saw, with a full appreciation of what was involved, the slaughter of tribes friendly to Egypt by the Dervishes in the Sudan. During the 1886 winter, which he spent in Egypt with Valentine, he wrote to Lord Rosebery, then Foreign Minister, and Rosebery replied in a long letter dated March 7th:

> ... The situation indeed demands all the firmness and statesmanship of this country. I would rather, therefore, not look back at the unhappy past; nor am I anxious at present to administer any more nostrums to sorely overdosed Egypt.

That visit was to be the last time Sam saw Valentine, for on November 17th, 1887, quite unexpectedly, Valentine died of a heart attack. Belatedly the British government recognised that they had lost a valued servant and there were glowing testimonials to his services. Sir Evelyn Baring in addition wrote personally to Sam, saying how much he had valued his advice and friendship. He added; "His loss is most deeply felt here, and by no one more than myself."

Perhaps because of Valentine's death, Sam and Florence spent the winter of 1877 at Sandford for a change. It was not such a haven of peace and tranquillity as might be supposed from its comparative isolation. As his nephew Robin Baily wrote:

> He was consulted by everyone—proconsuls like Dufferin and Cromer, statesmen like Salisbury and Rosebery, explorers like Stanley and Burton and soldiers like Kitchener and Wingate. Roland Ward would ask his opinion about a "Head"; Cogswell and Harrison would send him a new rifle to test ... Interesting people at Sandford Orleigh were frequent.

The Prince of Wales was a personal friend and sent his two sons Eddy and George to stay for occasional weekends when they were midshipmen on the *Brittania*. On one occasion, when they climbed a rare tree and broke the branches, Sam gave them both a sound thrashing. Sometimes the Prince would call without warning and once when Sam was away he arrived at the front door at eleven in the morning. An agitated footman passed the news to a maid who ran upstairs to Florence in the linen room where she was busy with the laundry. On hearing who was waiting she replied calmly: "Oh, you go and tell the Prince that I am all 'dobs and durbies' and that I cannot attend to him till I have finished."

Florence was convinced that men needed feeding. She ate little herself, but she gorged her men-folk. Sam ate enormously and latterly suffered from gout. He took very little exercise in England, but when he was after tigers in India with only a snack lunch in his pocket his gout never affected him. His doctor, whom he had persuaded to prescribe port for his gout, once ventured to suggest more exercise, but this had no effect on Sam, and when Florence received a similar mild warning she replied tartly: "I am not a horse that I should be exercised."

Sam believed in treating everyone alike, whether Prince or gipsy. He would often spend hours at gipsy encampments simply because he enjoyed their company. He made friends with travelling circuses, with road makers and with tinkers. Sometimes he invited such people back to have a cup of tea. Florence accepted such occasions with good humour, as long as he took such visitors into the billiard room where the reek of lion skins and tiger hides was overpowering enough to absorb all other smells.

On the other hand, punctuality at Sandford Orleigh was absolute. The clocks all chimed together. There was no indulgence for lateness. When the gong boomed for dinner up got Sam and if no No.1 lady was present he would latch on to No. 2 and walk off with her to the dining room. When at last the poor breathless defaulter rustled in he would bow her to her seat with rather awesome ceremony.

He remained immensely strong right up to the last. His great nephew, the Rev. Cyril Marshall recalled:

> I was present when Samson, the professional strong man gave a show at Newton Abbot. Samson asked the audience if anyone would like to come on the stage and inspect the gear to see that all was above board. Sam climbed onto the stage. Samson had just broken a chain by flexing his biceps. Sam asked Samson to bind this same chain around his arm. When this was done Sam slowly flexed his arm and suddenly crack went the chain. Yet at the time he was getting on for seventy.

It was perhaps typical of Sam that, prepared for every eventuality, he kept a large pair of conger-tongs in his bedroom. These were used by local fishermen for keeping conger eels at a suitable distance when hauling them into their boats. They were fitted with handles at least three feet long and had powerful, sharpened teeth to pierce and grip the eels. His, however, were intended for burglars, if any should be rash enough to break into his house at night. His plan was to seize the wretched intruder with them and lead him quietly away to another place where the household would not be disturbed by any unseemly scuffle. Adventure prone as he was, it is only surprising that there is no record of them ever having been put to use, but any would-be burglars in that part of the world were probably aware of his reputation and took care to give Sandford Orleigh a wide berth.

In the Library, which he had made his study, there was a wide-ranging selection of books; travel, particularly connected with Africa, Imperial politics, naval matters and science were his main interests, but there were also a number of classic authors and some works of fiction. Near his writing table was his collection of sporting rifles. His armoury varied from the muzzle-loading "Baby" still bound with crocodile skin, to the latest .577, and he was ever ready to discourse on their merits.

Among the heads on the walls at Sandford Orleigh was a rare specimen presented to Sam by his nephew, Commander Julian Baker. It was a small, delicately shaped head of the short-horned buffalo found only on the West Coast of Africa, superbly mounted by Rowland Ward. When Julian was in command of the *Foam* on that station he landed at a convenient place and took the opportunity for a "stroll", accompanied by a native attendant with a spare rifle. He saw the buffalo, much the same size as a Jersey bull, at a range of about 100 yards and bowled it over cleanly with a shot through the shoulder. On approaching the supposedly dead animal he was met with a charge. His rifle missed fire and he was gored through the thigh and tossed onto the beast's head. With great presence of mind and agility he seized the other horn and managed to disengage his leg. Then lying on the ground he succeeded in pulling with his right hand on the left horn and thrusting with his left hand in the animal's nose in the opposite direction, thus preventing it from goring him further.

While he struggled with it thus, his attendant rushed forward, but afraid to fire in case he hit his master he was forced to cut its throat with a sweep of his knife. It then fell struggling and bleeding in its death throes across the prostrate commander. With some difficulty Julian Baker was then conveyed back to his ship. There he remained on the sick list for a matter of three months before he was fully recovered.

A somewhat similar feat was performed by an acrobatic Hindu priest whom Sam encountered in 1888 when camped at a village named Bertulla during his winter visit to India that year. Sam's interpreter had described the man as "a sort of Bishop" and thereafter he was always known as the Bishop. When Sam gave him some rupees, he noted: "He exhibited his gratitude by a voluntary exhibition of his powers as an acrobat, leaping to a great height, and turning somersaults, for which performance his dress was admirably adapted, as he had nothing on but ashes . . ."

Sam had hired two dogs named Cabre and Mora, which were great coursers. He was shooting black buck which were very hard to kill with certainty and great "bullet despisers", liable to get away and die miserably unless hit within a fatal mark of about 3 to 4 inches covering heart and lungs. Whenever a black buck was wounded the dogs enjoyed running it down. On one occasion Cabre, the fiercer of the two, was on the trail of a buck Sam had wounded and he was following on a fast elephant some way behind. He wrote:

> . . . we managed to keep the animals in view . . . The dog was about 100 yards in the rear, running beautifully. We turned the corner, passed the village, and almost immediately we saw a crowd, in the middle of which was the Bishop, holding the buck by the horns, in spite of its frantic struggles to escape. It appeared that the animal at full speed was passing by his temple directly towards the lake, and the acrobatic parson, with extraordinary agility, sprang across its path and seized it by the horns . . .

In 1889 Sam and Florence were in India for the winter again, but this time hunting tigers at Jabalpur. He was already working on his book, the last he wrote, entitled *Wild Beasts and Their Ways*. Although a serious work of natural history it is full of lively, human anecdotes of interest and humour, such as that concerning the "sporting Indian parson" known as the Bishop, which make it extremely good reading. There were two editions printed in 1890 and it was reprinted again in 1891.

In 1890 Sam and Florence were amongst the first to be invited to welcome Stanley back on his return from Africa. Stanley was able to prove that the reason Sam had miscalculated the size and shape of Lake Albert N'yanza was simply due to the atmospheric conditions in the equitorial regions, which were unique. Sam was one of the few people with whom Stanley appears to have been on good terms and he acknowledged Sam's fairmindedness.

In the same year, 1890, Sam's daughter Agnes died in childbirth. She had married the superintendant of the Mahagastotte tea estate, Antony Crawley Boevey, when on a visit to her aunt. Both Edith and Ethel were at Sandford Orleigh when this news arrived and Florence had the task of comforting the grief-stricken family.

In 1891 Sam was seventy but he remained vigorous, if affected by the gout when home in Devon. Only when he returned to India for the winter did he find the attacks no longer affecting him. The winters of 1891 and 1892 were thus both spent in India, although in 1892 it was partly spent in Egypt. He was still busy with letters to *The Times* and to Cromer and Rosebery and similar figures and life at Sandford Orleigh still continued to be of interest.

In 1893, however, he decided that perhaps he did not feel well enough to go abroad for the winter that year. In reply to an invitation to stay with the Countess of Stradbroke he wrote:

Sandford Orleigh; 5th October 1893:

Although your most kind invitation to Henham is more than an ordinary attraction, I really *dare not* accept it. It sounds strange to me to say, at last, "I dare not"; but I am thinking of others more than of myself. I will not bother other people, now that I am growing old. If I were once again at Henham, I fear I could not resist the same enjoyments which I had in olden times. This would most probably bring on an attack of gout; in which case I should be a burden to my friends and an encumberance to myself. Henham is too far off to get back here in case of such a calamity. We have, in fact, made up our minds not to go beyond the limits of our own country this winter. We have given up several other projected visits. I shall try "prudence" this year—a drug I have not always recognised through life.

I cannot tell you how my heart sinks when I acknowledge that "the spirit is willing but the flesh is weak". Those who were born in 1821 cannot be like those born at a later and more reasonable date. I have no fear of hot countries, but the cold keeps me in-doors. It is quite possible that I may be off next year,—perhaps to shoot lions in Somaliland, or on some such errand . . .

Until the 17th of November, when he went out shooting, he was in good health. On his return he complained of pains in the chest which did not yield to treatment and when an attack of gout followed his doctor ordered him to bed on December 11th. After three weeks of this he was still complaining of pains in his chest. Julian, his favourite nephew, who was visiting Sandford Orleigh for Christmas, realised the seriousness of his illness and on the 29th slipped off to London to get a doctor without telling Florence in case she became alarmed. On his return he found he was too late. Sam died of a heart attack in Florence's arms on the night of the 30th of December, 1893.

12

Conclusion

When news of Sam's unexpected death became known the tributes to his achievements were as fulsome as might be expected. His work as explorer, soldier and administrator, in Egypt and the Sudan, his ability as an author and his unique experience as a hunter and naturalist were all lauded in the obituary columns of the newspapers. Personal tributes from friends such as Stanley, Lord Wharncliffe and numerous others swelled the requiem.

Surprisingly, perhaps, Sam had chosen to be cremated and his ashes were placed beside his father in the family vault at Grimley near Worcester, on 5th January 1894. Almost immediately the work of composing an official biography was set in hand. His friend Douglas Murray, correspondent of *The Times* in Cairo for many years, and A. Silva White were appointed his official biographers. Their book, *Sir Samuel Baker: A Memoir*, was published by Macmillan in 1895.

For a further twenty three years Florence remained at Sandford Orleigh, continuing to live exactly as she had while Sam was alive, except that the regular holidays abroad were abandoned. The house, however, remained precisely as it had always been, the routine unchanging with the passing years. All his trophies and his collection of weapons remained in position lovingly cared for and dusted. Any members of the Baker family were welcome, but of course particularly Julian, heir to Sandford Orleigh and its contents and in course of time promoted to Admiral.

In effect the house remained a shrine to Sam's memory, although, as it should have been in those circumstances, it was still a happy place and is remembered as such by those who visited it while Florence was still alive. Essentially Sam was a happy man and he was fortunate in having two extremely happy marriages, although his wives were of such very different mould. After Florence's death on March 11th, 1916, during the dark years of the First World War, the house and its contents were sold and his trophies dispersed. Although he left no son, it would have pleased Sam to know that a grand-daughter was to marry one of her Baker cousins so that he was to have great-grandsons in direct line with the Baker name.

Considering the life he had led it is remarkable that Sam died in bed at the comparatively mature age of seventy-two. He might well have been killed many times as a young man in Ceylon before he had learned the ways of wild animals. In his first year of exploration in the Sudan he admitted later to taking indefensible risks while hunting lions and other game. Subsequently, during his exploration of Central Africa, while penetrating to the Albert N'yanza, he only survived by sheer luck and will-power. While serving under the Khedive suppressing the slave trade he appeared to have a charmed life. Later, during his big-game-hunting excursions round the world, in North America and India, there were numerous occasions when his life was endangered.

Yet it was basically owing to a surfeit of good living and insufficient regular exercise that he died when he did, possibly some ten years or more earlier than might otherwise have been the case had he adhered to a more sensible régime. To this extent Florence, his devoted companion, was unwittingly the cause of his demise. She also prevented him returning to Central Africa, where he might indeed have shared a similar fate to Gordon, but where it is equally possible that he might have triumphed yet again, earning himself a notable place in history in the process.

Had he and Valentine worked together in 1883 as Gordon proposed they might well have triumphed over the Mahdi's forces and re-taken the Sudan. As it was the process was not completed until Kitchener defeated the forces of the Khalifa, who succeeded the Mahdi, at Omdurman in 1898. Of course it is always possible, even probable, that Queen Victoria would personally have vetoed such a plan involving the Bakers, just as she almost certainly vetoed Valentine's appointment to command the forces in Egypt. She was always implacable as far as the Baker family were concerned and even the prospect of extending the British Empire yet again might not have been sufficient to sway the balance as far as she was concerned.

Sam's later years of quiet domesticity, even if interspersed with excursions abroad, were a period of leg-shackled inaction, however comfortable, compared with his earlier life. At the time of his death he was remembered principally as an explorer, the discoverer with others of the sources of the Nile, and as as an administrator successful in suppressing the slave trade on the White Nile. On both grounds he was also recognised as the foremost authority in Britain on the Sudan. As a widely read author he was also given due recognition. Yet, although recognised as a great hunter and naturalist, the sporting side of his life, which in truth was his driving passion, was not so fully appreciated. This was the century when many great hunters and naturalists were writing, from Audubon in North America to Oswell and Selous in Africa; there were many in the same field and this neglect is perhaps understandable.

In many ways it is principally as a big-game hunter and early conservationist that he should be remembered, for there has never been another of his like in any century. In 850 B.C. the Assyrian King Ashurnisipal II boasted of killing 450 lions, 390 wild bulls, 200 ostriches and 30 elephants, but this of course was in conjunction with a concourse of hunters. Kubla Khan in 1298 hunted with 10,000 huntsmen on either hand from a canopied platform carried by four elephants, killing vast numbers of animals of all kinds. Count Gaston III of Foix and Bearn in the 1300s in Europe hunted bear, stags, wolves and boars, hunting with hounds and huntsmen and single-handed. Not even he compared with Sam, who was capable of hunting boar and elk singlehanded with his hounds and knife and equally capable of killing several elephants before breakfast, running among them with a single-barrelled muzzle-loader.

Throughout the nineteenth century, in the hundred years when more animals were slaughtered than in any other, no man had such a wide knowledge of wildlife at first hand. Few men had ranged the world as he had, or had the opportunity or skill to study such a variety of animals. This was the period of the hunter-naturalist when few would have been content as he often was merely to touch the trigger and allow an animal to depart unharmed, satisfied that he could have "bagged" it had he so wished.

In many ways Sam was far in advance of his time, just as he was also in many ways a product of his age, at times arrogant and insular, yet also humble, humorous, honest and interested in everything about him, whether human, animal or natural. It was above all his interest in nature which ruled his life and his curiosity about natural matters which must strike the observer most, whether in Ceylon, North America, India, Africa or England.

He attempted in his earlier days to explain the difference in his view between a sportsman and one who killed other than for sport. He wrote:

> Now the actual killing of an animal, the death itself, is not sport, unless the circumstances connected with it are such as to create that peculiar feeling which can only be expressed in the word "sport". This feeling cannot exist in the heart of a butcher. He would as soon slaughter a fine buck by tying him to a post and knocking him down as he would shoot him in his native haunts—the actual moment of death,

> the fact of killing, is his enjoyment. To a true sportsman the enjoyment of the sport increases in proportion to the wildness of the country. Catch a six-pound trout in a quiet millpond in a populous manufacturing neighbourhood . . . it may be sport. But catch a similar fish far from the haunts of man, in a boiling rocky torrent . . . and you cease to think the former fish worth catching . . . If you see no difference in the excitement you are not a sportsman.

He wrote elsewhere amplifying his views on sport and sportsmen thus:

> The love of sport is a feeling inherent in most Englishmen, and whether in the chase, or with the rod or gun, they far excel all other nations . . . The character of the nation is beautifully displayed in all our rules for hunting, shooting, fishing, fighting, etc.; a feeling of fair play pervades every amusement. Who would shoot a hare in a form? Who would net a trout stream? Who would hit a man when down? . . . I would always encourage the love of sport in a lad; guided by the spirit of fair play, it is a feeling that will make him above doing a mean thing in every station of life, and will give him real feelings of humanity. I have had great experience in the characters of *thorough* sportsmen, who are generally straightforward, honourable men, who would scorn to take a dirty advantage of man or animal. In fact all *real* sportsmen that I have met have been tender hearted men—who shun cruelty to an animal and are easily moved by a tale of distress. With these feelings, sport is an amusement worthy of a man, and this noble taste has been extensively developed since the opportunities of travelling have been of late years so wonderfully improved . . .

There speaks the Victorian born in the Georgian era who started shooting with muzzle loaders and who travelled round the Cape in sailing ships before graduating to steam ships on the Suez Canal to reach India. He wrote simply because he thought simply. When he spoke of shooting he knew the effects of both muzzle-loaders and breech-loaders. When he stalked the few remaining bison in the Rocky Mountains he was content merely to raise his rifle and touch the trigger, aware that he might have killed had he so wished. He was satisfied with the skill of the stalk and the interest of observing the animal in its natural habitat. Not even Florence's velvet chains of domestic bliss could curb this side of his nature and she was far too wise to try. The greatest hunter of his day, he was also amongst the early conservationists, aware that the slaughter had to stop while there was some game left.

Bibliography

By Samuel White Baker:
Eight Years in Ceylon: Longmans 1853
With Rifle and Hound in Ceylon: Longmans 1855
The Albert N'yanza, Great Basin of the Nile: Macmillan; 2 vols: 1866
The Nile Tributaries of Abyssinia: Macmillan. 1867
Ismailia: Macmillan 2 vols: 1874
Cyprus as I saw it 1879: Macmillan. 1879
Wild Beasts and Their Ways: Macmillan 1890
Cast up by the Sea: Macmillan; 1868
True Tales for my Grandsons: Macmillan; 1883
Diaries: Property Dr. John R. Baker in Royal Geographical Society Library
Letters: Dr. John R. Baker: Colonel Valentine Baker, etc.
Wharncliffe Letters: property of Rt. Hon. Earl of Wharncliffe, Sheffield City
    Libraries.
Articles; The Field, etc; pamphlets and lectures: etc.
Sir Samuel Baker: A Memoir: T. Douglas Murray and A. Silva White:
    Macmillan: 1895
Baker of the Nile: Dorothy Middleton: Falcon Press: 1949
The Nile Quest: Sir H.H. Johnston: Lawrence and Bullen: 1903
Great African Travellers: William H.G. Kingston; Routledge; 1874
African Discovery: An Anthology: Marjorie Perham and J. Simmons: Faber &
    Faber: 1942
The White Nile. Alan Moorhead: Hamish Hamilton. 1960
Proceedings of the Royal Geographical Society
Grant Letters: National Library of Scotland

Index

 THE PERFECT VICTORIAN HERO

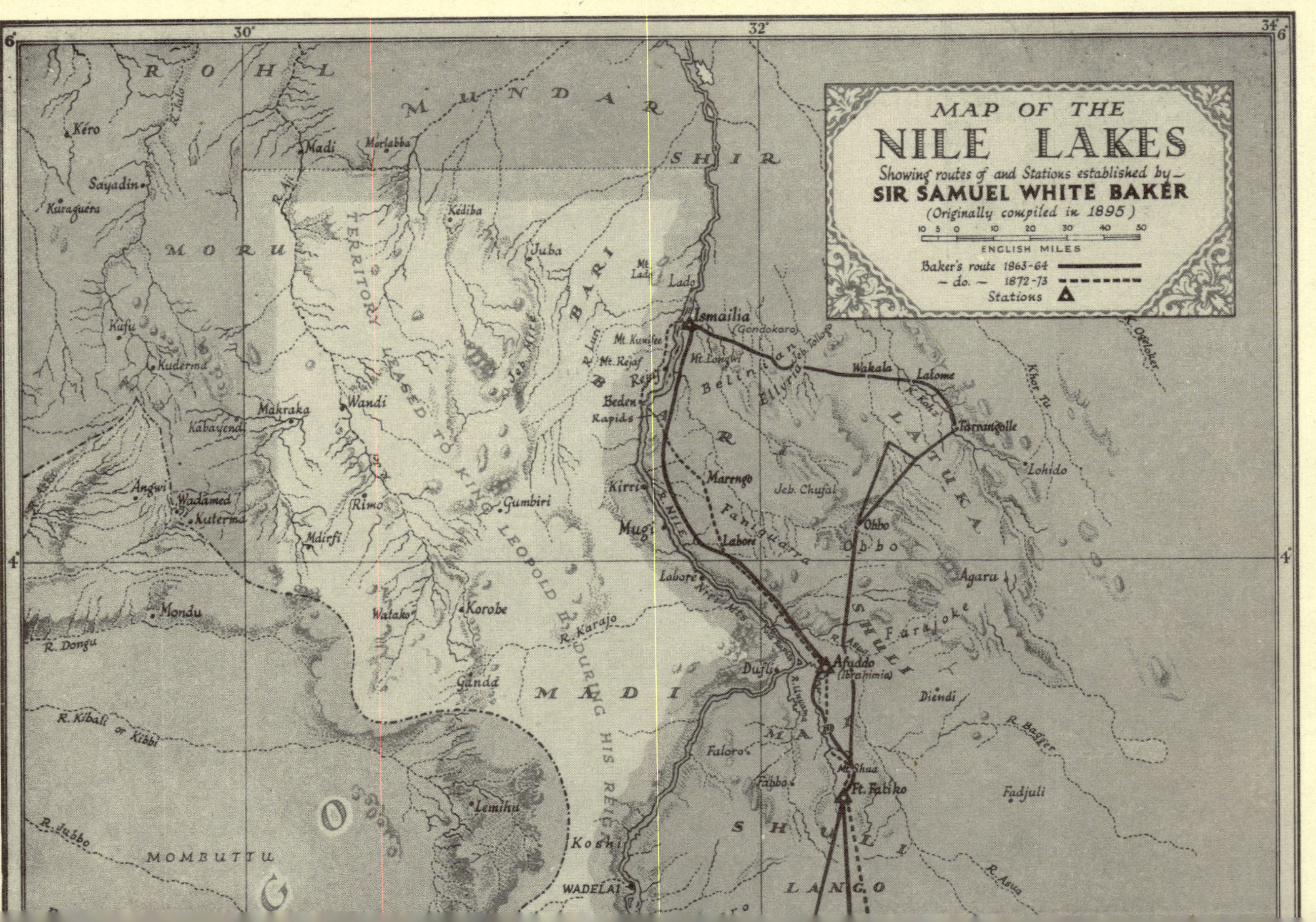

MAP OF THE
NILE LAKES
Showing routes of and Stations established by
SIR SAMUEL WHITE BAKER
(Originally compiled in 1895)
ENGLISH MILES
Baker's route 1863-64
– do. – 1872-73
Stations
ROHL
MUNDARI
SHIR
Kéro
Madi
Morlabba
Sayadin
Kuraguera
MORU
Kédiba
Kufu
Juba
Kuderma
BARI
Mt. Lado
Lado
Ismailia
(Gondokoro)
Mt. Kunlee
Mt. Longwi
Mt. Rejaf
Rejaf
Wakala
Lalome
Belinian
Ellyria
Jeb. Tollgs
Torrangolle
Beden
Rapids
LATUKA
Khor Tu
Makraka
Wandi
Marengo
Jeb. Chufal
Lohido
Kabayendi
Kirri
Faniguarra
Ohbo
Angwi
Wadamed
Rimo
Gumbiri
Labori
Ohbo
Kuterma
Mugi
Agaru
Mdirfi
Labore
Farijoke
SHULI
Mondu
Watako
Korobe
R. Karajo
Dufli
Afuddo
(Ibrahimia)
R. Dongu
GANDA
MADI
MIA
Diendi
R. Basser
R. Kibali
or Kibbi
Faloro
Mt. Shua
Fabbo
Ft. Fatiko
Fadjuli
Lemihu
TERRITORY LEASED TO KING LEOPOLD II. DURING HIS REIGN
MOMBUTTU
Koshi
SHULI
WADELAI
LANGO
R. Yubbo
R. Asua
K. Ogeloker